THE GOSPELS
IN MODERN ENGLISH

By J. B. PHILLIPS

LETTERS TO YOUNG CHURCHES
A translation of the New Testament Epistles

YOUR GOD IS TOO SMALL

THE GOSPELS *translated into Modern English*

THE
GOSPELS

translated into Modern English

by

J. B. PHILLIPS

New York
THE MACMILLAN COMPANY
1957

TRANSLATOR'S PREFACE

THERE is a peculiar difficulty in translating the Gospels of
the New Testament into modern English. In the first
place, the task is generally undertaken by Christians, who are
necessarily acquainted with the unsurpassable cadences and
rhythms of the Authorised Version, and consequently find it
almost impossible to relinquish forms of expression which are
mostly archaic and often obscure. One is therefore tempted
to suppose that the best translation into modern English
would be made by someone quite unfamiliar with the Authorised Version, but with a good knowledge of the Greek *koine*
(the colloquial language of that time) and a proper command
of the ordinary English of today. Such a person, being completely uninfluenced by traditional reverence, would be able
to give us as nearly as possible a modern English equivalent
of the simple unpolished Greek of the first three Gospels
(and, as some would say, of John's Gospel * as well).

Further, although most people, however great their reverence for the New Testament may be, do not hold a word-by-
word theory of inspiration, yet when they approach the four
Gospels, and what may be the *ipsissima verba* of Christ, they
unconsciously seek this kind of translation. (Such reverence
for the actual words of Holy Writ was shown in those older
editions of the Bible which printed in italics words which
were necessary for the sense, but which were not actually
present in the Greek and Hebrew!) But in reading a modern
work translated from a foreign language into English, we are

---

* There is a significant example of the disagreement of scholars
over the Greek of John's Gospel, quoted in Professor C. C. Torrey's
The Origin of the Gospels: "The late J. H. Moulton, a most accom-
plished grammarian, speaks of Jn.'s 'uneasy movement in the region
of unfamiliar idiom,' and concludes that 'the linguistic evidence all
goes to show that the author of the Fourth Gospel was a man who,
while cultured to the last degree, wrote Greek after the fashion of
men of quite elementary attainment.' Side by side with this may be
put the verdict of Schmiedel, that this evangelist 'abounds in subtle
variations' in his vocabulary and in his use of tenses; and that these
distinctions are natural to one 'so long habituated to Greek as to be
able to play on its words and utilise to the utmost its minute differences of grammatical expression.' "

not in the least concerned with a word-for-word version: all
we want is to know accurately the thought of the author and,
if possible, to recapture something of the style of the original
work. We do not care if a sentence be inverted or expanded
or re-arranged, so long as we are confident that a conscien-
tious translator is faithfully conveying the meaning of his
author to our minds and hearts.

Unfortunately this kind of translation, which is real translation, becomes almost impossible when we approach the four
Gospels. Most people refuse to believe that the majesty and
dignified simplicity of the Authorised Version, however
lovely in themselves, are no more a part of the original
message than the scarlet and blue and gold illumination on
a medieval manuscript. Yet, though we may not like it,
there is in fact very little sublime simplicity or simple
grandeur in the original Greek of the four Gospels. We face
a queer paradox—that the earliest and most reliable accounts
of the life of the very Son of God Himself were written in a
debased language which had lost its classical beauty.

There is a further difficulty. Throughout the centuries
these four documents have been subjected to a closer and
more meticulous examination of the texts and their variations than any other historical records whatsoever. Subtle
meanings are extracted where almost certainly no subtlety
was intended, and single Greek words are sometimes made to
bear an undue significance. Worse still, it is only too easy to
"read back" into comparatively simple language the results
of centuries of acute doctrinal conflict.

Since, then, there is considerable disagreement among
scholars over many points of translation, and since no one has
written *koine* for many centuries, the best method to adopt
in making a fair translation of the Gospel records would
appear to be:

(1) To "forget" completely the majesty and beauty of the
Authorised Version.

(2) To translate the Greek text as one would translate any
other document from a foreign language, with the same
conscientiousness but also with the same freedom in
conveying, as far as possible, the meaning and style
of the original writer.

The following version is a modest attempt to translate the Gospels on these lines.

I should like to acknowledge useful comments and criticisms from many friends, and especially to thank the Rev. R. Selby Wright, the Rev. J. P. H. Hobson, the Rev. G. H. G. Hewitt, the Rev. Professor C. F. D. Moule, H. Caiger, Esq., F.R.C.S.; and H. V. Gosling, Esq., Ph.D., who, though living in Canada, has been a most useful critic, supplying me with books at present unobtainable in this country. I must make it clear, however, that none of the above must be taken as responsible for the decisions I have had to make in translation.

Finally, I should like to thank most warmly Margery Hopkins and Joan Carter, who have given me invaluable secretarial help.

I append a short list of recommended books which may be of service to those who want to make a further study of the New Testament.

J. B. PHILLIPS.

REDHILL, 1952.
SURREY,
ENGLAND.

BOOKS RECOMMENDED FOR NEW TESTAMENT STUDY

ORIGINS:

The New Testament: a Conspectus — J. W. Hunkin (Macmillan)

*Introducing the New Testament — A. M. Hunter (Westminster)

The New Testament—Its Writers and Their Messages — C. F. Hunter (Methodist Bookroom, London) (out of print)

*A Fresh Approach to the New Testament — H. G. G. Herklots (Abingdon - Cokesbury)

About the Gospels — C. H. Dodd (Cambridge)

*The Gospels—a Short Introduction — Vincent Taylor (Epworth)

COMMENTARIES:

A New Commentary on Holy Scripture (Section on the Gospels) — (Macmillan)

The Century Bible—(R.V.) (Each of the Gospels separately) — (T. C. & E. C. Jack, Edinburgh)

(ST. JOHN ONLY)

†The Fourth Gospel — Sir E. Hoskyns (Faber)

Readings in St. John's Gospel — Wm. Temple (St. Martin's Press)

TRANSLATIONS:

The Four Gospels — C. C. Torrey (Harper)

The Four Gospels in One Story — F. W. Crofts (Longmans)

The New Testament: An American Translation — Edgar J. Goodspeed (University of Chicago Press)

TEXT:

The Four Gospels in Parallel — Herschel (S.P.C.K.)

A Synopsis of the First Three Gospels — Albert Huck (J. C. B. Moir, Tübingen)

Greek New Testament, or   (British and Foreign Bible
                                  Society, 1949)
Oxford Greek Testament   Edited by A. Souter
                                  (Oxford, 1947)

* Specially recommended to beginners in N.T. Study.
† For the advanced student only.

CONTENTS

THE GOSPEL OF
MATTHEW

Early tradition ascribed this Gospel to the apostle Matthew, but scholars nowadays almost all reject this view.

The author, whom we still can conveniently call Matthew, has plainly drawn on the mysterious "Q," which may have been a collection of oral traditions. He has used Mark's Gospel freely, though he has rearranged the order of events and has in several instances used far fewer words for what is plainly the same story. The style is lucid, calm and "tidy." Matthew writes with a certain judiciousness as though he himself had carefully digested his material and is convinced not only of its truth but of the divine pattern that lies behind the historic facts.

Matthew is quite plainly a Jew who has been convinced of Jesus' messianic claim. It is probable that he is writing primarily for fellow Jews. The frequent references to the Old Testament, the sense that Jesus' primary mission is to the "lost sheep" of the house of Israel and the implication that the Church, founded on the rock of Peter's faith, is the new Israel all bear the marks of a converted Jew writing for fellow Jews. He attempts to convey a logical conviction that the new teaching was not only prophesied in the old but does in fact supersede it in the divine plan.

If Matthew wrote, as is now generally supposed, somewhere between 85 and 90, this Gospel's value as a Christian document is enormous. It is, so to speak, a second generation view of Jesus Christ the Son of God and the Son of Man. It is being written at that distance in time from the great Event where sober reflection and sturdy conviction can perhaps give a better balanced portrait of God's unique revelation of Himself than could be given by those who were so close to the Light that they were partly dazzled by it.

THE ANCESTRY OF JESUS CHRIST

THE genealogy of Jesus Christ may be traced from Abraham, through forty-two generations, to Joseph the husband of Mary, Jesus' mother—fourteen generations from Abraham to David, fourteen from David to the Deportation to Babylon, and fourteen more from Babylon to Christ himself.

HIS BIRTH IN HUMAN HISTORY

1
18 The birth of Jesus Christ happened like this. When Mary was engaged to Joseph, just before their marriage, she was discovered to be pregnant—by the Holy Spirit. Whereupon Joseph, her future husband, who was a good man and did not want to see her disgraced, planned to break off the engagement quietly. But while he was turning the matter over in his mind an angel of the Lord appeared to him in a dream and said, "Joseph, son of David, do not be afraid to take Mary as your wife! What she has conceived is conceived through the Holy Spirit, and she will give birth to a son, whom you will call Jesus ('the Saviour') for it is he who will save his people from their sins."

All this happened to fulfil what the Lord had said through the prophet—

Behold, the virgin shall be with child, and shall bring forth a son, and they shall call his name Immanuel (which means "God with us").

Joseph woke up and did what the angel had told him. He married Mary, but had no intercourse with her until she had given birth to a son. And he gave him the name Jesus.

HEROD, SUSPICIOUS OF THE NEW-BORN KING, TAKES VINDICTIVE PRECAUTIONS

2
1 Jesus was born in Bethlehem, in Judaea, in the days when Herod was king of the province. Not long after his birth there arrived from the east a party of astrologers making for Jerusalem and enquiring as they went, "Where is the child born to be King of the Jews? For we saw his star in the east and we have come here to pay homage to him."

When King Herod heard about this he was deeply perturbed, as indeed were all the other people living in Jerusalem. So he got all the Jewish Scribes * and Chief Priests together and asked them where "Christ" should be born. Their reply was: "In Bethlehem, in Judaea. for this is what the prophet wrote about the matter—

And thou, Bethlehem, land of Judah,
Art in no wise least among the princes of Judah:
For out of thee shall come forth a governor,
Which shall be shepherd of my people Israel."

Then Herod summoned the wise men to meet him privately and questioned them closely as to the exact time when the star appeared. Then he sent them off to Bethlehem saying, "When you get there, search for this little child with the utmost care. And when you have found him come back and tell me—so that I may go and worship him too."

The wise men listened to the King and then went on their way to Bethlehem. And now the star, which they had seen in the east, went in front of them as they travelled until at last it shone immediately above the place where the little child lay. The sight of the star filled them with indescribable joy.

So they went into the house and saw the little child with his mother Mary. And they fell on their knees and worshipped him. Then they opened their treasures and presented him with gifts—gold, incense and myrrh.

Then, since they were warned in a dream not to return to Herod, they went back to their own country by a different route.

After they had gone the angel of the Lord appeared to Joseph in a dream and said, "Get up now, take the little child and his mother and escape to Egypt. Stay there until I tell you. For Herod means to seek out the child and kill him."

So Joseph got up, and took the child and his mother with him, and in the middle of the night set off for Egypt, where he remained until Herod's death.

This again is a fulfilment of the Lord's word spoken

* See Appendix, Note 1.

through the prophet—

Out of Egypt did I call my son.

When Herod saw that he had been fooled by the wise men he was furiously angry. He issued orders, and killed all the male children of two years and under in Bethlehem and the surrounding district—basing his calculation on his careful questioning of the wise men. Then Jeremiah's prophecy was fulfilled:

A voice was heard in Ramah,
Weeping and great mourning,
Rachel weeping for her children;
And she would not be comforted, because they are not.

JESUS IS BROUGHT TO NAZARETH

2
19 But after Herod's death an angel of the Lord again appeared to Joseph in a dream and said, "Now get up and take the infant and his mother with you and go into the land of Israel. For those who sought the child's life are dead."

So Joseph got up and took the little child and his mother with him and journeyed towards the land of Israel. When he heard that Archelaus was now reigning as King of Judaea in the place of his father Herod he was afraid to enter the country. But he received warning in a dream to turn aside into the district of Galilee and came to live in a small town called Nazareth—thus fulfilling the old prophecy,

He shall be called a Nazarene.

"THE PROPHESIED ELIJAH": JOHN THE BAPTIST

3
1 In due course John the Baptist arrived, preaching in the Judaean desert. "You must change your hearts—for the Kingdom of Heaven has arrived!"

This was the man whom the prophet Isaiah spoke about in the words:

The voice of one crying in the wilderness,
Make ye ready the way of the Lord,
Make his paths straight.

John wore clothes of camel-hair with a leather belt round his waist, and lived on locusts and wild honey. The people of

Jerusalem and of all Judaea and the Jordan district flocked to him, and were baptized by him in the river Jordan, publicly confessing their sins.

But when he saw many Pharisees and Sadducees * coming for baptism he said: "Who warned you, you serpent's brood, to escape from the wrath to come? Go and do something to show that your hearts are really changed. Don't go thinking that you can say to yourselves 'We are Abraham's children,' for I tell you that God could produce children of Abraham out of these stones.

"The axe is already at the root of the tree, and the tree that fails to produce good fruit will be cut down and thrown into the fire. It is true that I baptize you with water as a sign that your hearts are changed, but the One Who follows me is far stronger than I am—I am not good enough to carry his sandals. He will baptize you with the fire of the Holy Spirit. He comes all ready to separate the wheat from the chaff and very thoroughly will he clear his threshing-floor—the wheat he will collect into the granary and the chaff he will burn with a fire that cannot be put out."

JOHN BAPTIZES JESUS

Then Jesus came from Galilee to the Jordan to be baptized **3** by John. But John tried to stop him. "I need you to baptize **13** *me*," he said. "Surely *you* must not come to me?" But Jesus replied, "It is right for us to meet all the Law's demands— let it be so now."

Then John agreed to his baptism. Jesus came straight out of the water afterwards, and suddenly the heavens opened and he saw the Spirit of God coming down like a dove and resting upon him. And a Voice came out of Heaven saying, "This is my dearly-loved Son, in Whom I am well pleased."

JESUS FACES TEMPTATION ALONE IN THE DESERT

Then Jesus was led by the Spirit up into the desert, there **4** to be tempted by the devil. After a fast of forty days and **1** nights he was very hungry.

"If you really are the Son of God," said the tempter, coming to him, "tell these stones to turn into loaves."

* See Appendix, Note 1.

Jesus answered, "The Scripture says *'Man shall not live by bread alone, but by every word that proceedeth out of the mouth of God.'*"

Then the devil took him to the holy city, and set him on the highest ledge of the Temple. "If you really are the Son of God," he said, "throw yourself down. For the Scripture says—

He shall give his angels charge concerning thee:
And on their hands they shall bear thee up,
Lest haply thou dash thy foot against a stone."

"Yes," retorted Jesus, "and the Scripture also says *'Thou shalt not tempt the Lord thy God.'*"

Once again the devil took him to a very high mountain, and from there showed him all the kingdoms of the world and their magnificence. "Everything there I will give you," he said to him, "if you will fall down and worship me."

"Away with you, Satan!" replied Jesus, "the Scripture says,

Thou shalt worship the Lord thy God, and him only shalt thou serve."

Then the devil left him alone, and angels came to him and took care of him.

JESUS BEGINS HIS MINISTRY, IN GALILEE, AND CALLS HIS FIRST DISCIPLES

4
12   Now when Jesus heard that John had been arrested he went back to Galilee. He left Nazareth and came to live in Capernaum, a lake-side town in the Zebulun-Naphtali territory. In this way Isaiah's prophecy came true:

The land of Zebulun and the land of Naphtali,
Toward the sea, beyond Jordan,
Galilee of the Gentiles,
The people which sat in darkness
Saw a great light,
And to them which sat in the region and shadow of death,
To them did light spring up.

From that time Jesus began to preach and to say, "You

must change your hearts—for the Kingdom of Heaven has arrived."

While he was walking by the lake of Galilee he saw two brothers, Simon (Peter) and Andrew, casting their large net into the water. They were fishermen, so Jesus said to them,

"Follow me and I will teach you to catch men!"

At once they left their nets and followed him.

Then he went further on and saw two more men, also brothers, James and John. They were aboard the boat with their father Zebedee repairing their nets, and he called them. At once they left the boat, and their father, and followed him.

JESUS TEACHES, PREACHES AND HEALS

Jesus now moved about through the whole of Galilee, teaching in their synagogues and preaching the good news about the new Kingdom, and healing every disease and disability among the people. His reputation spread throughout Syria, and people brought to him all those who were ill, suffering from all kinds of diseases and pains—including the devil-possessed, the insane and paralysed. He healed them, and was followed by enormous crowds from Galilee, the Ten Towns, Jerusalem, Judaea and from beyond the River Jordan.

JESUS PROCLAIMS THE NEW VALUES
OF THE KINGDOM

When Jesus saw the vast crowds he went up the mountainside and after he had sat down his disciples came to him.

Then he began his teaching by saying to them,

"How happy are the humble-minded, for they already own the Kingdom of Heaven!

"How happy are those who know what sorrow means, for they will be given courage and comfort!

"Happy are those who claim nothing, for the whole earth will belong to them!

"Happy are those who are hungry and thirsty for goodness, for they will be fully satisfied!

"Happy are the kind-hearted, for they will have kindness shown to them!

"Happy are the pure in heart, for they will see God!

"Happy are those who make peace, for they will be known as sons of God!

"Happy are those who have suffered persecution for the cause of goodness, for the Kingdom of Heaven belongs to them!

"And what happiness will be yours when people blame you and ill-treat you and say all kinds of slanderous things against you for my sake! Be glad then, yes, be tremendously glad—for your reward in Heaven is magnificent. They persecuted the prophets before your time in exactly the same way.

"You are the earth's salt. But if the salt should become tasteless, what can make it salt again? It is completely useless and can only be thrown out of doors and stamped under foot.

"You are the world's light—it is impossible to hide a town built on the top of a hill. Men do not light a lamp and put it under a bucket. They put it on a lamp-stand and it gives light for everybody in the house.

"Let your light shine like that in the sight of men. Let them see the good things you do and praise your Father in Heaven.

CHRIST'S AUTHORITY SURPASSES THAT
OF THE LAW

5
17 "You must not think that I have come to abolish the Law or the prophets; I have not come to abolish them but to complete them. Indeed, I assure you that, while Heaven and earth last, the Law will not lose a single dot or comma until its purpose is complete. This means that whoever now relaxes one of the least of these commandments and teaches men to do the same will himself be called least in the Kingdom of Heaven. But whoever teaches and practises them will be called great in the Kingdom of Heaven. For I tell you your goodness must be a far better thing than the goodness of the Scribes and Pharisees before you can set foot in the Kingdom of Heaven at all!

"You have heard that it was said to the people in the old days, 'Thou shalt not murder,' and anyone who does so must stand his trial. But I say to you that anyone who is angry with his brother must stand his trial; anyone who contemp-

tuously calls his brother a fool * must face the Supreme Court;
and anyone who looks down on his brother as a lost soul is
heading straight for the fire of destruction.

"So that if, while you are offering your gift at the altar, you
should remember that your brother has something against
you, you must leave your gift there before the altar and go
away. Make your peace with your brother first, then come
and offer your gift. Come to terms quickly with your opponent while you have the chance, or else he may hand you over
to the judge and the judge in turn hand you over to the officer
of the court and you will be thrown into prison. Believe me,
you will never get out again till you have paid out your last
cent.

"You have heard that it was said to the people in the old
days, '*Thou shalt not commit adultery.*' But I say to you that
every man who looks at a woman lustfully has already committed adultery with her—in his heart.

"Yes, if your right eye leads you astray pluck it out and
throw it away; it is better for you to lose one of your members than that your whole body should be thrown on to the
rubbish-heap.

"Yes, if your right hand leads you astray cut it off and
throw it away; it is better for you to lose one of your members
than that your whole body should go to the rubbish-
heap.

"It also used to be said that whoever divorces his wife
must give her a proper certificate of divorce. But I say to
you that whoever divorces his wife except on the ground of
unchastity is making her commit adultery. And whoever
marries the woman who has been divorced also commits
adultery.

"Again, you have heard that the people in the old days
were told—'*Thou shalt not forswear thyself, but shalt perform
unto the Lord thine oaths,*' but I say to you, 'Don't use an
oath at all. Don't swear by Heaven, for it is God's throne,
nor by the earth for it is His footstool, nor by Jerusalem for
it is the Great King's city. No, and don't swear by your
own head—you cannot make a single hair, white or black!
Whatever you have to say let your 'yes' be a plain 'yes'

* See Appendix, Note 2.

and your 'no' be a plain 'no'—anything more than this is wrong.

"You have heard that it used to be said '*An eye for an eye and a tooth for a tooth,*' but I tell you, Don't resist the man who wants to do you harm. If a man hits your right cheek, turn the other one to him as well. If a man wants to sue you for your cloak, let him have it and your outer cloak as well. If anybody forces you to go a mile with him, do more—go two miles with him. Give to the man who asks anything from you, and don't turn away from the man who wants to borrow.

"You have heard that it used to be said '*Thou shalt love thy neighbor and hate thine enemy,*' but I tell you love your enemies, and pray for those who persecute you, so that you may be sons of your Heavenly Father. For He makes His sun rise on evil men as well as good, and He sends His rain on honest and dishonest alike.

"For if you love only those who love you, what credit is that to you? Even tax-collectors do that! And if you exchange greetings with your own circle, are you doing anything exceptional? Even the pagans do that much. No, you must be perfect, like your Heavenly Father.

THE NEW LIFE IS NOT A MATTER OF
OUTWARD SHOW

6   "Beware of doing your acts of charity conspicuously or you
1   will miss the reward of your Heavenly Father.

"So, when you do good to other people, don't hire a trumpeter to go in front of you—like those play-actors in the synagogues and streets who make sure that men admire them. Believe me, they have had all the reward they are going to get! No, when you do a good deed, don't even let your left hand know what your right hand is doing, so that your kindness may be secret. Your Father Who sees all secrets will reward you.

"And then, when you pray, don't be like the play-actors. They love to stand and pray in the synagogues and at street-corners so that people may see them at it. Believe me, they have had all the reward they are going to get. But when you pray, go into your own room, shut your door and pray to your Father privately. Your Father who sees all private things

will reward you. And when you pray don't rattle off long
prayers like the pagans who think they will be heard because
they use a lot of words. Don't be like them. After all God,
Who is your Father, knows your needs before you ask Him.
Pray like this—

Our Heavenly Father, may your Name be honoured;
May your Kingdom come, and your Will be done on earth
   as it is in Heaven.
Give us today the bread we need,
Forgive us what we owe to you, as we have also forgiven
   those who owe anything to us.
Keep us clear of temptation, and save us from evil.

FORGIVENESS OF FELLOW-MAN IS ESSENTIAL

"For if you forgive other people their failures, your   6
Heavenly Father will also forgive you. But if you refuse to   14
forgive other people, your Heavenly Father will not forgive
you your failures.

"And when you fast, don't look miserable, like those play-
actors! For they deliberately disfigure their faces so that
people may see that they are fasting. Believe me, they have
had all their reward. No, when you fast, brush your hair and
wash your face so that nobody knows that you are fasting—
let it be a secret between you and your Father. And your
Father who knows all secrets will reward you.

PUT YOUR TRUST IN GOD ALONE

"Don't pile up treasures on earth, where moth and rust can   6
spoil them and thieves can break in and steal. But keep your   19
treasure in Heaven where there is neither moth nor rust to
spoil it and nobody can break in and steal. For you may be
sure your heart will be wherever you keep your treasure.

"The eye is the lamp of the body. If your eye is clear and
true, your whole body will be full of light. But if your eye is
neither clear nor true, your whole body will be full of darkness. If all the light you have is darkness, it is dark indeed!

"No one can be loyal to two masters. He is bound to hate
one and love the other, or despise one and support the other.
You cannot serve God and the power of money at the same
time. That is why I say to you, don't worry about living

—wondering what you are going to eat or drink, or what you are going to wear. Surely life is more important than food, and the body more important than the clothes you wear. Look at the birds in the sky. They never sow nor reap nor store away in barns, and yet your Heavenly Father feeds them. Aren't you much more valuable to him than they are? Can any of you, however much he worries, make himself an inch taller? Consider how the wild flowers grow. They neither work nor weave, but I tell you that even Solomon in all his glory was not arrayed like one of these! Now if God gives such clothes to the flowers of the field, which are alive today and burnt in the stove tomorrow, is He not much more likely to clothe you, you 'little-faiths'?

"So don't worry and don't keep saying, 'What shall we eat, what shall we drink or what shall we wear?'! That is what pagans are always looking for; your Heavenly Father knows that you need them all. Set your heart on His Kingdom and His goodness, and all these things will come to you as a matter of course.

"Don't worry at all then about tomorrow. Tomorrow can take care of itself! One day's trouble is enough for one day.

THE COMMON SENSE BEHIND RIGHT BEHAVIOUR

7   "Don't criticise people, and you will not be criticised. For
1   you will be judged by the way you criticise others, and the measure you give will be the measure you get.

"Why do you look at the speck of sawdust in your brother's eye and fail to notice the plank in your own? How can you say to your brother, 'Let me get the speck out of your eye,' when there is a plank in your own? You fraud! Take the plank out of your own eye first, and then you can see clearly enough to remove your brother's speck of dust.

"You must not give holy things to dogs, nor must you throw your pearls before pigs—or they may trample them underfoot and turn and attack you.

"Ask and it will be given to you. Search and you will find. Knock and the door will be opened for you. The one who asks will always get; the one who is searching will always find, and the door is opened to the man who knocks.

"If any of you were asked by his son for bread would you be likely to give him a stone, or if he asks for a fish would you give him a snake? If you then, for all your evil, quite naturally give good things to your children, how much more likely is it that your Heavenly Father will give good things to those who ask Him?

"Treat other people exactly as you would like to be treated by them—this is the essence of all true religion.

"Go in by the narrow gate. For the wide gate has a broad road which leads to disaster and there are many people going that way. The narrow gate and the hard road lead out into life and only a few find it.

LIVING, NOT PROFESSING, IS WHAT MATTERS

"Be on your guard against false religious teachers, who come to you dressed up as sheep but are really greedy wolves. You can tell them by their fruit. Do you pick a bunch of grapes from a thorn-bush or figs from a clump of thistles? Every good tree produces good fruit, but a bad tree produces bad fruit. A good tree is incapable of producing bad fruit, and a bad tree cannot produce good fruit. The tree that fails to produce good fruit is cut down and burnt. So the fruit that men produce must be the test.   7   15

"It is not everyone who keeps saying to me 'Lord, Lord' who will enter the Kingdom of Heaven, but the man who actually does my Heavenly Father's Will.

"In 'that Day' many will say to me, 'Lord, Lord, didn't we preach in your name, didn't we cast out devils in your name, and do many great things in your name?' Then I shall tell them plainly, 'I have never known you. Go away from me, you have worked on the side of evil!'

TO FOLLOW CHRIST'S TEACHING MEANS THE ONLY REAL SECURITY

"Everyone then who hears these words of mine and puts them into practice is like a sensible man who built his house on the rock. Down came the rain and up came the floods, while the winds blew and roared upon that house—and it did not fall because its foundations were on the rock.   7   24

"And everyone who hears these words of mine and does not follow them can be compared with a silly man who built his house on the sand. Down came the rain and up came the floods, while the winds blew and battered that house till it collapsed—down it came with a terrific crash."

When Jesus had finished these words the crowd were astonished at the power behind his teaching. For his words had a ring of authority, quite unlike those of their Scribes.

JESUS CURES LEPERS, AND HEALS MANY

8 Large crowds followed him when he came down from the
1 mountain. There was a leper who came and knelt in front of him. "Sir," he said, "if you want to, you can make me clean." Jesus stretched out his hand and placed it on the leper saying, "Of course I want to. You are clean!" And, at once, he was clear of the leprosy.

"Mind you say nothing to anybody," Jesus told him. "Go straight off and show yourself to the priest and make the offerings for your recovery that Moses prescribed, as evidence to the authorities."

Then as he was coming into Capernaum a centurion approached. "Sir," he implored him, "my slave is in bed at home paralysed and in dreadful pain."

"I will come and heal him," said Jesus to him.

"Sir," replied the centurion, "I'm not important enough for you to come under my roof. Just give the order, and my servant will be healed. I'm a man under authority myself, and I have soldiers under me. I can say to one man 'Go' and I know he'll go, or I can say 'Come here' to another and I know he'll come—or I can say to my servant 'Do this' and he'll always do it."

When Jesus heard this, he was astonished. "Believe me," he said to those who were following him, "I haven't found faith as great as this even in Israel! I tell you that many people will come from east and west and sit at my table with Abraham, Isaac and Jacob in the Kingdom of Heaven. But those who should have belonged to the Kingdom will be banished to the darkness outside, where there will be tears and gnashing of teeth."

Then he said to the centurion, "Go home now, and everything will happen as you have believed it will."

And his servant *was* healed at that actual moment.

Then, on coming into Peter's house Jesus saw that Peter's

mother-in-law had been put to bed with a high fever. He
touched her hand and the fever left her. And then she got
up and began to see to their needs.

When evening came they brought to him many who were
possessed by evil spirits, which he expelled with a word.
Indeed he healed all who were ill. Thus was fulfilled Isaiah's
prophecy—

Himself took our infirmities and bare our diseases.

When Jesus had seen the great crowds around him he gave
orders for departure to the other side of the lake. But before
they started one of the Scribes who had come to Jesus said
to him, "Master, I will follow you wherever you go."

"Foxes have earths, birds in the sky have nests, but the Son
of Man has nowhere to lay his head," replied Jesus.

Another of his disciples said, "Lord, let me first go and bury
my father."

But Jesus said to him, "Follow me, and let the dead bury
their own dead."

JESUS SHOWS HIS MASTERY OVER THE
FORCES OF NATURE

When he was aboard the boat, his disciples followed him.   8
Before long a terrific storm sprang up and the boat was awash   23
with the waves. Jesus was sleeping soundly and the disciples
went forward and woke him up.

"Lord, save us!" they cried. "We are drowning!"

"What are you so frightened about, you little-faiths?" he
replied.

Then he got to his feet and rebuked the wind and the waters
and there was a great calm. The men were filled with astonishment and kept saying, "Whatever sort of man is this—
why, even the wind and the waves do what he tells them!"

When he arrived on the other side (which is the Gerasenes'
country) he was met by two devil-possessed men who came
out from among the tombs. They were so violent that nobody
dared to use that road.

"What have you got to do with us, Jesus, you Son of God?"
they yelled at him. "Have you come to torture us before the
proper time?"

It happened that in the distance there was a large herd of

pigs feeding. So the devils implored him, "If you throw us out, give us leave to go off into the herd of pigs!"

"Then go!" said Jesus.

And the devils came out of the two men and went into the pigs. Then quite suddenly the whole herd rushed madly down a steep cliff into the lake and were drowned.

The swineherds took to their heels, and ran to the town. There they poured out the whole story, not forgetting what had happened to the two men who had been devil-possessed. Whereupon the whole town went out to meet Jesus, and as soon as they saw him implored him to leave their territory.

JESUS HEALS IN HIS OWN TOWN

9
1 So Jesus re-embarked on the boat, crossed the lake, and came to his own town. There some people arrived bringing him a paralytic lying flat on his bed. When Jesus saw the faith of those who brought him he said to the paralytic, "Cheer up, my son! Your sins are forgiven."

At once some of the Scribes thought to themselves, "This man is blaspheming," but Jesus realised what they were thinking, and said to them, "Why must you have such evil thoughts in your minds? Do you think it is easier to say to this man 'Your sins are forgiven' or 'Get up and walk'? But to make it quite plain that the Son of Man has full authority on earth to forgive sins—Get up!" he said to the paralytic, "pick up your bed and go home." And the man got to his feet and went home. When the crowds saw what had happened they were filled with awe and praised God for giving such power to men.

JESUS CALLS A "SINNER" TO BE HIS DISCIPLE

9
9 Jesus left there and as he passed on he saw a man called Matthew sitting at his desk in the tax-collector's office.

"Follow me!" he said to him—and the man got to his feet and followed him.

Later, as Jesus was in the house sitting at the dinner-table, a good many tax-collectors and other disreputable people came on the scene and joined him and his disciples. Some Pharisees noticed this and said to the disciples, "Why does your Master have his meals with tax-collectors and sinners?" But Jesus heard it and replied,

"It is not the fit and flourishing who need the doctor, but those who are ill! Suppose you go away and learn what this means: 'I desire mercy and not sacrifice.' In any case I did not come to invite the 'righteous' but the 'sinners.'"

HE EXPLAINS THE JOY AND STRENGTH OF
THE NEW ORDER

Then John's disciples approached him with the question, "Why is it that we and the Pharisees observe the fasts, but your disciples do nothing of the kind?" 9 14

"Can you expect wedding-guests to be miserable while they have the bridegroom with them?" replied Jesus. "The day will come when they will lose the bridegroom—and then they will certainly fast.

"Nobody sews a patch of unshrunken cloth on to an old coat, for the patch will pull away from the coat and the hole will be worse than ever. Nor do people put new wine into old wineskins—otherwise the skins burst, the wine is spilt and the skins are ruined. But they put new wine into new skins and both are preserved."

JESUS HEALS A YOUNG GIRL, AND SEVERAL
OTHERS IN NEED

While he was saying these things to them an official came up to him and, bowing low before him, said, 9 18

"My daughter has just this moment died. Please come and lay your hand on her and she will come to life!"

At this Jesus got to his feet and followed him, accompanied by his disciples. And on the way a woman who had had a hæmorrhage for twelve years approached him from behind and touched the edge of his cloak.

"If only I can touch his cloak," she kept saying to herself, "I shall be all right."

But Jesus turned right round and saw her.

"Cheer up, my daughter," he said, "your faith has made you well!" And the woman was completely cured from that moment.

Then when Jesus came into the official's house and noticed the flute-players and the noisy crowd he said, "Will you please all go away; the little girl is not dead, she is fast asleep."

This was met with scornful laughter. But when the crowd

had been sent out Jesus came right into the room, took hold
of her hand, and the girl got up. And this became the talk
of the whole district.

As Jesus passed on his way two blind men followed him
with the cry, "Have pity on us, Son of David!" And when
he had gone inside the house these two came up to him.

"Do you believe I can do it?" he said to them.

"Yes, Lord," they replied.

Then he touched their eyes, saying, "You have believed
and you will not be disappointed."

Then their sight came back, and Jesus sternly warned
them, "Don't let anyone know about this." Yet when they
got outside they spread the story throughout the whole
district.

Later, when Jesus and his party were coming out they
brought to him a dumb man who was also devil-possessed.
And when the devil had been ejected the dumb man began
to talk. The crowds were simply amazed and said, "Nothing
like this has ever been seen in Israel." But the Pharisees'
comment was, "He throws out these devils because he is in
league with the Devil himself."

JESUS IS TOUCHED BY THE PEOPLE'S NEED

9
35 Jesus now travelled through all the towns and villages,
teaching in their synagogues, proclaiming the gospel of the
Kingdom, and healing all kinds of illness and disability. As
he looked at the vast crowds he was deeply moved with pity
for them, for they were as bewildered and miserable as a flock
of sheep with no shepherd.

"The harvest is great enough," he remarked to his disciples, "but the reapers are few. So you must pray to the Lord
of the Harvest to send men out to reap it."

JESUS SENDS OUT THE TWELVE WITH DIVINE POWER

10
1 Jesus called his twelve disciples to him and gave them
authority to expel evil spirits and heal all kinds of disease
and infirmity. The names of the Twelve Apostles were:

First, Simon, called Peter, with his brother Andrew;
James and his brother John, sons of Zebedee;
Philip and Bartholomew,

Thomas, and Matthew the tax-collector,
James, the son of Alphaeus, and Thaddaeus,
Simon the Patriot, and Judas Iscariot, who later turned
  traitor.

These were the twelve that Jesus sent out, with these instructions: "Don't turn off into any of the heathen roads, and
don't go into any Samaritan town. Concentrate on the lost
sheep of the house of Israel. As you go proclaim that the
Kingdom of Heaven has arrived. Heal the sick, raise the
dead, cure the lepers, throw out devils—give, as you have
received, without any charge whatever.

"Don't take any gold or silver or even coppers to put in
your purse; nor any baggage for the journey, nor even a
change of clothes, or sandals or a staff—the workman is worth
his keep!

"Wherever you go, whether it is into a town or a village,
find out someone who is respected, and stay with him until
you leave. As you enter his house give it your blessing. If
the house deserves it, the peace of your blessing will come to
it. But if it doesn't, your peace will return to you.

"And if anywhere no one will have you nor even listen
to what you have to say, leave that house or town and once
outside it shake off the dust of that place from your feet.
Believe me, Sodom and Gomorrah will fare better in the Day
of Judgment than that town.

HE WARNS THEM OF TROUBLES THAT LIE AHEAD

"Look, I am sending you out like sheep with wolves all 10
round you! So be as wise as serpents and yet as harmless as 16
doves. But be on your guard against men. For they will
take you to the courts and flog you in their synagogues.
You will be brought into the presence of governors and kings
because of me—to give your witness to them and to the
heathen.

"But when they do arrest you, never worry about how
you are to speak or what you are to say. You will be told at
the time what you are to say. For it will not be really you
who are speaking but the Spirit of your Father speaking
through you.

"Brothers are going to betray their brothers to death, and

fathers their children. Children are going to betray their parents and have them executed. You yourselves will be universally hated because of my name. But the man who endures to the very end will be safe and sound.

"But when they persecute you in one town make your escape to the next. Believe me, you will not have covered the towns of Israel before the Son of Man arrives. The disciple is not superior to his teacher any more than the servant is superior to his master, for what is good enough for the teacher is good enough for the disciple as well, and the servant will not fare better than his master. If men call the Master of the Household the 'Prince of Evil,' what sort of names will they give to his servants? But never let them frighten you, for there is nothing covered up which is not going to be exposed nor anything private which will not be made public. The things I tell you in the dark you must say in the day-light, and the things you hear in your private ear you must proclaim from the house-tops.

THEY SHOULD REVERENCE GOD BUT HAVE
NO FEAR OF MAN

10
28
"Never be afraid of those who can kill the body but are powerless to kill the soul! Far better to stand in awe of the One Who has the power to destroy body and soul in the fires of destruction!

"Two sparrows sell for a cent, don't they? Yet not a single sparrow falls to the ground without your Father's knowledge. But in your case the hairs of your head are all numbered. Never be afraid, then—you are far more valuable than sparrows.

"Every man who publicly acknowledges me I shall acknowledge in the presence of my Father in Heaven, but the man who disowns me before men I shall disown before my Father in Heaven.

THE PRINCE OF PEACE COMES TO
BRING DIVISION

10
34
"Never think I have come to bring peace upon the earth. No, I have not come to bring peace but a sword! Yes, I have come to set a man against his own father, a daughter against her own mother, and a daughter-in-law against her mother-

in-law. A man's enemies will be those who live in his own house.

"Anyone who puts his love for father or mother above his love for me does not deserve to be mine, and he who loves son or daughter more than me is not worthy of me, and neither is the man who refuses to take up his cross and follow my way. The man who has found his own life will lose it, but the man who has thrown it away for my sake will find it.

"Whoever welcomes you, welcomes me; and whoever welcomes me is welcoming the One Who sent me.

"Whoever welcomes a prophet just because he is a prophet will get a prophet's reward. And whoever welcomes a good man just because he is a good man will get a good man's reward. Believe me, anyone who gives even a drink of water to one of these little ones, just because he is my disciple, will by no means lose his reward."

When Jesus had finished giving his twelve disciples these instructions he went on from there to preach and teach in the towns in which they lived.

JOHN ENQUIRES ABOUT CHRIST: CHRIST SPEAKS ABOUT JOHN

John the Baptist was in prison and when he heard what 11
Christ was doing he sent a message through his own disciples 2
asking the question, "Are you the One Who was to come or are we to look for somebody else?"

Jesus gave them this reply, "Go and tell John what you see and hear—that blind men are recovering their sight, cripples are walking, lepers being healed, the deaf hearing, the dead being brought to life and the Good News is going to those in need. *And happy is the man who never loses his faith in me*."

As John's disciples were going away Jesus began talking to the crowd about John:

"What did you go out into the desert to look at? A reed waving in the breeze? No? Then what was it you went out to see? Was it a man dressed in fine clothes? But the men who wear fine clothes live in the courts of kings! But what did you really go to see—a prophet? Yes, I tell you, a prophet and even more than a prophet! This is the man of whom the Scripture says—

Behold, I send my messenger before thy face,
Who shall prepare thy way before thee.

"Believe me, no one greater than John the Baptist has ever arisen from all mankind, and yet a humble member of the Kingdom of Heaven is greater than he.

"From the days of John the Baptist until now the Kingdom of Heaven has been thrown wide open and eager men rush in to take it by storm. For the Law and all the Prophets foretold it till the time of John and—if you can believe it—John himself is the 'Elijah' who must come before the Kingdom. The man who has ears to hear must use them!

"But how can I show what this generation is like? It is like children sitting in the market-place calling out to their friends, 'We played at weddings for you but you wouldn't dance, and we played at funerals and you wouldn't cry!' For John came in the strictest austerity and people say, 'He's crazy!' Then the Son of Man came, enjoying life, and people say, 'Look, a drunkard and a glutton—the bosom-friend of the tax-collector and the sinner.' Ah well, Wisdom stands or falls by the way her children behave."

JESUS DENOUNCES APATHY—AND THANKS
GOD THAT SIMPLE MEN UNDERSTAND
HIS MESSAGE

11
20
Then Jesus began reproaching the towns where most of his miracles had taken place because their hearts were unchanged.

"Alas for you, Chorazin! Alas for you, Bethsaida! For if Tyre and Sidon had seen the demonstrations of God's power which you have seen they would have repented long ago in sackcloth and ashes. Yet I tell you this, that it will be more bearable for Tyre and Sidon in the Day of Judgment than for you.

"And as for you, Capernaum, are you built up to heaven? You are more likely to fall down into hell! If Sodom had seen the miracles that you have seen, Sodom would be standing today. Yet I tell you now that it will be more bearable for the land of Sodom in the Day of Judgment than for you."

At this same time Jesus said, "O Father, Lord of Heaven and earth, I thank you for hiding these things from the clever

and intelligent and for showing them to mere children. Yes, I
thank You, Father, that this was Your Will."

Then he said: "Everything has been put in my hands by my
Father, and nobody knows the Son except the Father. Nor
does anyone know the Father except the Son—and the man
to whom the Son decides to reveal Him.

"Come to me all of you who are weary and over-burdened
and I will give you rest! Put on my yoke and learn from me.
For I am gentle and humble in heart and you will find rest
for your souls. For my yoke is easy and my burden is light."

JESUS REBUKES THE SABBATARIANS

It happened then that Jesus passed through the wheatfields 12
on the Sabbath day. His disciples were hungry and began 1
picking the ears of wheat and eating them. But the Pharisees
saw them do it.

"There, you see," they remarked to Jesus, "your disciples
are doing what the Law forbids them to do on the Sabbath."

"Haven't any of you read what David did when he and his
companions were hungry?" replied Jesus, "—how he went
into the House of God and ate the Presentation Loaves, which
he and his followers were not allowed to eat since only
priests can do so?

"Haven't any of you read in the Law that every Sabbath
day priests in the Temple can break the Sabbath and yet
remain blameless? I tell you that there is something more
important than the Temple here. If you had grasped the
meaning of the Scripture '*I desire mercy and not sacrifice,*'
you would not have been so quick to condemn the innocent!
For the Son of Man is master even of the Sabbath."

Leaving there he went into their synagogue, where there
happened to be a man with a shrivelled hand.

"Is it right to heal anyone on the Sabbath day?" they asked
him—hoping to bring a charge against him.

"If any of you had a sheep which fell into a ditch on the
Sabbath day, would he not get hold of it and pull it out?" re-
plied Jesus. "How much more valuable is a man than a sheep?
You see, it is right to do good deeds on the Sabbath day."

Then Jesus said to the man, "Stretch your hand right out!"
He did stretch it right out, and it was restored as sound as
the other.

But the Pharisees went out and held a meeting against Jesus and discussed how they could get rid of him altogether.

JESUS RETIRES TO CONTINUE HIS WORK

12   But Jesus knew of this and he left the place.

15   Large crowds followed him and he healed them all, with the strict injunction that they should not make him conspicuous by their talk, thus fulfilling Isaiah's prophecy:

Behold, my servant whom I have chosen;
My beloved in whom my soul is well pleased:
I will put my Spirit upon him,
And he shall declare judgment to the Gentiles.
He shall not strive, nor cry aloud:
Neither shall any one hear his voice in the streets.
A bruised reed shall he not break,
And smoking flax shall he not quench,
Till he send forth judgment unto victory.
And in his name shall the Gentiles hope.

Then a devil-possessed man who could neither see nor speak was brought to Jesus. He healed him, and the one who had been both blind and dumb began to see and speak. At this the whole crowd went wild with excitement, and people kept saying, "Can this be the Son of David?"

THE PHARISEES DRAW AN EVIL CONCLUSION,
AND JESUS REBUKES THEM

12   But the Pharisees on hearing this remark said to each
24   other, "This man is only expelling devils because he is in league with Beelzebub, the prince of devils."

Jesus knew what they were thinking and said to them, "Any kingdom divided against itself is bound to collapse, and no town or household divided against itself can last for long. If it is Satan who is expelling Satan, then he is divided against himself—so how do you suppose that his kingdom can continue? And if I expel devils because I am an ally of Beelzebub, what alliance do your sons make when they do the same thing? They can settle that question for you! But if I am expelling devils by the Spirit of God, *then the Kingdom of God has swept over you unawares!* How do you suppose anyone could get into a strong man's house and

steal his property unless he first tied up the strong man? But
if he did that, he could ransack the whole place.

"The man who is not on my side is against me, and the
man who does not gather with me is really scattering. That
is why I tell you that men may be forgiven for every sin and
blasphemy, but blasphemy against the Spirit cannot be forgiven. A man may say a word against the Son of Man and
be forgiven, but whoever speaks against the Holy Spirit cannot be forgiven either in this world or in the world to come!

"You must choose between having a good tree with good
fruit or a rotten tree with rotten fruit. For you can tell a tree
at once by its fruit.

"You serpent's brood, how can you say anything good out
of your evil hearts? For a man's words depend on what fills
his heart. A good man gives out good—from the goodness
stored in his heart; a bad man gives out evil—from his store
of evil. I tell you that men will have to answer at the Day
of Judgment for every idle thing they say—for it is your
words that will acquit you, and your words that will condemn
you!"

JESUS REFUSES TO GIVE A SIGN

Then some of the Scribes and Pharisees said, "Master, we
want to see a sign from you." 12
38

"It is only an evil and unfaithful generation that craves
for a sign," replied Jesus, "and no sign will be given to it—
except the sign of the prophet Jonah. For just as Jonah was
in that great fish's belly for three days and nights, so will the
Son of Man be in the heart of the earth for three days and
nights. The men of Nineveh will stand up with this generation in the Judgment and will condemn it. For they did
repent when Jonah preached to them; and you have something greater than Jonah with you now! The Queen of the
South will stand up in the Judgment with this generation and
will condemn it. For she came from the ends of the earth to
listen to the wisdom of Solomon, and you have something
greater than the wisdom of Solomon with you now!

THE DANGER OF SPIRITUAL EMPTINESS

"When the evil spirit goes out of a man it wanders through
waterless places looking for rest and never finding it. Then 12
43

it says, 'I will go back to the house where I came from.'
When it arrives it finds it unoccupied, but cleaned and all in
order. Then it goes and collects as companions seven other
spirits more evil than itself, and they all go in and make themselves at home. The last state of that man is worse than the
first—and that is just what will happen to this evil generation."

JESUS AND HIS RELATIONS

12
46 While he was still talking to the crowds, his mother and
his brothers happened to be standing outside waiting to
speak to him. Somebody told him, "Look, your mother and
your brothers are outside wanting to speak to you." But
Jesus replied to the one who told him, "Who is my mother,
and who are my brothers?"; then with a gesture of his hand
towards his disciples he went on, "There! There are my
mother and brothers. For whoever does the will of my
Heavenly Father is brother and sister and mother to me."

JESUS TELLS THE PARABLE OF THE SEED

13
1 It was on the same day that Jesus went out of the house
and sat down by the lake-side. Such great crowds collected
round him that he got aboard a small boat and sat down while
all the people stood on the beach. He spoke to them at great
length in parables, and began:

"There was once a man who went out to sow. In his sow-
ing some of the seeds fell by the roadside and the birds
swooped down and gobbled them up. Some fell on stony
patches where they had very little soil. They sprang up
quickly in the shallow soil, but when the sun came up they
were scorched by the heat and withered away because they
had no roots. Some seeds fell among thorn-bushes and the
thorns grew up and choked the life out of them. But some
fell on good soil and produced a crop—some a hundred times
what had been sown, some sixty and some thirty times. The
man who has ears to hear should use them!"

At this the disciples approached him and asked, "Why do
you talk to them in parables?"

"Because you have been given the chance to understand
the secrets of the Kingdom of Heaven," replied Jesus, "but
they have not. You see, when a man has something he gets
more given to him till he has plenty. But if he has nothing

even his nothing will be taken away from him. This is why I speak to them in these parables; for they are going through life with their eyes open, but seeing nothing, and with their ears open, but understanding nothing of what they hear. They are the living fulfilment of Isaiah's prophecy which says:

By hearing ye shall hear, and shall in no wise understand;
And seeing ye shall see, and shall in no wise perceive;
For this people's heart is waxed gross,
And their ears are dull of hearing,
And their eyes they have closed;
Lest haply they should perceive with their eyes,
And hear with their ears,
And understand with their heart,
And should turn again,
And I should heal them.

"But you are fortunate enough to have eyes that see and ears that hear! Believe me, a great many prophets and good men have longed to see the things you are seeing and never saw them. Yes, and they longed to hear the things which you are hearing and never heard them.

"Now listen to the parable of the sower. When a man hears the message of the Kingdom and does not grasp it, the evil one comes and snatches away what was sown in his heart. This is like the seed sown by the roadside. The seed sown on the stony patches represents the man who hears the message and eagerly accepts it. But it has not taken root in him and does not last long—the moment trouble or persecution arises he has no more use for the message. The seed sown among the thorns represents the man who hears the message all right, and then the worries of this life and the deceptive pleasure of wealth choke the life out of it and so it produces no 'crop' in his life. But the seed sown on good soil is the man who both hears and understands the message. His life shows a good crop, a hundred, sixty or thirty times what was sown."

GOOD AND EVIL GROW SIDE BY SIDE IN THIS PRESENT WORLD

Then he put another parable before them. "The Kingdom 13 of Heaven," he said, "is like a man who sowed good seed in 24 his field. But while his men were asleep his enemy came and sowed weeds among the wheat, and went away. When the crop came up and ripened, the weeds appeared as well. Then the owner's servants came up to him and said, 'Sir, didn't you sow good seed in your field? Where did all these weeds come from?' 'Some blackguard has done this to spite me,' he replied. 'Do you want us then to go out and pull them all up?' said the servants. 'No,' he returned, 'if you pull up the weeds now, you would pull up the wheat with them. Let them both grow together till the harvest. And at harvest-time I shall tell the reapers, "Collect all the weeds first and tie them up in bundles ready to burn, but collect the wheat and store it in my barn." ' "

THE KINGDOM'S POWER OF GROWTH, AND
WIDESPREAD INFLUENCE

13 Then he put another parable before them: "The Kingdom
31 of Heaven is like a speck of mustard seed which a man took and sowed in his field. As a seed it is the smallest of them all, but it grows to be the biggest of all plants. It becomes a tree, big enough for birds to come and nest in its branches."

This is another of the parables he told them: "The Kingdom of Heaven is like yeast, taken by a woman and put into three basins of flour until the whole lot has risen."

All these things Jesus spoke to the crowd in parables, and he did not speak to them at all without using parables—to fulfil the prophecy:

I will open my mouth in parables;
I will utter things hidden from the foundation of the world.

JESUS AGAIN EXPLAINS A PARABLE TO
HIS DISCIPLES

13 Later, he left the crowds and went indoors, where his
36 disciples came and said, "Please explain to us the parable of the weeds in the field."

"The one who sows the good seed is the Son of Man," replied Jesus. "The field is the whole world. The good seed? That is the sons of the Kingdom, while the weeds are the sons of the evil one. The blackguard who sowed them is the Devil. The harvest is the end of this world. The reapers are angels.

"Just as weeds are gathered up and burned in the fire so will it happen at the end of this world. The Son of Man will send out his angels and they will uproot from the Kingdom everything that is spoiling it, and all those who live in defiance of its laws, and will throw them into the blazing furnace, where there will be tears and gnashing of teeth. Then the good will shine out like the sun in their Father's Kingdom. The man who has ears should use them!

MORE PICTURES OF THE KINGDOM OF HEAVEN

"Again, the Kingdom of Heaven is like some treasure 13 which has been buried in a field. A man finds it and buries 44 it again, and goes off overjoyed to sell all his possessions to buy himself that field.

"Or again, the Kingdom of Heaven is like a merchant searching for fine pearls. When he has found a single pearl of great value, he goes and sells all his possessions and buys it.

"Or the Kingdom of Heaven is like a big net thrown into the sea collecting all kinds of fish. When it is full, the fishermen haul it ashore and sit down and pick out the good ones for the barrels, but they throw away the bad. That is how it will be at the end of this world. The angels will go out and pick out the wicked from among the good and throw them into the blazing furnace, where there will be tears and bitter regret.

"Have you grasped all this?"

"Yes," they replied.

"You can see then," returned Jesus, "how every one who knows the Law and becomes a disciple of the Kingdom of Heaven is like a householder who can produce from his store both the new and the old."

JESUS IS NOT APPRECIATED IN HIS
NATIVE TOWN

When Jesus had finished these parables he left the place, 13 and came into his own country. Here he taught the people 53 in their own synagogue, till in their amazement they said, "Where does this man get this wisdom and these powers? He's only the carpenter's son. Isn't Mary his mother, and aren't James, Joseph, Simon and Judas his brothers? And aren't all his sisters living here with us? Where did he get all this?" And they were deeply offended with him.

But Jesus said to them, "No prophet goes unhonoured except in his own country and in his own home!"

And he performed very few miracles there because of their lack of faith.

HEROD'S GUILTY CONSCIENCE

14   About this time Herod, governor of the province, heard
1   the reports about Jesus and said to his men, "This must be John the Baptist: he has risen from the dead. That is why miraculous powers are at work in him."

For previously Herod had arrested John and had him bound and put in prison, all on account of Herodias, the wife of his brother Philip. For John had said to him, "It is not right for you to have this woman." Herod wanted to kill him for this, but he was afraid of the people, since they all thought John was a prophet. But during Herod's birthday celebrations Herodias' daughter delighted him by dancing before his guests, so much so that he swore to give her anything she liked to ask. And she, prompted by her mother, said, "I want you to give me, here and now, on a dish, the head of John the Baptist!" Herod was aghast at this, but because he had sworn in front of his guests, he gave orders that she should be given what she had asked. So he sent men and had John beheaded in the prison. Then his head was carried in on a dish and presented to the young girl who handed it to her mother. Later John's disciples came, took his body and buried it. Then they went and told the news to Jesus. When he heard it he went away by boat to a deserted place, quite alone.

JESUS FEEDS A TIRED AND HUNGRY CROWD

14   Then the crowds heard of his departure and followed him
13b   out of the towns on foot. When Jesus emerged from his retreat he saw a vast crowd and was very deeply moved and cured the sick ones among them. As evening fell his disciples came to him and said, "We are right in the wilds here and it is very late. Send away these crowds now, so that they can go into the villages and buy themselves food."

"There's no need for them to go away," returned Jesus. "You give them something to eat!"

"But we haven't anything here," they told him, "except five loaves and two fish." To which Jesus replied, "Bring them here to me."

He told the crowd to sit down on the grass. Then he took the five loaves and two fish in his hands, and, looking up to Heaven, he thanked God, broke the loaves and passed them to his disciples who handed them to the crowd. Everybody ate and was satisfied. Afterwards they collected twelve baskets full of pieces which were left over. Those who ate numbered about five thousand men, apart from the women and children.

JESUS AGAIN SHOWS HIS POWER OVER THE
FORCES OF NATURE

Directly after this Jesus insisted on his disciples getting 14 aboard their boat and going on ahead to the other side, while 22 he himself sent the crowds home. And when he had sent them away he went up the mountain quite alone, to pray. When it grew late he was there by himself while the boat was by now a long way from the shore at the mercy of the waves, for the wind was dead against them. In the small hours Jesus went out to them, walking on the water of the lake. When the disciples caught sight of him walking on the water they were terrified. "It's a ghost!" they said, and screamed with fear. But at once Jesus spoke to them. "It's all right! It's I myself, don't be afraid!"

"Lord, if it's really you," said Peter, "tell me to walk towards you on the water."

"Come on, then," replied Jesus.

And Peter stepped down from the boat and did walk on the water, making for Jesus. But when he saw the fury of the wind he panicked and began to sink, calling out, "Lord, save me!" At once Jesus reached out and caught him, saying, "You little-faith! What made you lose your nerve like that?" Then, when they were both aboard the boat, the wind dropped. The whole crew came then and knelt down before Jesus crying, "You are indeed the Son of God!"

When they had crossed over to the other side of the lake,

they landed at Gennesaret, and when the men of that place
had recognised him, they sent word to the whole surrounding country and brought all the diseased to him. They implored him to let them "touch just the edge of his cloak,"
and all those who did so were cured.

SUPERFICIAL AND TRUE CLEANLINESS

15   Then some of the Scribes and Pharisees from Jerusalem
1 came and asked Jesus, "Why do your disciples break our
ancient tradition and eat their food without washing their
hands properly first?"

"Tell me," replied Jesus, "why does your tradition break
God's commandment? For God said, '*Honour thy father and
thy mother,*' and '*He that speaketh evil of father or mother,
let him die the death.*' But you say that if a man tells his
parents, 'Whatever use I might have been to you is now given
to God,' then he owes no further duty to his parents. And so
your tradition empties the commandment of God of all its
meaning. You hypocrites! Isaiah described you beautifully
when he said:

This people honoureth me with their lips;
But their heart is far from me.
But in vain do they worship me,
Teaching as their doctrines the precepts of men."

Then he called the crowd to him and said, "Listen, and
understand this thoroughly! It is not what goes *into* a man's
mouth that makes him common or unclean. It is what comes
out of a man's mouth that makes him unclean."

15   Later his disciples came to him and said, "Do you know
12 that the Pharisees are deeply offended by what you said?"

"Every plant which my Heavenly Father did not plant
will be pulled up by the roots," returned Jesus. "Let them
alone. They are blind guides, and when one blind man leads
another blind man they will both end up in the ditch!"

"Explain this parable to us," broke in Peter.

"Are even you too still unable to grasp things like this?"
replied Jesus. "Don't you see that whatever goes *into* the
mouth passes into the stomach and then out of the body
altogether? But the things that come *out* of a man's mouth
come from his heart and mind, and it is they that really

make a man unclean. For it is from a man's mind that evil thoughts arise—murder, adultery, lust, theft, perjury and blasphemy. These are the things which make a man unclean, not eating without washing his hands properly."

A GENTILE'S FAITH IN JESUS

Jesus left that place and retired into the Tyre and Sidon 15 district. There a Canaanite woman from these parts came to 21 him crying at the top of her voice,

"Lord, have pity on me! My daughter is in a terrible state —a devil has got into her!"

Jesus made no answer, and the disciples came up to him and said, "Do send her away—she's still following us and calling out."

"I was only sent," replied Jesus, "to the lost sheep of the house of Israel."

Then the woman came and knelt at his feet. "Do please help me, Lord," she said.

"It is not right, you know," Jesus replied, "to take the children's food and throw it to the dogs."

"Yes, Lord, I know, but even the dogs live on the scraps that fall from their master's table!"

"You certainly don't lack faith," returned Jesus, "it shall be as you wish."

And at that moment her daughter was cured.

JESUS HEALS AND FEEDS VAST CROWDS
OF PEOPLE

Jesus left there, walked along the shore of the lake of 15 Galilee, then climbed the hill and sat down. And great crowds 29 came to him, bringing with them people who were lame, blind, dumb, maimed and many others. They simply put them down at his feet and he healed them. The result was that the people were astonished at seeing dumb men speak, maimed men healed, lame men walking about and blind men having recovered their sight. And they praised the God of Israel.

But Jesus quietly called his disciples to him. "My heart goes out to this crowd," he said. "They've stayed with me three days now and have no more food. I don't want to send them home without anything or they will collapse on the way."

"Where could we find enough food to feed such a crowd in this deserted spot?" the disciples replied.

"How many loaves have you got?" asked Jesus.

"Seven, and a few small fish."

Then Jesus told the crowd to sit down comfortably on the ground. And when he had taken the seven loaves and the fish into his hands, he broke them with a prayer of thanksgiving and gave them to the disciples to pass on to the people. Everybody ate and was satisfied, and they picked up seven baskets full of pieces left over. Those who ate numbered four thousand men apart from women and children. Then Jesus sent the crowds home, boarded the boat and arrived at the district of Magdala.

JESUS AGAIN REFUSES TO GIVE A SIGN

16   Once the Pharisees and the Sadducees arrived together to
1   test him, and asked him to give them a sign from Heaven. But he replied, "When the evening comes you say, 'Ah, fine weather—the sky is red.' In the morning you say, 'There will be a storm today, the sky is red and threatening.' Yes, you know how to interpret the look of the sky but you have no idea how to interpret the signs of the times! A wicked and unfaithful age insists on a sign; and it will not be given any sign at all but that of the prophet Jonah." And he turned on his heel and left them.

HE IS MISUNDERSTOOD BY THE DISCIPLES

16   Then his disciples came to him on the other side of the lake,
5   forgetting to bring any bread with them. "Keep your eyes open," said Jesus to them, "and be on your guard against the 'yeast' of the Pharisees and Sadducees!" But they were arguing with each other, and saying, "We forgot to bring the bread." When Jesus saw this he said to them, "Why all this argument among yourselves about not bringing any bread, you little-faiths? Don't you understand yet, or have you forgotten the five loaves and the five thousand, and how many baskets you took up afterwards; or the seven loaves and the four thousand and how many baskets you took up then? I wonder why you don't yet understand that I wasn't talking about bread at all when I told you to beware of the yeast of the Pharisees and Sadducees." Then they grasped

the fact that he had not told them to beware of yeast in the ordinary sense but of the teaching of the Pharisees and Sadducees.

PETER'S BOLD AFFIRMATION

When Jesus reached the Caesarea-Philippi district he asked 16
his disciples a question. "Who do people say the Son of Man 13
is?"

"Well, some say John the Baptist," they told him. "Some say Elijah, others Jeremiah or one of the prophets."

"But what about you?" he said to them. "Who do you say that I am?"

Simon Peter answered, "You? You are Christ, the Son of the Living God!"

"Simon, son of Jonah, you are a fortunate man indeed!" said Jesus, "for it was not your own nature but my Heavenly Father Who has revealed this truth to you! Now I tell you that you are Peter the rock, and it is on this rock that I am going to found my Church and the gates of Hell will be powerless against it. I will give you the keys of the Kingdom of Heaven; whatever you bind on earth will be held bound in Heaven and whatever you loose on earth will be held loosed in Heaven!" Then he impressed on his disciples that they should not tell anyone that he was Christ.

JESUS SPEAKS ABOUT HIS PASSION, AND
THE COST OF FOLLOWING HIM

From that time onwards Jesus began to explain to his dis- 16
ciples that he would have to go to Jerusalem, and endure 21
much suffering from the elders, Chief Priests and Scribes, and finally be killed; and be raised to life again on the third day.

Then Peter took him on one side and started to remonstrate with him over this. "God bless you, Master! Nothing like this must happen to you!" Then Jesus turned round and said to Peter, "Out of my way, Satan! . . . you stand right in my path, Peter, when you look at things from man's point of view and not from God's."

Then Jesus said to his disciples, "If anyone wants to follow in my footsteps he must give up all right to himself, take up his cross and follow me. For the man who wants to save his life will lose it; but the man who loses his life for my sake

will find it. For what good is it for a man to gain the whole
world at the price of his own soul? What could a man offer
to buy back his soul once he had lost it?

"For the Son of Man will come in the glory of his Father
and in the company of His angels and then he will repay
every man for what he has done. Believe me, there are some
standing here today who will know nothing of death till they
have seen the Son of Man coming as King."

THREE DISCIPLES GLIMPSE THE GLORY
OF CHRIST

17   Six days later Jesus chose Peter, James and his brother
1   John, to accompany him up a high mountain where they were
quite alone. There his whole appearance changed before their
eyes, his face shining like the sun and his clothes as white as
light. Then Moses and Elijah were seen talking to Jesus.

"Lord," exclaimed Peter, "it is wonderful for us to be
here! If you like I could make three shelters, one each for
you and Moses and Elijah——"

But while he was still talking a bright cloud overshadowed
them all and a Voice came out of the cloud:

"This is My dearly loved Son in Whom I am well pleased.
Hear His words!"

When they heard this Voice the disciples fell on their
faces, overcome with fear. Then Jesus came up to them and
touched them.

"Get up and don't be frightened," he said. And as they
raised their eyes there was no one to be seen but Jesus himself.

On the way down from the mountain Jesus warned them
not to tell anyone about what they had seen until after the
Son of Man should have risen from the dead. Then the disciples demanded, "Why is it, then, that the Scribes always
say Elijah must come first?"

"Yes, Elijah does come first," replied Jesus, "and begins
the world's reformation. But I tell you that Elijah has come
already and men did not recognise him. They did what they
liked with him, and they will do the same to the Son of
Man."

Then they realised that he had been referring to John the
Baptist.

JESUS HEALS AN EPILEPTIC BOY

When they returned to the crowds again a man came and   17
knelt in front of Jesus. "Lord, do have pity on my son," he   14
said, "for he is a lunatic and is in a terrible state. He is always
falling into the fire or into the water. I did bring him to
your disciples but they couldn't cure him."

"You really are an unbelieving and difficult people," Jesus
returned. "How long must I be with you, and how long must
I put up with you? Bring him here to me!"

Then Jesus reprimanded the evil spirit and it went out of
the boy, who was cured from that moment.

Afterwards the disciples approached Jesus privately and
asked, "Why weren't we able to get rid of it?"

"Because you have so little faith," replied Jesus. "I assure
you that if you have as much faith as a grain of mustard-
seed you can say to this mountain, 'Up you get and move
over there!' and it will move—you will find nothing is impossible."

As they went about together in Galilee, Jesus told them,
"The Son of Man is going to be handed over to the power
of men, and they will kill him. And on the third day he will
be raised to life again." This greatly distressed the disciples.

JESUS PAYS THE TEMPLE-TAX—IN
AN UNUSUAL WAY!

Then when they arrived at Capernaum the Temple tax-   17
collectors came up and said to Peter, "Your master doesn't   24
pay Temple-tax, we presume?"

"Oh yes, he does!" replied Peter. Later when he went into
the house Jesus anticipated what he was going to say. "What
do *you* think, Simon?" he said. "Who do the kings of this
world get their rates and taxes from—their own people or
from others?"

"From others," replied Peter.

"Then the family is exempt," Jesus told him. "Yet we don't
want to give offence to these people, so go down to the lake
and throw in your hook. Take the first fish that bites, open
his mouth and you'll find a coin. Take that and give it to
them, for both of us."

JESUS COMMENDS THE SIMPLICITY
OF CHILDREN

18   It was at this time that the disciples came to Jesus with
1   the question, "Who is really greatest in the Kingdom of
Heaven?" Jesus called a little child to his side and set him
on his feet in the middle of them all. "Believe me," he said,
"unless you change your whole outlook and become like little
children you will never enter the Kingdom of Heaven. It
is the man who can be as humble as this little child who is
'greatest' in the Kingdom of Heaven.

"Anyone who welcomes one child like this for my sake is
welcoming me. But if anyone leads astray one of these little
children who believe in me he would be better off thrown
into the depths of the sea with a mill-stone hung round his
neck! Alas for the world with its pitfalls! In the nature of
things there must be pitfalls, yet alas for the man who is
responsible for them!

THE RIGHT WAY MAY MEAN COSTLY SACRIFICE

18   "If your hand or your foot is a hindrance to you, cut it off
8   and throw it away. It is a good thing to go into Life maimed
or crippled—rather than to have both hands and feet and be
thrown on to the everlasting fire. Yes, and if your eye leads
you astray, tear it out and throw it away. It is a good thing
to go one-eyed into Life—rather than to have both your
eyes and be thrown on the fire of the rubbish-heap.

"Be careful that you never despise a single one of these
little ones—for I tell you that they have angels who see my
Father's face continually in Heaven.

"What do you think? If a man has a hundred sheep and
one wanders away from the rest, won't he leave the ninety-
nine on the mountain-side and set out to look for the one
who has wandered away? Yes, and if he should chance to
find it I assure you he is more delighted over that one than
he is over the ninety-nine who never wandered away. You
can understand then that it is never the Will of your Father
in Heaven that a single one of these little ones should be lost.

RECONCILIATION MUST ALWAYS BE ATTEMPTED

18   "But if your brother wrongs you, go and have it out with
15   him at once—just between the two of you. If he will listen

to you, you have won him back as your brother. But if he
will not listen to you, take one or two others with you so that
everything that is said may have the support of two or three
witnesses. And if he still won't pay any attention, tell the
matter to the church. And if he won't even listen to the
church then he must be to you just like a pagan—or a tax-
collector!

THE CONNECTION BETWEEN EARTHLY CONDUCT
AND SPIRITUAL REALITY

"Believe me, whatever you bind upon earth will be held 18
bound in Heaven, and whatever you loose on earth will be 18
held loosed in Heaven.

"And I tell you once more that if two of you on earth agree
in asking for anything it will be granted to you by my
Heavenly Father. For wherever two or three people come
together in my name, I am there, right among them!"

THE NECESSITY FOR FORGIVENESS

Then Peter approached him with the question, "Master, 18
how many times can my brother wrong me and I must for- 21
give him? Would seven times be enough?"

"No," replied Jesus, "not seven times, but seventy times
seven! For the Kingdom of Heaven is like a king who
decided to settle his accounts with his servants. When he
had started calling in his accounts, a man was brought to
him who owed him thousands of dollars. And when it was
plain that he had no means of repaying the debt, his master
gave orders for him to be sold as a slave, and his wife and
children and all his possessions as well, and the money to be
paid over. At this the servant fell on his knees before
his master, 'Oh, be patient with me!' he cried, 'and I will pay
you back every penny!' Then his master was moved with
pity for him, set him free and cancelled the debt.

"But when this same servant had left his master's presence,
he found one of his fellow-servants who owed him a few
dollars. He grabbed him and seized him by the throat,
crying, 'Pay up what you owe me!' At this his fellow-servant
fell down at his feet, and implored him, 'Oh, be patient with
me, and I will pay you back!' But he refused and went
out and had him put in prison until he should repay the
debt.

"When the other fellow-servants saw what had happened, they were horrified and went and told their master the whole incident. Then his master called him in.

"'You wicked servant!' he said. 'Didn't I cancel all that debt when you begged me to do so? Oughtn't you to have taken pity on your fellow-servant as I, your master, took pity on you?' And his master in anger handed him over to the jailers till he should repay the whole debt. This is how my Heavenly Father will treat you unless you each forgive your brother from your heart."

THE DIVINE PRINCIPLE OF MARRIAGE

19 When Jesus had finished talking on these matters, he left
1 Galilee and went on to the district of Judaea on the far side of the Jordan. Vast crowds followed him there, and he cured them.

Then the Pharisees arrived with a test-question.

"Is it right," they asked, "for a man to divorce his wife on any grounds whatever?"

"Haven't you read," he answered, "that the One Who created them from the beginning made them male and female and said: *'For this cause shall a man leave his father and mother, and shall cleave to his wife; and the twain shall become one flesh?'* So they are no longer two separate people but one. No man therefore must separate what God has joined together."

"Then why," they retorted, "did Moses command us to give a written divorce-notice and dismiss the woman?"

"It was because you knew so little of the meaning of love that Moses allowed you to divorce your wives! But that was not the original principle. I tell you that anyone who divorces his wife on any grounds except her unfaithfulness and marries some other woman commits adultery."

His disciples said to him, "If that is a man's position with his wife, it is not worth getting married!"

"It is not everybody who can live up to this," replied Jesus, "—only those who have a special gift. For some are incapable of marriage from birth, some are made incapable by the action of men, and some have made themselves so for the sake of the Kingdom of Heaven. Let the man who can accept what I have said accept it."

JESUS WELCOMES CHILDREN

Then some little children were brought to him, so that   19
he could put his hands on them and pray for them. The   13
disciples frowned on the parents' action but Jesus said,

"You must let little children come to me, and you must
never stop them. The Kingdom of Heaven is made of little
children like these!" Then he laid his hands on them and
went on his way.

JESUS SHOWS THAT KEEPING THE
COMMANDMENTS IS NOT ENOUGH

Then it happened that a man came up to him and   19
said, "Master, what good thing must I do to secure eternal   16
life?"

I wonder why you ask me about what is good?" Jesus
answered him. "Only One is good. But if you want to enter
that life you must keep the commandments."

"Which ones?" he asked.

"*Thou shalt do no murder, Thou shalt not commit adultery, Thou shalt not steal, Thou shalt not bear false witness,
Honour thy father and thy mother: and Thou shalt love thy
neighbour as thyself*," replied Jesus.

"I have carefully kept all these," returned the young man.
"What is still missing in my life?"

Then Jesus told him, "If you want to be perfect, go now
and sell your property and give the money away to the poor
—you will have riches in Heaven. Then come and follow
me!"

When the young man heard that he turned away crest-
fallen, for he was very wealthy.

Then Jesus remarked to his disciples, "Believe me, a rich
man will find it very difficult to enter the Kingdom of
Heaven. Yes, I repeat, a camel could more easily squeeze
through the eye of a needle than a rich man get into the
Kingdom of God!"

The disciples were simply amazed to hear this, and said,
"Then who can possibly be saved?"

Jesus looked steadily at them and replied, "Humanly
speaking it is impossible; but with God anything is possible!"

JESUS DECLARES THAT SACRIFICE FOR THE
KINGDOM WILL BE REPAID

19   At this Peter exclaimed, "Look, we have left everything
27 and followed you. What is that going to be worth to us?"

"Believe me," said Jesus, "when I tell you that in the next
world, when the Son of Man shall sit down on his glorious
throne, you who have followed me will also sit on twelve
thrones and become judges of the twelve tribes of Israel.
Every man who has left houses or brothers or sisters or father
or mother or children or land for my sake will receive it all
back many times over, and will inherit eternal life. But
many who are first now will be last then—and the last first!

"For the Kingdom of Heaven is like a farmer going out
early in the morning to hire labourers for his vineyard. He
agreed with them on a wage of a dollar a day and sent
them to work. About nine o'clock he went out and saw some
others standing about in the market-place with nothing to
do. 'You go to the vineyard too,' he said to them, 'and I
will pay you a fair wage.' And off they went. At about midday and again at about three o'clock in the afternoon he went
out and did the same thing. Then about five o'clock he went
out and found some others standing about. 'Why are you
standing about here all day doing nothing?' he asked them.
'Because no one has employed us,' they replied. 'You go off
into the vineyard as well, then,' he said.

"When evening came the owner of the vineyard said to his
foreman, 'Call the labourers and pay them their wages, beginning with the last and ending with the first.' So those
who were engaged at five o'clock came up and received a
dollar a man. But when the first to be employed came
they reckoned they would get more, but they also received
a dollar a man. As they took their money they grumbled
at the farmer and said, 'These last fellows have only put in
one hour's work and you've treated them exactly the same
as us who have gone through all the hard work and heat of
the day!'

"But he replied to one of them, 'My friend, I'm not being
unjust to you. Wasn't our agreement for a dollar a day?
Take your money and go home. It is my wish to give the
late-comer as much as I give you. May I not do what I like

with what belongs to me? Must you be jealous because I am generous?'

"So, many who are last now will be first then and first last."

JESUS' FINAL JOURNEY TO JERUSALEM

Then, as he was going up to Jerusalem, Jesus took the 20 twelve disciples aside and spoke to them as they walked 17 along. "Listen, we are now going up to Jerusalem and the Son of Man will be handed over to the Chief Priests and the Scribes—and they will condemn him to death. They will hand him over to the heathen to ridicule and flog and crucify. And on the third day he will be raised!"

At this point the mother of the sons of Zebedee arrived with her sons and knelt in front of Jesus to ask him a favour.

"What is it you want?" he asked her.

"Please say that these two sons of mine may sit one on each side of you when you are King!" she said.

"You don't know what it is you are asking," replied Jesus. "Can you two drink what I have to drink?"

"Yes, we can," they answered.

"Ah, you will indeed 'drink my drink,'" Jesus told them, "but as for sitting on either side of me, that is not for me to grant—that belongs to those for whom my Father has planned it."

When the other ten heard of this incident they were highly indignant with the two brothers.

But Jesus called them to him and said,

"You know that the rulers of the heathen lord it over them and that their great ones have absolute power? But it must not be so among you. No, whoever among you wants to be great must become the servant of you all, and if he wants to be first among you he must be your slave—just as the Son of Man did not come to be served but to serve, and to give his life to set many others free."

HE RESTORES SIGHT TO TWO BLIND MEN

A great crowd followed them as they were leaving Jericho, 20 and two blind men who were sitting by the roadside, hearing 29 that it was Jesus who was passing by, cried out, "Have pity on us, Lord, you Son of David!" The crowd tried to hush them up, but this only made them cry out more loudly still, "Have pity on us, Lord, you Son of David!"

Jesus stood quite still and called out to them, "What do you want me to do for you?"

"Lord, do something to make us see!"

And Jesus, deeply moved with pity, touched their eyes. At once they could see again, and they followed him.

JESUS' FINAL ENTRY INTO JERUSALEM

21 As they approached Jerusalem and came to Bethphage
1 and the Mount of Olives, Jesus sent two disciples ahead telling them, "Go into the village in front of you and you will at once find there an ass tethered, and a colt with her. Untie them and bring them to me. Should anyone say anything to you, you are to say, 'Their master needs them,' and he will send them immediately."

All this happened to fulfil the prophet's saying—

Tell ye the daughter of Zion,
Behold, thy King cometh unto thee,
Meek, and riding upon an ass,
And upon a colt the foal of an ass.

So the disciples went off and followed Jesus' instructions. They brought the ass and the colt, and put their cloaks on them, and Jesus took his seat. Then most of the crowd spread their own cloaks on the road, while others cut down branches from the trees and spread them in his path. The crowds who went in front of him and the crowds who followed behind him all shouted, "God save the Son of David! Blessed is the man who comes in the Name of the Lord! Heaven bless him!"

And as he entered Jerusalem a shock ran through the whole city. "Who *is* this?" men cried. "This is Jesus the prophet," replied the crowd, "the man from Nazareth in Galilee!"

Then Jesus went into the Temple and drove out all the buyers and sellers there. He overturned the tables of the money-changers and the benches of those who sold doves, crying—

"It is written, '*My house shall be called a house of prayer.*' But you have turned it into a thieves' kitchen!"

And there in the Temple the blind and the lame came to him, and he healed them. But when the Chief Priests and the Scribes saw the wonderful things he had done, and that children were shouting in the Temple the words, "God save the Son of David," they were highly indignant. "Can't you hear what these children are saying?" they asked Jesus.

"Yes," he replied, "and haven't you ever read the words, *'Out of the mouth of babes and sucklings thou hast perfected praise'?"* And he turned on his heel and went out of the city to Bethany, where he spent the night.

HIS STRANGE WORDS TO THE FIG-TREE

In the morning he came back early to the city and felt hungry. He saw a fig-tree growing by the side of the road but when he got to it he discovered there was nothing on it but leaves. 21
18

"No more fruit shall ever grow on you!" he said to it, and all at once the fig-tree withered away. When the disciples saw this happen they were simply amazed. "How on earth did the fig-tree wither away quite suddenly like that?" they asked.

"Believe me," replied Jesus, "if you have faith and have no doubts in your heart, you will not only do this to a fig-tree but even if you should say to this mountain, 'Get up and throw yourself into the sea,' it will happen! Everything you ask for in prayer, if you have faith, you will receive."

JESUS MEETS A QUESTION WITH A
COUNTER-QUESTION

Then when he had entered the Temple and was in the middle of teaching, the Chief Priests and Jewish elders came up to him and said, "What authority have you for what you're doing, and who gave you permission?" 21
23

"I am also going to ask you one question," Jesus replied to them, "and if you answer it I will tell you what authority I have for what I do. John's baptism, now, did it come from Heaven or was it purely human?"

At this they began arguing among themselves, "If we say, 'It came from Heaven,' he will say to us, 'Then why didn't you believe in him?' If on the other hand we should say, 'It

was purely human'—well, frankly, we are afraid of the
people—for all of them consider John was a prophet."

So they answered Jesus, "We do not know."

"Then I will not tell you by what authority I do these
things!" returned Jesus. "But what is your opinion about
this? There was a man with two sons. He went to the first
and said, 'Go and work in my vineyard today, my son.' He
said, 'All right, sir'—but he never went near it. Then the
father approached the second son with the same request. He
said, 'I won't.' But afterwards he changed his mind and
went. Which of these two did what their father wanted?"

"The second one," they replied.

"Yes, and I tell you that tax-collectors and prostitutes are
going into the Kingdom of God in front of you!" retorted
Jesus. "For John came to you as a saint, and you did not
believe him—yet the tax-collectors and the prostitutes did!
And, even after seeing that, you would not change your
minds and believe him.

JESUS TELLS A POINTED STORY

21
33
"Now listen to another story. There was once a man, a
land-owner, who planted a vineyard, fenced it round, dug
out a hole for the wine-press and built a watch-tower.
Then he let it out to farm-workers and went abroad. When
the vintage-time approached he sent his servants to the
farm-workers to receive his share of the proceeds. But they
took the servants, beat up one, killed another, and drove off
a third with stones. Then he sent some more servants, a
larger party than the first, but they treated them just the
same. Finally he sent his own son, thinking, 'They will
respect my son.' Yet when the farm-workers saw the son
they said to each other, 'This fellow is the future owner.
Come on, let's kill him and we shall get everything that would
have gone to him!' So they took him, threw him out of the
vineyard and killed him. Now when the owner of the vineyard returns, what will he do to those farm-workers?"

"He will kill those scoundrels without mercy," they replied, "and will let the vineyard out to other tenants, who
will pay him his share at the proper time."

"And have you never read these words of Scripture," said
Jesus to them:

The stone which the builders rejected,
The same was made the head of the corner:
This was from the Lord,
And it is marvellous in our eyes?

"Here, I tell you, lies the reason why the Kingdom of God is going to be taken away from you and given to a people who will produce its proper fruit."

When the Chief Priests and the Pharisees heard his parables they realized that he was speaking about them. They tried to think of a way of getting him arrested, but they were afraid of the crowds, who regarded him as a prophet.

THE KINGDOM IS NOT TO BE LIGHTLY DISREGARDED

Then Jesus began to talk to them again in a series of parables. **22**
1

"The Kingdom of Heaven," he said, "is like a king who arranged a wedding for his son. He sent his servants to summon those who had been invited to the festivities, but they refused to come. Then he tried again; he sent some more servants, saying to them, 'Tell those who have been invited, "Here is my wedding-breakfast all ready, my bullocks and fat cattle have been slaughtered and everything is prepared. Come along to the festivities."' But they took no notice of this and went off, one to his farm, and another to his business. As for the rest, they got hold of the servants, treated them disgracefully, and finally killed them. At this the king was very angry and sent his troops and killed those murderers and burned down their city. Then he said to his servants, 'The wedding feast is quite ready, but those who were invited were not good enough for it. So go off now to all the street corners and invite everyone you find there to the feast.' So the servants went out on to the streets and collected together all that they found, bad and good alike. And the hall became filled with guests. Then the king came in to have a look at them as they sat there, and he noticed a man not dressed for a wedding. 'How did you come in here, my friend,' he said to him, 'without being properly dressed for the wedding?' And the man was speechless. Then the king said to the ushers, 'Tie him up and throw him into the

darkness outside. He can weep and gnash his teeth there!'
For many are invited but few are chosen."

A CLEVER TRAP—AND A PENETRATING
ANSWER

22   Then the Pharisees went off and discussed how they could
15 trap him in argument. Eventually they sent their disciples
with some of the Herod-party to say this, "Master, we
know that you are an honest man who teaches the way
of God faithfully and that you are not swayed by men's
opinion of you. Obviously you don't care for human
approval. Now tell us—*Is it right to pay taxes to Caesar or
not?*"

But Jesus knowing their evil intention said, "Why try this
trick on me, you frauds! Show me the money you pay the
tax with." They handed him a coin, and he said to them,
"Whose face is this and whose name is in the inscription?"

"Caesar's," they said.

"Then give to Caesar," he replied, "what belongs to
Caesar and to God what belongs to God!"

This reply staggered them and they left him alone and
went away.

JESUS EXPOSES THE IGNORANCE OF
THE SADDUCEES

22   On the same day some Sadducees (who deny that there
23 is any resurrection) approached Jesus with this question:
"Master, Moses said if a man should die without any children,
his brother should marry his widow and raise up a family for
him. Now, we have a case of seven brothers. The first one
married and died, and since he had no family he left his wife
to his brother. The same thing happened with the second
and the third, right up to the seventh. Last of all the woman
herself died. Now in this 'resurrection,' whose wife will she
be of these seven men—for she belonged to all of them?"

"You are very wide of the mark," replied Jesus to them,
"for you are ignorant of both the Scriptures and the power of
God. For in the Resurrection there is no such thing as marrying or being married—men live like the angels in Heaven.
And as for the matter of the resurrection of the dead,
haven't you ever read what was once said to you by God

Himself, 'I am the God of Abraham, the God of Isaac and the God of Jacob'? God is not a God of the dead but of the living!" When the crowds heard this they were astounded at his teaching.

THE GREATEST COMMANDMENTS IN THE LAW

When the Pharisees heard that he had silenced the Sad- 22 ducees they came up to him in a body, and one of them, an 36 expert in the Law, put this test-question: "Master, what are we to consider the Law's greatest commandment?"

Jesus answered him, " 'Thou shalt love the Lord thy God with all thy heart, and with all thy soul and with all thy mind.' This is the first and great commandment. And there is a second like it: 'Thou shalt love thy neighbour as thyself.' The whole of the Law and the prophets depends on these two commandments."

JESUS PUTS AN UNANSWERABLE QUESTION

Then Jesus asked the assembled Pharisees this question: 22 "What is your opinion about Christ? Whose son is he?" 41

"The Son of David," they answered.

"How then," returned Jesus, "does David when inspired by the Spirit call him Lord? He says—

The Lord said unto my *Lord*,
Sit thou on my right hand,
Till I put thine enemies underneath thy feet?

If David then calls him Lord, how can he be his son?"

Nobody was able to answer this and from that day on no one dared to ask him any further questions.

HE PUBLICLY WARNS PEOPLE AGAINST
THEIR RELIGIOUS LEADERS

Then Jesus addressed the crowds and his disciples. "The 23 Scribes and the Pharisees teach the Mosaic Law," he told 1 them, "so you must do what they tell you and follow their instructions. But you must not imitate their lives! For they preach and do not practise. They pile up back-breaking burdens and lay them on other men's shoulders—yet they themselves will not lift a finger to shift them. Their whole lives are planned with an eye to effect. They increase the size of their phylacteries * and lengthen the tassels of their robes; they love seats of honour at dinners and front places in the synagogues. They love to be greeted with respect in public places and to have men call them 'Rabbi!' Don't you ever be called 'Rabbi'—you have only one Teacher, and all of you are brothers. And don't call any human being 'father' —for you have one Father and He is in Heaven. And you must not let people call you 'leaders'—you have only one Leader, Christ! The only 'superior' among you is the one who serves the others. For every man who promotes himself will be humbled, and every man who learns to be humble will find promotion.

"But alas for you, you Scribes and Pharisees, play-actors that you are! You lock the doors of the Kingdom of Heaven in men's faces; you will not go in yourselves and you will not allow those at the door to go inside.

"Alas for you, you Scribes and Pharisees, play-actors! You scour sea and land to make a single convert, and then you turn him into twice as much a son of perdition as yourselves.

"Alas for you, you blind leaders! You say, 'If anyone swears by the Temple it doesn't count, but if he swears by the gold of the Temple he is bound by his oath.' You blind idiots, which is the more important, the gold or the Temple which sanctifies the gold? And you say, 'If anyone swears by the altar it doesn't count, but if he swears by the gift placed on the altar he is bound by his oath.' Have you no eyes— which is more important, the gift, or the altar which sanctifies the gift? Any man who swears by the altar is swearing by the altar and whatever is offered upon it; and anyone who swears by the Temple is swearing by the Temple and by Him Who dwells in it; and anyone who swears by Heaven is swearing by the Throne of God and by the One Who sits upon that Throne.

"Alas for you, Scribes and Pharisees, you utter frauds! For you pay your tithe on mint and aniseed and cummin, and neglect the things which carry far more weight in the Law— justice, mercy and good faith. These are the things you should have observed—without neglecting the others. You call yourselves leaders, and yet you can't see an inch before

---

* Phylacteries: strips of parchment inscribed with texts from the Law, worn on the arm and forehead.

your noses. You filter out a mosquito and swallow a camel.

"What miserable frauds you are, you Scribes and Pharisees! You clean the outside of the cup and the dish, while the inside is full of greed and self-indulgence. Can't you see, Pharisee? First wash the inside of a cup or a plate, and then you can polish the outside.

"Alas for you, you hypocritical Scribes and Pharisees! You are like white-washed tombs, which look fine on the outside but inside are full of dead men's bones and all kinds of rottenness. In the same way you appear like good men on the outside—but inside you are a mass of pretence and wickedness.

"What miserable frauds you are, you Scribes and Pharisees! You build tombs for the prophets, and decorate monuments for good men of the past, and then say, 'If we had lived in the times of our ancestors we should never have joined in the killing of the prophets.' Yes, 'your ancestors'—*that* shows you to be sons indeed of those who murdered the prophets. Go ahead then, and finish off what your ancestors tried to do. You serpents, you viper's brood, how do you think you are going to avoid being condemned to the rubbish-heap? Listen to this: 'I send unto you prophets and wise and learned men; and some of these you will kill and crucify, others you will flog in your synagogues and hunt from town to town.' So that on your hands is all the innocent blood spilt on this earth, from the blood of Abel the good to the blood of Zachariah, Barachiah's son, whom you murdered between the sanctuary and the altar. Yes, I tell you that all this will be laid at the doors of this generation.

JESUS MOURNS OVER JERUSALEM, AND FORETELLS ITS DESTRUCTION

"Oh, Jerusalem, Jerusalem! You murder the prophets and 23 stone the messengers that are sent to you. How often have I 37 longed to gather your children round me like a bird gathering her brood together under her wings—and you would never have it. Now all you have left is your house—deserted. I tell you that you will never see me again till the day when you cry, 'Blessed is He Who comes in the Name of the Lord!'"

Then Jesus went out of the Temple and was walking away

when his disciples came up and drew his attention to its buildings. "You see all these?" replied Jesus. "I tell you every stone will be thrown down till there is not a single one left standing upon another."

And as he was sitting on the slope of the Mount of Olives his disciples came to him privately and said, "Tell us, when will this happen? What will be the signal for your coming and the end of this world?"

"Be careful that no one misleads you," returned Jesus, "for many men will come in my name saying 'I am Christ,' and they will mislead many. You will hear of wars and rumours of wars—don't let yourselves be alarmed. All these things have to happen, but that is not the end. For one nation will rise in arms against another, and one kingdom against another, and there will be famines and earthquakes in different parts of the world. But all that is only the beginning of the birth-pangs. For then comes the time when men will hand you over to persecution, and kill you. And the hatred of all nations will fall on you because you bear my name. Then comes the time when men will lose their faith and will betray and hate each other. Yes, and many false prophets will arise, and many people will be misled; and because of the spread of wickedness the love of most men will grow cold, though the man who holds out to the end will be saved. This good news of the Kingdom will be proclaimed to men all over the world as a witness to the heathen, and then only will the end come.

JESUS PROPHESIES A FUTURE OF SUFFERING

24
15
"When the time comes, then, that you see the 'abomination of desolation' prophesied by Daniel 'standing in the sacred place'—the reader should note this—then is the time for those in Judaea to escape to the hills. A man on his house top must not waste time going into his house to collect anything; a man at work in the fields must not go back home to fetch his clothes. Alas for the pregnant, alas for those with tiny babies at that time. Pray God that you may not have to make your escape in the winter or on the Sabbath day, for then there will be great misery, such as has never happened from the beginning of the world and will never happen again! Yes, if those days had not been cut short no human being

would survive. But for the sake of God's people tho
are to be shortened.

"If anyone says to you then, 'Look, here is Chr
'There He is!' don't believe it. False Christs an
prophets are going to appear and will produce grea
and wonders to mislead, if it were possible, even God's own
people. Listen, I am warning you. So that if people say to
you, 'There He is, in the desert!' you are not to go out there.
If they say, 'Here He is, in this inner room!' don't believe it.
For as lightning flashes across from east to west so will the
Son of Man's coming be. 'Wherever there is a dead body,
there the vultures will flock.'

AT THE END OF TIME THE SON OF MAN WILL RETURN

"Immediately after the misery of those days the sun will
be darkened, the moon will fail to give her light, the stars will
fall from the sky, and the powers of heaven will be shaken.
Then the Sign of the Son of Man will appear in the sky, and
all the nations of the earth will wring their hands as they
see the Son of Man coming on the clouds of the sky in all His
power and splendour. And He will send out His angels with
a loud trumpet-call and they will gather together His chosen
from the four winds—from one end of the heavens to the
other.

"Learn what the fig-tree can teach you. As soon as its
branches grow full of sap and produce leaves you know that
summer is near. So when you see all these things happening
you may know that He is near, at your very door! Believe
me, this generation will not disappear till all this has taken
place. Earth and sky will disappear, but my words—never!
But about that actual day and time no one knows—not even
the angels of Heaven, only my Father. For just as things
were in the days of Noah so will they be at the coming of the
Son of Man. In those days before the Flood people were eating, drinking, marrying and being married up till the very
day that Noah went into the ark, and knew nothing about the
Flood until it came and destroyed them all. So will it be at
the coming of the Son of Man. Two men will be in the field;
one is taken and one is left behind. Two women will be grind-
ing at the hand-mill; one is taken and one is left behind. You

24
29

must be on the alert then, for you do not know when your
Master is coming. You can be sure of this, however, that if
the householder had known what time of night the burglar
would arrive, he would have been ready for him and would
not have allowed his house to be broken into. That is why
you must always be ready, for you do not know what time
the Son of Man will arrive.

VIGILANCE IS ESSENTIAL

24
45   "Who then is the faithful and sensible servant, whom his
master put in charge of his household to give the others their
food at the proper time? Well, he is fortunate if his master
finds him doing that duty on his return! Believe me, he will
promote him to look after all his property. But if he should
be a bad servant who says to himself, 'My master takes his
time about returning,' and should begin to beat his fellow-
servants and eat and drink with drunkards, that servant's
master will return suddenly and unexpectedly, and will
utterly expose him and send him to join all the other
hypocrites—to his bitter sorrow and regret!

"In those days the Kingdom of Heaven will be like ten
bridesmaids who took their lamps and went out to meet the
bridegroom. Five of them were sensible and five were silly.
The silly ones took their lamps but did not take any oil with
them. But the sensible ones brought their lamps and oil in
their flasks as well. Then, as the bridegroom was a very long
time, they all grew drowsy and dropped off to sleep. But in
the middle of the night there came a shout, 'Wake up, here
comes the bridegroom! Out you go to meet him!' Then up
got all the bridesmaids and attended to their lamps. The
silly ones said to the sensible ones, 'Please give us some of
your oil—our lamps are going out!' 'Oh no,' returned the
sensible ones, 'there might not be enough for all of us. Better
go to the oil-shop and buy some for yourselves.' But while
they had gone off to buy the oil the bridegroom arrived, and
those bridesmaids who were ready went in with him for the
festivities and the door was shut behind them. Later on the
rest of the bridesmaids came and said, 'Oh please, sir, open
the door for us!' But he replied, 'I tell you I don't know
you!' So be on the alert—for you do not know the day or
the time.

LIFE IS HARD FOR THE FAINT-HEARTED

"It is just like a man going abroad who called his household   25
servants together before he went and handed his property   14
over to them to manage. He gave one five thousand dollars,
another two thousand and another one thousand—according
to their respective abilities. Then he went away.

"The man who had received five thousand dollars went
out at once and by doing business with this sum he made
another five thousand. Similarly the two thousand dollar
man made another two thousand. But the man who had
received one thousand dollars went off and dug a hole in
the ground and hid his master's money.

"Some years later the master of these servants arrived and
went into the accounts with them. The one who had the five
thousand dollars came in and brought him an additional
five thousand with the words, 'You gave me five thousand
dollars, sir; look, I've increased it by another five thousand.'
'Well done!' said his master, 'you're a sound, reliable servant.
You've been trustworthy over a few things, now I'm going
to put you in charge of much more. Come in and share
your master's rejoicing.' Then the servant who had received
two thousand dollars came in and said, 'You gave me two
thousand dollars, sir; look, here's two thousand more that
I've managed to make by it.' 'Well done!' said his master,
'you're a sound, reliable servant. You've been trustworthy
over a few things, now I'm going to put you in charge of
many. Come in and share your master's pleasure.'

"Then the man who had received the one thousand came
in and said, 'Sir, I always knew you were a hard man, reaping
where you never sowed and collecting what you never
threshed—so I was scared and I went off and hid your
thousand dollars in the ground. Here is your money,
intact.'

" 'You're a wicked lazy servant!' his master told him.
'You say you knew that I reap where I never sowed and
collect what I never threshed? Then you ought to have put
my money in the bank, and then when I came I should at
any rate have got back what belongs to me with interest.
Take his thousand dollars away from him and give it to the
man who now has the ten thousand!' (For the man who has

something will have more given to him and will have plenty.
But as for the man who has nothing, even his 'nothing' will
be taken away.) 'And throw this useless servant into the
darkness outside, where he can weep and wail over his
stupidity.'

THE FINAL JUDGMENT

25   "But when the Son of Man comes in his splendour with all
31   his angels with him, then he will take his seat on his glorious
throne. All the nations will be assembled before him and he
will separate men from each other like a shepherd separating
sheep from goats. He will place the sheep on his right hand
and the goats on his left.

"Then the King will say to those on his right: 'Come, you
who have won my Father's blessing! Take your inheritance
—the Kingdom reserved for you since the foundation of the
world! For I was hungry and you gave me food. I was
thirsty and you gave me a drink. I was lonely and you made
me welcome. I was naked and you clothed me. I was ill and
you came and looked after me. I was in prison and you came
to see me there.'

"Then the true men will answer him: 'Lord, when did
we see *you* hungry and give you food? When did we see *you*
thirsty and give you something to drink? When did we see
you lonely and make you welcome, or see *you* naked and
clothe you, or see *you* ill or in prison and go to see you?'

"And the King will reply, 'I assure you that whatever you
did for the humblest of my brothers you did for me.'

"Then he will say to those on his left, 'Out of my presence,
cursed as you are, into the eternal fire prepared for the
devil and his angels! For I was hungry and you gave me
nothing to eat. I was thirsty and you gave me nothing to
drink. I was lonely and you never made me welcome. When
I was naked you did nothing to clothe me; when I was sick
and in prison you never cared about me.'

"Then they too will answer him, 'Lord, when did we ever
see *you* hungry, or thirsty, or lonely, or naked, or sick, or in
prison, and failed to look after you?'

"Then the King will answer them with these words, 'I
assure you that whatever you failed to do to the humblest
of my brothers you failed to do to me.'

"And these will go off to eternal punishment, but the true men to eternal life."

JESUS ANNOUNCES HIS COMING DEATH

When Jesus had finished all this teaching he spoke to his 26
disciples, "Do you realize that the Passover will begin in two 1
days' time; and the Son of Man is going to be betrayed and
crucified?"

AN EVIL PLOT—AND AN ACT OF LOVE

At that very time the Chief Priests and elders of the people 26
were assembled in the Court of Caiaphas, the High Priest, 3
and were discussing together how they might get hold of
Jesus by some trick and kill him. But they kept on saying,
"It must not be during the Festival or there might be a riot."

Back in Bethany, while Jesus was in the house of Simon
the leper, a woman came to him with an alabaster flask of
most expensive perfume, and poured it on his head as he was
at table. The disciples were indignant when they saw this,
and said, "What is the point of such wicked waste? Couldn't
this perfume have been sold for a lot of money and the proceeds given to the poor?" Jesus knew what they were saying
and spoke to them, "Why must you make this woman feel
uncomfortable? She has done a beautiful thing for me. You
have the poor with you always, but you will not always have
me. When she poured this perfume on my body, she was preparing it for my burial. I tell you plainly that wherever the
gospel is preached in the whole world, this act of hers will
also be told in memory of her."

THE BETRAYAL IS ARRANGED

After this, one of the twelve, Judas Iscariot by name, 26
approached the Chief Priests. "What would you give me," 14
he said to them, "if I hand him over to you?" They settled
with him for thirty silver coins, and from then on he looked
for a convenient opportunity to betray Jesus.

THE LAST SUPPER

On the first day of Unleavened Bread the disciples came 26
to Jesus with the question, "Where do you want us to make 17
our preparations for you to eat the Passover?"

"Go into the city," Jesus replied, "to a certain man there and say to him, 'The Master says, "My time is near. I am going to keep the Passover with my disciples at your house."'" The disciples did as Jesus had instructed them and prepared the Passover. Then late in the evening he took his place at table with the Twelve and during the meal he said, "I tell you plainly that one of you is going to betray me." They were deeply distressed at this and began to say to him in turn, "Surely, Lord, I am not the one?" And his answer was, "The man who has dipped his hand into the dish with me is the man who will betray me. It is true that the Son of Man will follow the road foretold by the Scriptures, but alas for the man through whom he is betrayed! It would be better for that man if he had never been born." And Judas who actually betrayed him spoke to him, "Master, am I the one?"

"As you say!" replied Jesus.

In the middle of the meal Jesus took a loaf and after blessing it he broke it into pieces and gave them to the disciples. "Take and eat this," he said, "it is my body." Then he took a cup and, after thanking God, he gave it to them with the words, "Drink this, all of you, for it is my blood, the blood of the New Agreement shed to set many free from their sins. I tell you I will drink no more wine until I drink it fresh with you in my Father's Kingdom." Then they sang a hymn together and went out to the Mount of Olives. There Jesus said to them, "Tonight every one of you will lose his faith because of me. For the Scripture says, *'I will smite the shepherd, and the sheep of the flock shall be scattered abroad.'* But after I have risen I shall go before you into Galilee!"

At this Peter exclaimed, "Even if everyone should lose his faith through you, I never will!"

"I tell you, Peter," replied Jesus, "that tonight, before the cock crows, you will disown me three times."

"Even if it means dying with you I will never disown you," said Peter. And all the disciples made the same protest.

THE PRAYER IN GETHSEMANE

26
36   Then Jesus came with the disciples to a place called Gethsemane and said to them, "Sit down here while I go over there and pray." Then he took with him Peter and the two

sons of Zebedee and began to be in terrible distress. "My heart is in bitter anguish," he told them, "stay here and keep watch with me." Then he walked on a little way and fell on his face and prayed, "Oh, my Father, if it is possible let this cup pass from me—yet it must not be what I want, but what You want."

Then he came back to the disciples and found them fast asleep. He spoke to Peter, "Couldn't you three keep awake with me for a single hour? Watch and pray, all of you, that you may not have to face temptation. Your spirit is willing, but human nature is weak."

Then he went away a second time and prayed, "My Father, if it is not possible for this cup to pass from me without my drinking it, then Your Will must be done."

And he came and found them asleep again, for they could not keep their eyes open. So he left them and went away again and prayed for the third time using the same words as before. Then he came back to his disciples and spoke to them, "Are you still going to sleep and take your ease? In one moment you will see the Son of Man betrayed into the hands of evil men. Wake up, let us be going! Look, here comes my betrayer!"

THE BETRAYAL

And while the words were still on his lips Judas, one of the Twelve, arrived with a great crowd armed with swords and staves, sent by the Chief Priests and Jewish elders. (The traitor himself had given them a sign, "The one I kiss will be the man. Get him!")   26

47

Without any hesitation he walked up to Jesus. "Greetings, Master!" he cried and kissed him affectionately. "Judas, my friend," replied Jesus, "*what made you come here?*"

Then the others came up, seized hold of Jesus and held him. One of Jesus' disciples drew his sword, slashed at the High Priest's servant and cut off his ear. At this Jesus said to him, "Put your sword back into its proper place. All those who take the sword die by the sword. Don't you realize that I could appeal to my Father, and He would at once send more than twelve legions of angels to defend me? But then, how would the Scriptures be fulfilled which say that all this must take place?"

Then Jesus spoke to the crowds around him. "So you've come out with your swords and staves to capture me like a bandit, have you? I have been sitting in front of you day after day while I taught in the Temple and you never laid a finger on me. But all this is happening as the prophets said it would." And at this point all the disciples deserted him and made their escape.

JESUS BEFORE THE HIGH PRIEST

26
57
The men who had seized Jesus took him off to Caiaphas the High Priest in whose house the Scribes and elders were assembled. Peter followed him at a safe distance right up to the High Priest's courtyard. Then he went inside and sat down with the servants and waited to see the end.

Meanwhile the Chief Priests, the elders and the whole Council did all they could to find false evidence against Jesus to get him condemned to death. They failed completely. Even after a number of perjurers came forward they still failed. In the end two of these stood up and said, "This man said, 'I can pull down the Temple of God and rebuild it in three days.'" Then the High Priest got to his feet and addressed Jesus, "Have you no answer? What about the evidence of these men against you?" But Jesus was silent. Then the High Priest said to him, "I command you by the living God, to tell us on your oath if you are Christ, the Son of God." Jesus said to him, "I am. Yes, and I tell you that in the future you will see the Son of Man sitting at the right hand of Power and coming on the clouds of Heaven."

At this the High Priest tore his robes and cried, "That was blasphemy! We've no more need of witnesses? Look, you've heard the blasphemy—what's your verdict now?" And they replied, "He deserves to die."

Then they spat in his face and knocked him about, and some slapped him, crying, "Prophesy, you Christ, who was that who hit you?"

PETER DISOWNS HIS MASTER

26
69
All this time Peter was sitting outside in the courtyard, and a maidservant came up to him and said, "Weren't you with Jesus, the man from Galilee?" But he denied it before them all, saying, "I don't know what you're talking about." Then when he had gone out into the porch, another

maid caught sight of him and said to those who were there,
"This man, too, was with Jesus the man from Nazareth."
And again he denied it with an oath—"I don't know the
man!" A few minutes later those who were standing about
came up to Peter and said to him, "You certainly are one of
them, you know; it's obvious from your accent." At that he
began to curse and swear—"I tell you I don't know the
man!" Immediately, as the cock crew, the words of Jesus
came back into Peter's mind—"Before the cock crows you
will disown me three times." And he went outside and wept
bitterly.

When the morning came, all the Chief Priests and elders of
the people met in council to decide how they could get Jesus
executed. Then they marched him off with his hands tied,
and handed him over to Pilate the Governor.

THE REMORSE OF JUDAS

Then Judas, who had betrayed him, saw that he was con-   27
demned and in his remorse returned the thirty silver coins   3
to the Chief Priests and elders, with the words, "I was wrong
—I have betrayed an innocent man to death."

"And what has that got to do with us?" they replied.
"That's your affair."

And Judas flung down the silver in the Temple and went
outside and hanged himself. But the Chief Priests picked up
the money and said, "It is not legal to put this into the
Temple treasury. It is, after all, blood-money." So, after a
further consultation, they purchased with it the Potter's
Field to be a burial-ground for foreigners, which is why it is
called "the Field of Blood" to this day. And so the words of
Jeremiah the prophet came true:

> And they took the thirty pieces of silver, the price of
> him that was priced, whom certain of the children of
> Israel did price: and they gave them for the potter's field,
> as the Lord appointed me.

JESUS BEFORE PILATE

Meanwhile Jesus stood in front of the Governor, who asked   27
him, "Well, you—*are* you the King of the Jews?"   11

"Yes, I am," replied Jesus.

While the Chief Priests and elders were making their accusations, he made no reply at all. So Pilate said to him, "Can't you hear the evidence they're bringing against you?" But to the Governor's amazement, Jesus did not answer a single one of their accusations.

Now it was the custom at festival-time for the Governor to release any prisoner whom the people chose. And it happened that at this time there was in prison a notorious prisoner called Barabbas. So when they assembled to make their usual request, Pilate said to them, "Which one do you want me to set free, Barabbas or Jesus called Christ?" For he knew very well that the latter had been handed over to him through sheer malice. And indeed while he was actually sitting in court his wife sent a message to him—"Don't have anything more to do with that good man! I went through agonies dreaming about him last night!" But the Chief Priests and elders persuaded the mob to ask for Barabbas and demanded Jesus' execution. Then the Governor spoke to them, "Which of these two are you asking me to release?"

"Barabbas!" they cried.

"Then what am I to do with Jesus who is called Christ?" said Pilate.

"Have him crucified!" they all told him. At this Pilate said, "Why, what is his crime?" But their voices rose to a roar, "Have him crucified!" When Pilate realised that nothing more could be done but that there would soon be a riot, he took a bowl of water and washed his hands before the crowd, saying, "I take no responsibility for the death of this man. You must see to it yourselves." To this the whole crowd replied, "Let his blood be on us and on our children!" Whereupon Pilate released Barabbas for them, but he had Jesus flogged, and handed over for crucifixion.

Then the Governor's soldiers took Jesus into the Governor's palace and collected all the guard around him. There they stripped him and put a scarlet cloak on him. They twisted some thorn-twigs into a crown and put it on his head and put a stick into his right hand. They bowed low before him and jeered at him with the words, "Hail, Your Majesty, king of the Jews!" Then they spat on him, took the stick and hit him on the head with it. And when they had finished their fun, they stripped the cloak off again, put his own clothes on him and led him off for crucifixion. On their way out of the city they met a man called Simon, a native of Cyrene in Africa, and they compelled him to carry Jesus' cross.

THE CRUCIFIXION

Then when they came to a place called Golgotha (which 27 means Skull Hill) they offered him a drink of wine mixed 33 with some bitter drug, but when he had tasted it he refused to drink. And when they had nailed him to the cross they shared out his clothes by drawing lots.

Then they sat down to keep guard over him. And over his head they put a placard with the charge against him:

THIS IS JESUS, THE KING OF THE JEWS

Now two bandits were crucified with Jesus at the same time, one on each side of him. The passers-by nodded their heads knowingly and called out to him in mockery, "Hi, you who could pull down the Temple and build it up again in three days—why don't you save yourself? If you are the Son of God, step down from the cross!" The Chief Priests also joined the Scribes and elders in jeering at him, saying, "He saved others, but he can't save himself! If this is the King of Israel, why doesn't he come down from the cross now, and we will believe him! He trusted in God . . . let God rescue him if He will have anything to do with him! For he said, 'I am God's son.' " And even the bandits who were crucified with him hurled abuse at him.

Then from midday until three o'clock darkness spread over the whole countryside, and then Jesus cried with a loud voice, "My God, my God, why did You forsake me?" Some of those who were standing there heard these words which Jesus spoke in Aramaic (*Eli, Eli, lama sabachthani?*), and said, "This man is calling for Elijah!" And one of them ran off and fetched a sponge, soaked it in vinegar and put it on a long stick and held it up for him to drink. But the others said, "Let him alone! Let's see if Elijah will come and save him." But Jesus gave one more great cry, and died.

And the sanctuary curtain in the Temple was torn in two from top to bottom. The ground shook, rocks split and graves were opened. (A number of bodies of holy men who were asleep in death rose again. They left their graves after Jesus' resurrection and entered the Holy City and appeared to

many people.) And the centurion and his company who
were keeping guard over Jesus saw the earthquake and all
that was happening and were terrified. "Indeed he *was* a son
of God!" they said.

There were many women at the scene watching from a
distance. They had followed Jesus from Galilee to minister
to his needs. Among them was Mary of Magdala, Mary the
mother of James and Joses, and the mother of Zebedee's
sons.

JESUS IS BURIED AND THE TOMB IS GUARDED

27
57 That evening, Joseph, a wealthy man from Arimathaea,
who was himself a disciple of Jesus, went to Pilate and asked
for the body of Jesus, and Pilate gave orders for the body to
be handed over to him. So Joseph took it, and wrapped it
in clean linen and placed it in his own new tomb which
he had hewn in the rock. Then he rolled a large stone over
the doorway of the tomb and went away. But Mary from
Magdala and the other Mary remained there, sitting in front
of the tomb.

Next day, which was the day after the Preparation, the
Chief Priests went in a body with the Pharisees to Pilate and
said, "Sir, we have remembered that while this impostor was
alive, he said, 'After three days I shall rise again.' Will you
give the order then to have the grave closely guarded until
the third day, so that there can be no chance of his disciples
coming and stealing the body and telling people that he has
risen from the dead? We should then be faced with a worse
fraud than the first one."

"You have your guard," Pilate told them. "Go and make
it as safe as you can." And they went and made the grave
secure, putting a seal on the stone and leaving the soldiers
on guard.

THE FIRST LORD'S DAY: JESUS RISES

28
1 When the Sabbath was over, just as the first day of the
week was dawning, Mary from Magdala and the other Mary
went to look at the tomb, and at that moment there was a
great earthquake, for an angel of the Lord came down from
Heaven, rolled back the stone and took his seat upon it. His
appearance was dazzling like lightning and his clothes were

white as snow. The guards shook with terror at the sight of him and collapsed like dead men. But the angel spoke to the women, "Do not be afraid. I know that you are looking for Jesus Who was crucified. He is not here—He is risen, just as He said He would. Come and look at the place where He was lying. Then go quickly and tell His disciples that He has risen from the dead. And, listen, He goes before you into Galilee! And there you will see Him. Now I have told you my message." Then the women went away quickly from the tomb, their hearts filled with fear and great joy, and ran to give the news to His disciples. But quite suddenly, Jesus stood before them in their path, and said, "Peace be with you!" And they came up to Him and, clasping His feet, worshipped Him. Then Jesus said to them, "Do not be afraid. Go now and tell My brothers to go into Galilee and they shall see Me there."

And while they were on their way, some of the sentries went into the city and reported to the Chief Priests everything that had happened. They got together with the elders, and after consultation gave the soldiers a considerable sum of money and told them, "Your story must be that his disciples came after dark, and stole him away while you were asleep, and if by any chance this reaches the Governor's ears, we will put it right with him and see that you do not suffer for it." So they took the money and obeyed their instructions. The story was spread and is current among the Jews up to the present day.

JESUS GIVES HIS FINAL COMMISSION

But the Eleven went to the mountain in Galilee where 28
Jesus had arranged to meet them, and when they had seen 16
Him they worshipped Him, though some of them were doubtful. But Jesus came and spoke these words, "All power in Heaven and on earth has been given to Me. You, then, are to go and make disciples of all the nations and baptize them in the Name of the Father and of the Son and the Holy Spirit. Teach them to observe all that I have commanded you and, remember, I am with you always, to the end of the world."

THE GOSPEL OF
MARK

It is generally agreed that Mark's Gospel is the earliest. It probably appeared in 65, soon after the Great Fire of Rome which devastated a great part of the city in the winter of 64–65. The Christians were made the scapegoats of this disaster by the Emperor Nero, and it is quite probable that there is a definite connection between the appearance of this first-written Gospel and the monstrously false accusations which were being made against Christians. The original papyrus roll is traditionally supposed to have borne the title—"The Gospel of Jesus Christ the Son of God."

The author is generally thought to have been John Mark, a native of Jerusalem. The house of his mother Mary became one of the meeting places of the early Christians (Acts 12, 12). It has been suggested that perhaps John Mark is the mysterious young man who escaped from the soldiers' hands on the night of Jesus' arrest (Mark 14, 51). He is also linked with the early growth of the Church, working with Paul, Barnabas and Peter.

Eusebius, the fourth-century historian, quotes Papias (who wrote about 140) as saying that Mark was the "interpreter of Peter," and this seems to have been generally accepted by the early Church.

We may therefore reasonably assume that Mark, drawing on what Peter had told him personally, and being himself convinced of the Divinity of Christ, wrote down this Gospel, probably at Rome, with non-Jewish readers in mind. We notice, for instance, that he hardly quotes at all from the Old Testament, that he explains particular Jewish customs and that he translates any Aramaic expression by its Greek equivalent.

His style has no literary polish but it has the forceful vitality of the man who believes what he writes, and it is not without certain vivid flashes of realism. He draws with strong

*lines the portrait of a Man Who was thoroughly human
but unmistakably the Son of God.*

*The manuscript of Mark ends abruptly at 16, 8, and
nearly all scholars regard the subsequent verses as a later
addition.*

HOW IT BEGAN

THE Gospel of Jesus Christ, the Son of God, begins with
the fulfilment of this prophecy of Isaiah—

> Behold, I send my messenger before thy face,
> Who shall prepare thy way;
> The voice of one crying in the wilderness,
> Make ye ready the way of the Lord,
> Make his paths straight.

For John came and began to baptize men in the desert, proclaiming baptism as the mark of a complete change of heart
and of the forgiveness of sin. All the people of the Judaean
countryside and everyone in Jerusalem went out to him in
the desert and received his baptism in the river Jordan, publicly confessing their sins.

John himself was dressed in camel-hair, with a leather belt
round his waist, and he lived on locusts and wild honey. The
burden of his preaching was, "There is someone coming after
me who is stronger than I—indeed I am not good enough
to kneel down and undo his sandals. I have baptized you with
water, but he will baptize you with the Holy Spirit."

THE ARRIVAL OF JESUS

It was in those days that Jesus arrived from the Galilean
village of Nazareth and was baptized by John in the Jordan.
All at once, as he came up out of the water, he saw the
heavens split open, and the Spirit coming down upon him
like a dove. A Voice came out of Heaven, saying,

"You are My dearly-loved Son, in Whom I am well
pleased!"

Then the Spirit sent him out at once into the desert, and
there he remained for forty days while Satan tempted him.
During this time, no one was with him but wild animals and
only the angels were there to care for him.

JESUS BEGINS TO PREACH THE GOSPEL, AND
TO CALL MEN TO FOLLOW HIM

1   It was after John's arrest that Jesus came into Galilee,
14   proclaiming the Gospel of God, saying,

"The time has come at last—the Kingdom of God has arrived. You must change your hearts and minds and believe the Good News."

As he walked along the shore of the Lake of Galilee, he saw two fishermen, Simon and his brother Andrew, casting their nets into the water.

"Come and follow me, and I will teach you to catch men," he cried.

At once they dropped their nets, and followed him.

Then he went a little further along the shore and saw James the son of Zebedee, aboard a boat with his brother John, overhauling their nets. At once he called them, and they left their father Zebedee in the boat with the hired men, and went off after him.

JESUS BEGINS HEALING THE SICK

1   They arrived at Capernaum, and on the Sabbath day Jesus
21   walked straight into the synagogue and began teaching. They were amazed at his way of teaching, for he taught with the ring of authority, quite unlike the Scribes. All at once, a man in the grip of an evil spirit appeared in the synagogue shouting out,

"What have you got to do with us, Jesus from Nazareth? Have you come to kill us? I know who you are—you're God's Holy One!"

But Jesus cut him short and spoke sharply,

"Hold your tongue and get out of him!"

At this the evil spirit convulsed the man, let out a loud scream and left him. Everyone present was so astounded that people kept saying to each other.

"What on earth has happened? This new teaching has authority behind it. Why, he gives orders to evil spirits and they obey him!"

And his reputation spread like wild-fire through the whole Galilean district.

Then he got up and went straight from the synagogue to

the house of Simon and Andrew, accompanied by James and
John. Simon's wife's mother was in bed with a high fever,
and they lost no time in telling Jesus about her. He went up
to her, took her hand and helped her to her feet. The fever
left her, and she began to see to their needs.

When the evening came, as the sun was setting, they kept
bringing to him all who were sick or troubled by evil spirits.
The whole population of the town gathered round the doorway. And he healed great numbers of people who were suffering from all kinds of diseases. In many cases he expelled
evil spirits; but he would not allow them to say a word, for
they knew perfectly well who he was.

HE RETIRES FOR PRIVATE PRAYER

Then, in the early morning, while it was still dark, Jesus   1
got up, left the house and went off to a deserted place, and 35
there he prayed. Simon and his companions went in search
of him, and when they found him, they said,

"Everyone is looking for you."

"Then we will go somewhere else, to the neighbouring
towns," he replied, "so that I may tell my message there
too—that is why I have come."

So he continued preaching in their synagogues and expelling evil spirits throughout the whole of Galilee.

JESUS CURES LEPROSY

Then a leper came to Jesus, knelt in front of him and ap-   1
pealed to him,   40

"If you want to, you can make me clean."

Jesus was filled with pity for him, and stretched out his
hand and placed it on the leper, saying,

"Of course I want to—you are clean."

At once the leprosy left him and he was quite clean.
Jesus sent him away there and then, with the strict injunction,

"Mind you say nothing at all to anybody. Go straight off
and show yourself to the priest, and make the offerings for
your recovery which Moses prescribed, as evidence to the
authorities."

But he went off and began to talk a lot about it, circulating
his story far and wide. Consequently, Jesus was unable to

enter a town publicly and had to stay outside in unfrequented places. Yet the people still came to him from all quarters.

FAITH AT CAPERNAUM

2
1 When he re-entered Capernaum some days later, a rumour spread that he was in somebody's house. Such a large crowd collected that while he was giving them his message it was impossible even to get near the doorway. Meanwhile, a group of people arrived to see him, bringing with them a paralytic whom four of them were carrying. And when they found it was impossible to get near him because of the crowd, they removed the tiles from the roof over Jesus' head and let down the paralytic's mat through the opening. And when Jesus saw their faith, he said to the man on the mat,

"My son, your sins are forgiven."

But some of the Scribes were sitting there silently asking themselves,

"Why does this man talk such blasphemy? Who can possibly forgive sins but God?"

Jesus realised instantly what they were thinking, and said to them,

"Why must you argue like this in your minds? Which do you suppose is easier—to say to a paralysed man, 'Your sins are forgiven,' or 'Get up, pick up your mat and walk'? But to prove to you that the Son of Man has full authority to forgive sins on earth, I say to you,"—and here he spoke to the paralytic—"Get up, pick up your mat and go home."

At once the man sprang to his feet, picked up his mat and walked off in full view of them all. Everyone was amazed, praised God and said,

"We have never seen anything like this before."

Then Jesus went out again by the lake-side and the whole crowd came to him, and he continued to teach them.

JESUS NOW CALLS "A SINNER" TO
FOLLOW HIM

2
14 As Jesus went on his way, he saw Levi the son of Alphaeus sitting at his desk in the tax-office, and he said to him,

"Follow me!"

Levi got up and followed him. Later, when Jesus was sitting at dinner in Levi's house, a large number of tax-collectors and disreputable folk came in and joined him and his disciples. For there were many such people among his followers. When the Scribes and Pharisees saw him eating in the company of tax-collectors and outsiders, they remarked to his disciples,

"Why does he eat with tax-collectors and sinners?"

When Jesus heard this, he said to them,

"It is not the fit and flourishing who need the doctor, but those who are ill. I did not come to invite the 'righteous,' but the 'sinners.' "

THE QUESTION OF FASTING

The disciples of John and those of the Pharisees were fasting. They came and said to Jesus,

"Why do those who follow John or the Pharisees keep fasts but your disciples do nothing of the kind?"

Jesus told them,

"Can you expect wedding-guests to fast in the bridegroom's presence? Fasting is out of the question as long as they have the bridegroom with them. But the day will come when the bridegroom will be taken away from them—that will be the time for them to fast.

"Nobody," he continued, "sews a patch of unshrunken cloth on to an old garment. If he does, the new patch tears away from the old and the hole is worse than ever. And nobody puts new wine into old wineskins. If he does, the new wine bursts the skins, the wine is spilt and the skins are ruined. No, new wine must go into new wineskins."

JESUS REBUKES THE SABBATARIANS

One day he happened to be going through the wheatfield on the Sabbath day. And his disciples, as they made their way along, began to pick the ears of wheat. The Pharisees said to him,

"Look at that! Why should they do what is forbidden on the Sabbath day?"

Then he spoke to them,

"Have you never read what David did, when he and his companions were hungry? Haven't you read how he went into the House of God when Abiathar was High Priest, and ate the Presentation Loaves, which nobody is allowed to eat, except the priests—and gave some of the bread to his companions? The Sabbath," he continued, "was made for man's sake; man was not made for the sake of the Sabbath. That is why the Son of Man is master even of the Sabbath."

On another occasion when he went into the synagogue, there was a man there whose hand was shrivelled, and they were watching Jesus closely to see whether he would heal him on the Sabbath day, so that they might bring a charge against him. Jesus said to the man with the shrivelled hand,

"Stand up and come out here in front!"

Then he said to them,

"Is it right to do good on the Sabbath day, or to do harm? Is it right to save life or to kill?"

There was a dead silence. Then when he had looked round in anger at the faces surrounding him, for he was deeply distressed by their callousness, he said to the man,

"Stretch out your hand!"

And he stretched it out, and the hand was restored as sound as the other one. The Pharisees walked straight out and discussed with Herod's party how they could have Jesus put out of the way.

JESUS' ENORMOUS POPULARITY

3 Jesus now retired to the lake-side with his disciples. A
7 huge crowd of people followed him, not only from Galilee, but from Judaea, Jerusalem and Idumaea, some from the Trans-jordan district and from the neighbourhood of Tyre and Sidon. This vast crowd came to him because they had heard about the sort of things he was doing. So Jesus told his disciples to have a small boat kept in readiness for him, in case the people should crowd him too closely. For he healed so many people that all those who were in pain kept pushing forward to touch him with their hands. Evil spirits, as soon as they saw him, acknowledged his authority and screamed,

"You are the Son of God!"

But he warned them repeatedly that they must not make him known.

JESUS CHOOSES THE TWELVE APOSTLES

3 Later he went up on to the mountain-side and summoned
13 the men whom he wanted, and they went up to him. He

appointed a band of Twelve to be his companions, whom he could send out to preach, with power to drive out evil spirits. These were the Twelve he appointed:

Peter (which was the new name he gave Simon), James the son of Zebedee, and John his brother. (He gave them the name of Boanerges, which means the "Thunderers.") Andrew, Philip, Bartholomew, Matthew, Thomas, James the son of Alphaeus, Thaddaeus, Simon the Patriot, and Judas Iscariot, who betrayed him.

JESUS EXPOSES AN ABSURD ACCUSATION

Then he went indoors, but again such a crowd collected that it was impossible for them even to eat a meal. When his family heard of this, they set out to take charge of him, for they said, "He must be mad!"

The Scribes who had come down from Jerusalem were saying that he was possessed by Beelzebub, and that he drove out devils because he was in league with the prince of devils. So Jesus called them to him and spoke to them in a parable—

"How can Satan be the one who drives out Satan? If a kingdom is divided against itself, then that kingdom cannot last, and if a household is divided against itself, it cannot last either. And if Satan leads a rebellion against Satan—his days are certainly numbered. No one can break into a strong man's house and steal his property, without first tying up the strong man hand and foot. But if he did that, he could ransack the whole place.

"Believe me, all men's sins can be forgiven and all their blasphemies. But there can never be any forgiveness for blasphemy against the Holy Spirit. That is an eternal sin."

He said this because they were saying, "He is in the power of an evil spirit."

THE NEW RELATIONSHIPS IN THE KINGDOM

Then his mother and his brothers arrived. They stood outside the house and sent a message asking him to come out to them. There was a crowd sitting round him when the message was brought telling him, "Your mother and your brothers are outside looking for you."

Jesus replied, "And who are really my mother and my brothers?"

And he looked round at the faces of those sitting in a circle about him.

"Look!" he said, "my mother and my brothers are here. Anyone who does the Will of God is brother and sister and mother to me."

THE STORY OF THE SOWER

4   Then once again he began to teach them by the lake-side.
1   A bigger crowd than ever collected around him, so that he got into the little boat on the lake and sat down, while the crowd covered the ground right up to the water's edge. He taught them a great deal in parables, and in the course of his teaching he said,

"Listen! A man once went out to sow his seed and as he sowed, some seed fell by the roadside and the birds came and gobbled it up. Some of the seed fell among the rocks where there was not much soil, and sprang up very quickly because there was no depth of earth. But when the sun rose, it was scorched and because it had no root, it withered away. And some of the seed fell among thorn-bushes and the thorns grew and choked the life out of it, and it bore no crop. And there was some seed which fell on good soil, and when it grew, produced a crop which yielded thirty or sixty or even a hundred times as much as the seed."

Then he added,

"Every man who has ears should use them!"

Then when they were by themselves, his close followers and the Twelve asked him about the parables, and he told them,

"The secret of the Kingdom of God has been given to you. But to those who do not know the secret, everything is in a parable, so that

seeing they may see, and not perceive;
and hearing they may hear, and not understand;
lest haply they should turn again, and it should be forgiven them."

Then he continued,

"Do you really not understand this parable? Then how are you going to understand all the other parables? The man who sows sows the message. As for those who are by the roadside where the message is sown, as soon as they hear it Satan comes at once and takes away what has been sown in their minds. Similarly, the seed sown among the rocks represents those who hear the message without hesitation and accept it joyfully. But they have no real roots and do not last. When trouble or persecution arises because of the message, they give up their faith in disgust. Then there are the seeds which were sown among thorn-bushes. These are the people who hear the message, but the worries of this world and the false glamour of riches and all sorts of other ambitions creep in and choke the life out of what they have heard, and it produces no crop in their lives. As for the seed sown on good soil this means the men who hear the message and accept it and do produce a crop—thirty, sixty, even a hundred times as much as they received."

TRUTH IS MEANT TO BE USED

Then he said to them, 4

"Is a lamp brought into the room to be put under a bucket 21
or underneath the bed? Surely its place is on the lamp-stand. There is nothing hidden which is not meant to be made perfectly plain one day, and there are no secrets which are not meant one day to be common knowledge. If a man has ears he should use them!

"Be careful how you listen," he went on to them. "Whatever measure you use will be used towards you, and even more than that. For the man who has something will receive more. As for the man who has nothing, even his nothing will be taken away."

JESUS GIVES PICTURES OF THE KINGDOM'S GROWTH

Then he said, 4

"The Kingdom of God is like a man scattering seed on the 26
ground and then going to bed each night and getting up every morning, while the seed sprouts and grows up, though he has no idea how it happens. The earth produces a crop without any help from anyone: first a blade, then the ear of wheat, then the full-grown grain in the ear. And as soon as the crop is ready, he sends for the reapers without delay for the harvest-time has come."

Then he continued,

"What can we say the Kingdom of God is like? How shall we put it in a parable? It is like a tiny grain of mustard-seed which, when it is sown, is smaller than any seed that is ever sown. But after it is sown in the earth, it grows up and becomes bigger than any other plant. It shoots out great branches so that birds can come and nest in its shelter."

So he taught them his message with many parables such as their minds could take in. He did not speak to them at all without using parables, although in private he explained everything to his disciples.

JESUS SHOWS HIMSELF MASTER OF
NATURAL FORCES

4   On the evening of that day, he said to them,
35   "Let us cross over to the other side of the lake."

So they sent the crowd home and took him with them in the little boat in which he had been sitting, accompanied by other small craft. Then came a violent squall of wind which drove the waves aboard the boat until it was swamped. Jesus was in the stern asleep on the cushion. They awoke him with the words,

"Master, don't you care that we're drowning?"

And he woke up and said to the water,

"Hush now! Be still!"

The wind dropped and everything was very still.

"Why are you so frightened? What has happened to your faith?" he asked them.

But sheer awe swept over them, and they kept saying to each other,

"Who ever can he be?—even the wind and the waves do what he tells them!"

JESUS MEETS A VIOLENT LUNATIC

5   So they arrived on the other side of the lake in the country
1   of the Gerasenes. As Jesus was getting out of the boat, a man in the grip of an evil spirit rushed out to meet him from among the tombs where he was living. It was no longer possible to restrain him even with a chain. Indeed he had frequently been secured with fetters and lengths of chain, but

he had simply snapped them and no one could do anything with him. All through the night as well as in the day-time he screamed among the tombs and cut himself with stones. Now, as soon as he saw Jesus in the distance, he ran and knelt before him, yelling at the top of his voice,

"What have you got to do with me, Jesus, Son of the Most High God? For God's sake, don't torture me!"

For Jesus had already said, "Come out of this man, you evil spirit!"

Then he asked him,

"What is your name?"

"My name is Legion," he replied, "for there are many of us."

Then he begged and prayed him not to send "them" out of the country.

A large herd of pigs was grazing there on the mountain-side, and the evil spirits implored him, "Send us over to the pigs and we'll get into them!"

And Jesus allowed them to do this, and they came out of the man and made off and went into the pigs. The whole herd of about two thousand stampeded down the cliff into the lake and was drowned. The swineherds took to their heels and spread their story in the city and all over the countryside. Then the people came to see what had happened. As they approached Jesus, they saw the man who had been devil-possessed sitting there properly clothed and perfectly sane—the same man that had been possessed by "Legion"—and they were really frightened. Those who had seen the incident told them what had happened to the devil-possessed man and about the disaster to the pigs. Then they began to implore Jesus to leave their district. As he was embarking on the little boat, the man who had been possessed begged that he might go with him. But Jesus would not allow this.

"Go home to your own people," he told him, "and tell them what the Lord has done for you, and how kind he has been to you!"

So the man went off and began to spread throughout the Ten Towns the story of what Jesus had done for him. And they were all simply amazed.

FAITH IS FOLLOWED BY HEALING

5   When Jesus had crossed again to the other side of the
21   lake, a great crowd collected around him as he stood on the
shore. Then came a man called Jairus, one of the synagogue
presidents. And when he saw Jesus, he knelt before him,
pleading for his help.

"My little girl is dying," he said. "Will you come and put
your hands on her—then she will get better and live."

Jesus went off with him, followed by a large crowd jostling at his elbow. Among them was a woman who had had
a haemorrhage for twelve years and who had gone through
a great deal at the hands of many doctors, spending all her
money in the process. She had derived no benefit from them
but, on the contrary, was getting worse. This woman had
heard about Jesus and came up behind him under cover of
the crowd, and touched his cloak,

"For if I can only touch his clothes," she kept saying,
"I shall be all right."

The haemorrhage stopped immediately, and she knew in
herself that she was cured of her trouble. At once Jesus knew
intuitively that power had gone out of him, and he turned
round in the middle of the crowd and said,

"Who touched my clothes?"

His disciples replied,

"You can see this crowd jostling you. How can you ask,
'Who touched me'?"

But he looked all around at their faces to see who had done
so. Then the woman, scared and shaking all over because she
knew that she was the one to whom this thing had happened,
came and flung herself before him and told him the whole
story. But he said to her,

"Daughter, it is your faith that has healed you. Go home
in peace, and be free from your trouble."

While he was still speaking, messengers arrived from the
synagogue president's house.

"Your daughter is dead—there is no need to bother the
Master any further."

But when Jesus heard this, he said,

"Now don't be afraid, just go on believing!"

Then he allowed no one to follow him except Peter and

James and John, James's brother. They arrived at the president's house and Jesus noticed the hubbub and all the weeping and wailing, and as he went in, he said to the people in the house,

"Why are you making such a noise with your crying? The child is not dead; she is fast asleep."

They greeted this with a scornful laugh. But Jesus turned them all out, and taking only the father and mother and his own companions with him, went into the room where the child was. Then he took the little girl's hand and said to her in Aramaic,

"Wake up, little girl!"

At once she jumped to her feet and walked round the room, for she was twelve years old. This sight sent the others nearly out of their minds with joy. But Jesus gave them strict instructions not to let anyone know what had happened—and ordered food to be given to the little girl.

THE "PROPHET WITHOUT HONOUR"

Then he left that district and came into his own native town, followed by his disciples. When the Sabbath day came, he began to teach in the synagogue. The congregation were astonished and remarked,

"Where does he get all this from? What is this wisdom that he has been given—and what about these marvellous things that he can do? He's only the carpenter, Mary's son, the brother of James, Joses and Judas and Simon; and his sisters are living here with us!"

And they were deeply offended with him. But Jesus said to them,

"No prophet goes unhonoured—except in his own country or with his own relations or in his own home!"

And he could do nothing miraculous there apart from laying his hands on a few sick people and healing them; their lack of faith astonished him.

THE TWELVE ARE SENT OUT TO PREACH
THE GOSPEL

Then he made his way round the villages, continuing his teaching. He summoned the Twelve, and began to send them out in twos, giving them power over evil spirits. He in-

structed them to take nothing for the road except a staff—
no satchel, no bread and no money in their pockets. They
were to wear sandals and not to take more than one garment.
And he told them,

"Wherever you are, when you go into a house, stay there
until you leave that place. And wherever people will not welcome you or listen to what you have to say, leave them and
shake the dust off your feet as a protest against them!"

So they went out and preached that men should change
their whole outlook. They expelled many evil spirits and
anointed many sick people with oil and healed them.

HEROD'S GUILTY CONSCIENCE

6
14
All this came to the ears of King Herod, for Jesus' reputation was spreading, and people were saying that John the
Baptist had risen from the dead, and that was why he was
showing such miraculous powers. Others maintained that he
was Elijah, and others that he was one of the prophets of the
old days come back again. But when Herod heard of all this,
he said,

"It must be John whom I beheaded, risen from the
dead!"

For Herod himself had sent and arrested John and had
him bound in prison, all on account of Herodias, wife of his
brother Philip. He had married her, though John used to
say to Herod, "It is not right for you to possess your own
brother's wife." Herodias herself was furious with him for
this and wanted to have him executed, but she could not do
it, for Herod had a deep respect for John, knowing that he
was a just and holy man, and protected him. He used to
listen to him and be profoundly disturbed, and yet he enjoyed
hearing him.

Then a good opportunity came, for Herod gave a birthday
party for his courtiers and army commanders and for the
leading people in Galilee. Herodias' daughter came in and
danced, to the great delight of Herod and his guests. The
king said,

"Ask me anything you like and I will give it to you!"

And he swore to her,

"I will give you whatever you ask me, up to half of my
kingdom!"

And she went out and spoke to her mother,

"What shall I ask for?"

'And she said,

"*The head of John the Baptist!*"

The girl rushed back to the king's presence, and made her request.

"I want you to give me, this minute, the head of John the Baptist on a dish!" she said.

Herod was aghast, but because of his oath and the presence of his guests, he did not like to refuse her. So he sent one of the palace guardsmen straight away to bring him John's head. He went off and beheaded him in the prison, brought back his head on the dish, and gave it to the girl who handed it to her mother. When his disciples heard what had happened, they came and took away the body and put it in a tomb.

THE APOSTLES RETURN: THE HUGE CROWDS MAKE REST IMPOSSIBLE

The Apostles returned to Jesus and reported to him every detail of what they had done and taught.   6
                                                                    30

"Now come along to some quiet place by yourselves, and rest for a little while," said Jesus, for there were people coming and going incessantly so that they had not even time for meals. They went off in the boat to a quiet place by themselves, but a great many saw them go and recognised them, and people from all the towns hurried around the shore on foot to forestall them. When Jesus disembarked he saw the large crowd and his heart was touched with pity for them because they seemed to him like sheep without a shepherd. And he settled down to teach them about many things. As the day wore on, his disciples came to him and said,

"We are right in the wilds here and it is getting late. Let them go now, so that they can buy themselves something to eat from the farms and villages around here."

But Jesus replied,

"You give them something to eat!"

"You mean we're to go and spend ten dollars on bread? Is that how you want us to feed them?"

"What bread have you got?" asked Jesus. "Go and have a look."

And when they had found out, they told him,

"We have five loaves and two fish."

JESUS MIRACULOUSLY FEEDS FIVE
THOUSAND PEOPLE

6
39   Then Jesus directed the people to sit down in parties on the fresh grass. And they threw themselves down in groups of fifty and a hundred. Then Jesus took the five loaves and the two fish, and looking up to Heaven, thanked God, broke the loaves and gave them to the disciples to distribute to the people. And he divided the two fish among them all. Everybody ate and was satisfied. Afterwards they collected twelve baskets full of pieces of bread and fish that were left over. There were five thousand men who ate the loaves.

JESUS' MASTERY OVER NATURAL LAW

6
45   Directly after this, Jesus made his disciples get aboard the boat and go on ahead to Bethsaida on the other side of the lake, while he himself sent the crowds home. And when he had sent them all on their way, he went off to the mountainside to pray. When it grew late, the boat was in the middle of the lake, and he was by himself on land. He saw them straining at the oars, for the wind was dead against them. And in the small hours he went towards them, walking on the waters of the lake, intending to go past them. But when they saw him walking on the water, they thought he was a ghost, and screamed out. For they all saw him and they were absolutely terrified. But Jesus at once spoke quietly to them,

"It's all right, it is I myself; don't be afraid!"

And he climbed aboard the boat with them, and the wind dropped. But they were scared out of their wits. They had not had the sense to learn the lesson of the loaves. Even that miracle had not opened their eyes to see who he was.

And when they had crossed over to the other side of the lake, they landed at Gennesaret and tied up there. As soon as they came ashore, the people recognised Jesus and rushed all over the countryside and began to carry the sick around on their mats to wherever they heard that he was. Wherever he went, in villages or towns or farms, they laid down their sick right in the road-way and begged him that they might "just touch the edge of his cloak." And all those who touched him were healed.

JESUS EXPOSES THE DANGER OF MAN-MADE TRADITIONS

And now Jesus was approached by the Pharisees and some 7
of the Scribes who had come from Jerusalem. They had 1
noticed that his disciples ate their meals with "common"
hand—meaning that they had not gone through a ceremonial
washing. The Pharisees, and indeed all the Jews, will never eat
unless they have washed their hands in a particular way,
following a traditional rule. And they will not eat anything
bought in the market until they have first performed their
"sprinkling." And there are many other things which they
consider important, concerned with the washing of cups, jugs
and basins. So the Pharisees and the Scribes put this question
to Jesus,

"Why do your disciples refuse to follow the ancient tradition, and eat their bread with 'common' hands?"

Jesus replied,

"You hypocrites, Isaiah described you beautifully when he
wrote—

This people honoureth me with their lips,
But their heart is far from me.
But in vain do they worship me,
Teaching as doctrines the precepts of men.

You are so busy holding on to the traditions of men that you
let go the Commandment of God!"

Then he went on,

"It is wonderful to see how you can set aside the Commandment of God to preserve your own tradition! For Moses
said, 'Honour thy father and thy mother' and 'He that
speaketh evil of father or mother, let him die the death.' But
you say, 'if a man says to his father or his mother, Korban—
meaning, I have given God whatever duty I owed to you,'
then he need not lift a finger any longer for his father or
mother, so making the Word of God invalid for the sake of
the tradition which you hold. And this is typical of much of
what you do."

Then he called the crowd close to him again, and spoke to
them,

"Listen to me now, all of you, and understand this. There

is nothing outside a man which can enter into him and make him 'common.' It is the things which go out of a man that make him 'common'!"

Later, when he had gone indoors away from the crowd, his disciples asked him about this parable.

"Oh, are you as dull as they are?" he said. "Can't you see that anything that goes into a man from outside cannot make him 'common' or unclean? You see, it doesn't go into his heart, but into his stomach, and passes out of the body altogether, so that all food is clean enough. But," he went on, "whatever comes out of a man, that is what makes a man 'common' or unclean. For it is from inside, from men's hearts and minds, that evil thoughts arise—lust, theft, murder, adultery, greed, wickedness, deceit, sensuality, envy, slander, arrogance and folly! All these evil things come from inside a man and make him unclean!"

THE FAITH OF A GENTILE IS REWARDED

7
24
Then he got up and left the place and went off to the neighbourhood of Tyre. There he went into a house and wanted no one to know where he was. But it proved impossible to remain hidden. For no sooner had he got there, than a woman who had heard about him, and who had a daughter possessed by an evil spirit, arrived and prostrated herself before him. She was a Greek, a Syrophoenician by birth, and she asked him to drive the evil spirit out of her daughter. Jesus said to her,

"You must let the children have all they want first. It is not right, you know, to take the children's food and throw it to the dogs."

But she replied,

"Yes, Lord, I know, but even the dogs under the table eat what the children leave."

"If you can answer like that," Jesus replied, "you can go home! The evil spirit has left your daughter."

And she went back to her home and found the child lying quietly on her bed, and the evil spirit gone.

JESUS RESTORES SPEECH AND HEARING

7
31
Then once more Jesus left the neighbourhood of Tyre and passed through Sidon towards the Lake of Galilee, and crossed

the Ten Towns territory. Then they brought to him a man
who was deaf and unable to speak intelligibly, and they implored him to put his hand upon him. Jesus took him away
from the crowd by himself. Then he put his fingers in the
man's ears and touched his tongue with his own saliva. Then,
looking up to Heaven, he gave a deep sigh and said to him in
Aramaic,

"Open!"

And his ears were opened immediately and whatever tied
his tongue came loose and he spoke quite plainly. Jesus gave
instructions that they should tell no one about this happening, but the more he told them, the more they broadcast the
news. People were absolutely amazed, and kept saying,

"How wonderfully he has done everything! He even
makes the deaf hear and the dumb speak."

HE AGAIN FEEDS THE PEOPLE MIRACULOUSLY

About this time it happened again that a large crowd collected and had nothing to eat. Jesus called the disciples over
to him and said,

"My heart goes out to this crowd; they have been with me
three days now and they have no food left. If I send them
off home without anything, they will collapse on the way—
and some of them have come from a distance."

His disciples replied,

"Where could anyone find the food to feed them here in
this deserted spot?"

Then Jesus asked them,

"How many loaves have you got?"

"Seven," they replied.

So Jesus told the crowd to sit down comfortably on the
ground. Then he took the seven loaves into his hands, and
with a prayer of thanksgiving broke them, and gave them to
the disciples to distribute to the people. And they did so.
They had a few small fish as well, and after blessing them,
Jesus told the disciples to give these also to the people.
They ate and they were satisfied. Moreover, they picked up
seven baskets full of pieces left over. The people numbered
about four thousand. Jesus sent them home, and then he
boarded the boat at once with his disciples and went on to the
district of Dalmanutha.

JESUS REFUSES TO GIVE A "SIGN"

8 Now the Pharisees came out and began an argument with
11 him, wanting a sign from Heaven. Jesus gave a deep sigh,
and then said,

"What makes this generation want a sign? I can tell you
this, they will certainly not be given one!"

Then he left them and got aboard the boat again, and
crossed the lake.

The disciples had forgotten to take any food and had only
one loaf with them in the boat. Jesus spoke seriously to them,
"Keep your eyes open! Be on your guard against the 'yeast'
of the Pharisees and the 'yeast' of Herod!" And this sent
them into an earnest consultation among themselves because
they had brought no bread. Jesus knew it and said to them,

"Why all this discussion about bringing no bread? Don't you
understand or grasp what I say even yet? Are you like the people who *having eyes, do not see? and having ears, do not hear?*
Have you forgotten—when I broke five loaves for five thousand people, how many baskets full of pieces did you pick up?"

"Twelve," they replied.

"And when there were seven loaves for four thousand
people, how many baskets of pieces did you pick up?"

"Seven," they said.

"And does this still mean nothing to you?" he said.

JESUS RESTORES SIGHT

8 So they arrived at Bethsaida where a blind man was
22 brought to him, with the earnest request that he should
touch him. Jesus took the blind man's hand and led him outside the village. Then he moistened his eyes with saliva and
putting his hands on him, asked,

"Can you see at all?"

The man looked up and said,

"I can see people. They look like trees—only they are
walking about."

Then Jesus put his hands on his eyes once more and his
sight came into focus, and he recovered and saw everything
sharp and clear. And Jesus sent him off to his own house
with the words,

"Don't go into this village."

JESUS' QUESTION: PETER'S INSPIRED ANSWER

Jesus then went away with his disciples to the villages of   8
Caesarea Philippi. On the way he asked them,   27

"Who are men saying that I am?"

"John the Baptist," they answered. "But others say that
you are Elijah or, some say, one of the prophets."

Then he asked them,

"But what about you—who do you say that I am?"

"You are Christ!" answered Peter.

Then Jesus impressed it upon them that they must not
mention this to anyone.

JESUS SPEAKS OF THE FUTURE AND OF THE
COST OF DISCIPLESHIP

And he began to teach them that it was inevitable that the   8
Son of Man should go through much suffering and be com-   31
pletely repudiated by the elders and Chief Priests and Scribes,
and be killed, and after three days rise again. He told them
all this quite bluntly.

And this made Peter draw him on one side and take him
to task about what he had said. But Jesus turned and faced
his disciples and rebuked Peter.

"Out of my way, Satan!" he said. "Peter, you are not
looking at things from God's point of view, but from man's!"

Then he called his disciples and the people around him,
and said to them,

"If anyone wants to follow in my footsteps, he must give
up all right to himself, take up his cross and follow me. The
man who tries to save his life will lose it; it is the man who
loses his life for my sake and the Gospel's who will save it.
What good can it do a man to gain the whole world at the
price of his own soul? What can a man offer to buy back his
soul once he has lost it? Whoever is ashamed of me and my
words in this unfaithful and sinful generation, the Son of Man
will be ashamed of him when he comes in the Father's glory
with the holy angels around him."

JESUS FORETELLS HIS GLORY

Then he added,   9

"Believe me, there are some of you standing here who will   1 know nothing of death until you have seen the Kingdom of God coming in its power!"

Six days later, Jesus took Peter and James and John with him and led them up a high mountain where they were entirely alone. His whole appearance changed before their eyes, while his clothes became white like dazzling snow—whiter than any earthly bleaching could make them. Elijah and Moses appeared to the disciples and stood there in conversation with Jesus. Peter burst out to Jesus,

"Master, it is wonderful for us to be here! Shall we make three shelters—one for you, one for Moses and one for Elijah?"

He really did not know what to say, for they were very frightened. Then came a cloud which overshadowed them and a Voice came out of the cloud,

"This is My dearly-loved Son. Hear Him!"

Then, quite suddenly they looked all round them and saw nobody at all with them but Jesus. And as they came down from the mountain, he warned them not to tell anybody what they had seen till "the Son of Man should have risen again from the dead." They treasured this remark and tried to puzzle out among themselves what the "rising from the dead" could mean. Then they asked him this question,

"Why do the Scribes say that Elijah must come before Christ?"

"It is quite true," he replied, "that Elijah does come first, and begins the world's reformation. But what does the Scripture say about the Son of Man? This: that he must go through much suffering and have his claims rejected! Indeed I tell you that Elijah has come already and they did to him exactly what they wanted—just as the Scripture says of him."

JESUS HEALS AN EPILEPTIC BOY

9
14   Then as they rejoined the other disciples, they saw that they were surrounded by a large crowd and that some of the Scribes were arguing with them. As soon as the people saw Jesus, they ran forward excitedly to welcome him.

"What is the trouble?" Jesus asked them.

A man from the crowd answered,

"Master, I brought my son to you because he has a dumb spirit. Wherever he is, it gets hold of him, throws him down on the ground and there he foams at the mouth and grinds his teeth. It's simply wearing him out. I did speak to your disciples to get them to drive it out, but they hadn't got the power to do it."

Jesus answered them,

"Oh, what a faithless people you are! How long must I be with you before you will believe; how long must I bear your lack of faith? Bring him here to me."

So they brought the boy to him, and as soon as the spirit saw Jesus, it hurled the boy to the ground and there he writhed, foaming at the mouth.

"How long has he been like this?" Jesus asked the father.

"Ever since he was a child," he replied. "Again and again it has thrown him into the fire or into water to finish him off. But if you can do anything, please take pity on us and help us."

"If I can do anything!" retorted Jesus. "Everything is possible to the man who believes."

"I do believe," the boy's father burst out. "Help me to believe more!"

When Jesus noticed that a crowd was rapidly gathering, he spoke sharply to the evil spirit, with the words,

"I command you, deaf and dumb spirit, come out of this boy, and never go into him again!"

The spirit gave a loud scream and after a dreadful convulsion left him. The boy lay there like a corpse, so that most of the bystanders said, "He is dead."

But Jesus grasped his hands and lifted him up, and then he stood on his own feet. When he had gone home, Jesus' disciples asked him privately,

"Why were we unable to drive it out?"

"Nothing can drive out this kind of thing except prayer," replied Jesus.

JESUS PRIVATELY WARNS HIS DISCIPLES OF
HIS OWN DEATH

Then they left that district and went straight through Galilee. Jesus kept this journey secret for he was teaching his disciples that the Son of Man would be betrayed into the power of men, that they would kill him and that three days after his death he would rise again. But they were completely mystified by this saying, and were afraid to question him about it.

JESUS DEFINES THE NEW "GREATNESS"

9   So they came to Capernaum. And when they got indoors
33 he asked them,

"W. it were you discussing as we came along?"

They were silent, for on the way they had been arguing
about who should be the greatest. Jesus sat down and called
the Twelve, and said to them,

"If any man wants to be first, he must be last and servant
of all."

Then he took a little child and stood him in front of them
all, and putting his arms round him, said to them,

"Anyone who welcomes one little child like this for my
sake is welcoming me. And the man who welcomes me is
welcoming not only me but the One Who sent me!"

Then John said to him,

"Master, we saw somebody driving out evil spirits in your
name, and we stopped him, for he is not one who follows us."

But Jesus replied,

"You must not stop him. No one who does a miracle in
my name would readily say anything against me. For the
man who is not against us is on our side. In fact, I assure you
that the man who gives you a mere drink of water in my
name, because you are followers of mine, will most certainly
be rewarded. And I tell you too, that the man who disturbs
the faith of one of the humblest of those who believe in me
would be better off if he were thrown into the sea with a great
millstone hung round his neck!

ENTERING THE KINGDOM MAY MEAN
PAINFUL SACRIFICE

9   "Indeed, if it is your own hand that spoils your faith, you
43 must cut it off. It is better for you to enter Life maimed than
to keep both your hands and go to the rubbish-heap. If your
foot spoils your faith, you must cut it off. It is better for you
to enter Life on one foot than to keep both your feet and be
thrown on to the rubbish-heap. And if your eye leads you
astray, pluck it out. It is better for you to go one-eyed into
the Kingdom of God than to keep both eyes and be thrown
on to the rubbish-heap, where decay never stops and the fire
never goes out. For everyone will be salted with fire. Salt is

a very good thing; but if it should lose its saltiness, what can you do to restore its flavour? You must have salt in yourselves, and live at peace with each other."

THE DIVINE PURPOSE IN MARRIAGE

Then he got up and left Galilee and went off to the borders of Judaea and the Jordan. Again great crowds assembled to meet him, and again according to his custom, he taught them. Then some Pharisees arrived to ask him this test-question,

"Is it right for a man to divorce his wife?"

Jesus replied by asking them,

"What did Moses command you to do?"

"Moses allowed men to write a divorce-notice and then to dismiss her," they said.

"Moses gave you that commandment," returned Jesus, "because you know so little of the meaning of love. But from the beginning of the creation, God made them male and female. *'For this cause shall a man leave his father and mother, and shall cleave to his wife; and the twain shall become one flesh.'* So that in body they are no longer two people but one. Therefore man must never separate what God has joined together."

On reaching the house, his disciples questioned him again about this matter.

"Any man who divorces his wife and marries another woman," he told them, "commits adultery against his wife. And if she herself divorces her husband and marries someone else, she commits adultery."

HE WELCOMES SMALL CHILDREN

Then some people came to him bringing little children for him to touch. The disciples tried to discourage them. When Jesus saw this, he was indignant and told them,

"You must let little children come to me—never stop them! For the Kingdom of God is made of little ones like these. Indeed, I assure you that the man who does not accept the Kingdom of God like a little child will never enter it."

Then he took the children in his arms and laid his hands on them and blessed them.

JESUS SHOWS THE DANGER OF RICHES

10   As he began to take the road again, a man came running
17 up and fell at his feet, and asked him,

"Good Master, tell me please, what must I do to be sure
of eternal life?"

"I wonder why you call me good," returned Jesus. "No
one is good—only God. You know the commandments, 'Do
no murder, Do not commit adultery, Do not steal, Do not
bear false witness, Do not cheat, Honour thy father and
mother.' "

"Master," he replied, "I have carefully kept all these since
I was quite young."

Jesus looked steadily at him, and his heart warmed
towards him. Then he said,

"There is one thing you have missed. Sell everything you
have, give the money away to the poor—you will have
riches in Heaven. And then come and follow me."

At these words his face fell and he went away in deep distress, for he was very rich. Then Jesus looked round at them
all, and said to his disciples,

"How difficult it is for those who have great possessions to
enter the Kingdom of God!"

The disciples were staggered at these words, but Jesus
continued,

"Children, you don't know how hard it can be to get into
the Kingdom of Heaven. Why, a camel could more easily
squeeze through the eye of a needle than a rich man get into
the Kingdom of God."

At this their astonishment knew no bounds, and they said
to each other,

"Then who can possibly be saved?"

Jesus looked straight at them and said,

"Humanly speaking it is impossible, but with God everything is possible."

Then Peter burst out,

"But look, we have left everything and followed you!"

"I promise you," returned Jesus, "nobody leaves home or
brothers or sisters or mother or father or children or property
for my sake or the Gospel's without getting back a hundred
times over, now in this present life, homes and brothers and

sisters, mothers and children and land—though not without
persecution—and in the next world eternal life. But many
who are first now will then be last, and the last now will then
be the first."

THE LAST JOURNEY TO JERUSALEM BEGINS

They were now on their way going up to Jerusalem and   10
Jesus walked on ahead. They were puzzled and bewildered   32
at this but went on following him, with fear in their hearts.
Then once more he took the Twelve aside and began to tell
them what was going to happen to him.

"We are now going up to Jerusalem," he said, "as you can
see. And the Son of Man will be betrayed into the power of
the Chief Priests and Scribes. They are going to condemn him
to death and hand him over to pagans who will jeer at him
and spit at him and flog him and kill him. But after three
days he will rise again."

AN ILL-TIMED REQUEST

Then Zebedee's two sons James and John approached him,   10
saying,   35
"Master, we want you to grant us a special request."

"What do you want me to do for you?" answered Jesus.

"Give us permission to sit one on each side of you in the
glory of your kingdom!"

"You don't know what you are asking," Jesus said to
them. "Can you drink the cup I have to drink? Can you go
through the baptism I have to undergo?"

"Yes, we can," they replied.

Then Jesus told them,

"You will indeed drink the cup I am drinking, and you will
undergo the baptism by which I am being baptized! But as
to sitting on either side of me, that is not for me to give—
such places belong to those for whom they are prepared."

When the other ten heard about this, they began to be
highly indignant with James and John; so Jesus called them
all to him, and said,

"You know that the so-called rulers in the heathen world
lord it over them, and their great men have absolute power.
But it must not be so among you. No, whoever among you
wants to be great must become the servant of you all, and

if he wants to be first among you he must be your slave! For
the Son of Man himself did not come to be served but to
serve, and to give his life to set many others free."

Then they came to Jericho, and as he was leaving it accompanied by his disciples and a large crowd, Bartimaeus (that
is, the son of Timaeus), a blind beggar, was sitting in his
usual place by the side of the road. When he heard that it
was Jesus of Nazareth, he began to call out,

"Jesus, Son of David, have pity on me!"

Many of the people told him to keep quiet, but he shouted
all the more,

"Son of David have pity on me!"

Jesus stood quite still and said,

"Call him here."

So they called the blind man, saying,

"It's all right now, come along, he's calling you!"

At this he threw off his coat, jumped to his feet and came
to Jesus.

"What do you want me to do for you?" he asked him.

"Oh, Master, let me see again!"

"Go on your way then," returned Jesus, "your faith has
healed you."

And he recovered his sight at once and followed Jesus
along the road.

JESUS ARRANGES FOR HIS ENTRY
INTO THE CITY

11   Then when they came near to Jerusalem to Bethphage
1   and Bethany on the slopes of the Mount of Olives, he sent off
two of his disciples with these instructions,

"Go into the village just ahead of you and there you will
find a tethered colt on which no one has ever yet ridden.
Untie it, and bring it here. If anybody asks you, 'Why are
you doing this?' just say, 'The Lord needs it, and will send
it back immediately.' "

So they went off and found the colt tethered by a doorway
outside in the open street, and they untied it. Some of the
bystanders did say, "What are you doing, untying this colt?"
but they made the reply Jesus told them to make, and the
men raised no objection. So they brought the colt to Jesus,
threw their garments upon its back, and mounted him on it.

Many of the people spread out their garments in his path as
he rode along, and others put down straw which they had cut
from the fields. The whole crowd, both those who were in
front and those who were behind Jesus, shouted,

"God save Him!—God bless the One Who comes in the
Name of the Lord! Hurrah for the coming kingdom of our
father David! God save Him from on high!"

Jesus entered Jerusalem and went into the Temple and
looked round on all that was going on. And then, since it
was late in the day, he went out to Bethany with the Twelve.

On the following day when they had left Bethany, Jesus
felt hungry. He noticed a fig-tree in the distance covered
with leaves, and he walked up to it to see if he could find any
fruit on it. But when he got to it, he could find nothing but
leaves, for it was not yet time for the figs. Then Jesus spoke
to the tree,

"Nobody shall ever eat fruit from you!"

And the disciples heard him say it.

Then they came into Jerusalem and Jesus went into the
Temple and began to drive out those who were buying and
selling there. He over-turned the tables of the money-
changers and the benches of the dove-sellers, and he would
not allow the people to carry their water-pots through the
Temple. And he taught them and said,

"Doesn't the Scripture say, '*My house shall be called a
house of prayer for all nations*'? But you have turned it into
a thieves' kitchen!"

The Chief Priests and Scribes heard him say this and tried
to find a way of getting rid of him. But they were in fact
afraid of him, for his teaching had captured the imagination
of the people. And every evening he left the city.

JESUS TALKS OF FAITH, PRAYER AND
FORGIVENESS

One morning as they were walking along, they noticed that   11
the fig-tree had withered away right down to the roots. Peter   20
remembered it, and said,

"Master, look, the fig-tree that you cursed is all shrivelled
up!"

"Have faith in God," replied Jesus to them. "I tell you
that if anyone should say to this mountain, 'Get up and throw

yourself into the sea,' and without any doubt in his heart believe that what he says will happen, then it *will* happen! That is why I tell you, whatever you pray about and ask for, believe that you have received it and it will be yours. And whenever you stand praying, you must forgive anything that you are holding against anyone else, and your Heavenly Father will forgive you *your* sins."

JESUS' AUTHORITY IS DIRECTLY CHALLENGED

11 So they came once more to Jerusalem, and while Jesus was
27 walking in the Temple, the Chief Priests, elders and Scribes approached him, and asked,

"What authority have you for what you're doing? And who gave you permission to do these things?"

"I am going to ask you one question," replied Jesus, "and if you answer me, I will tell you what authority I have for what I do. The baptism of John, now—did it come from Heaven or was it purely human? Tell me that."

At this they argued with each other, "If we say from Heaven, he will say, 'then why didn't you believe in him?' but if we say it was purely human, well . . ." For they were frightened of the people, since all of them believed that John was a real prophet. So they answered Jesus,

"We do not know."

"Then I cannot tell you by what authority I do these things," returned Jesus.

JESUS TELLS A STORY, WITH A POINTED APPLICATION

12 Then he began to talk to them in parables.
1 "A man once planted a vineyard," he said, "fenced it round, dug out the hole for the wine-press and built a watch-tower. Then he let it out to some farm-workers and went abroad. At the end of the season he sent a servant to the tenants to receive his share of the vintage. But they got hold of him, knocked him about and sent him off empty-handed. The owner tried again. He sent another servant to them, but this one they knocked on the head and generally insulted. Once again he sent them another servant, but him they mur-dered. He sent many others and some they beat up and some

they murdered. He had one man left—his own son who was very dear to him. He sent him last of all to the tenants, saying to himself, 'They will surely respect my own son.' But they said to each other, 'This fellow is the future owner—come on, let's kill him, and everything that he would get will come to us!' So they got hold of him and murdered him, and threw his body out of the vineyard. What do you suppose the owner of the vineyard is going to do? He will come and destroy the men who were working his vineyard and will hand it over to others. Have you never read this Scripture—

The stone which the builders rejected,
The same was made the head of the corner;
This was from the Lord,
And it is marvellous in our eyes?"

Then they tried to get their hands on him, for they knew perfectly well that he had aimed this parable at them—but they were afraid of the people. So they left him and went away.

A TEST QUESTION

Later they sent some of the Pharisees and some of the Herod-party to trap him in an argument. They came up and said to him,

"Master, we know that you are an honest man and that you are not swayed by men's opinion of you. Obviously you don't care for human approval but teach the way of God with the strictest regard for truth—*is it right to pay tribute to Caesar or not: are we to pay or not to pay?*"

But Jesus saw through their cunning and said to them,

"Why try this trick on me? Bring me a coin and let me look at it."

So they brought one to him.

"Whose face is this?" asked Jesus, "and whose name is in the inscription?"

"Caesar's," they replied.

"Then give to Caesar what belongs to Caesar, and to God what belongs to God!"—a reply which staggered them.

JESUS REVEALS THE IGNORANCE OF
THE SADDUCEES

12   Then some of the Sadducees (a party which maintains that
18   there is no resurrection) approached him, and put this question to him,

"Master, Moses instructed us that if a man's brother dies
leaving a widow but no child, then the man should marry the
woman and raise children for his brother. Now there were
seven brothers, and the first one married and died without
leaving issue. Then the second one married the widow and
died leaving no issue behind him. The same thing happened
with the third, and indeed the whole seven died without leaving any child behind them. Finally the woman herself died.
Now in this 'resurrection,' when men rise up again, whose
wife is she going to be—for she was the wife of all seven of
them?"

Jesus replied, "Does not this show where you go wrong—
and how ignorant you are of both the Scriptures and the
power of God? When people rise from the dead they neither
marry nor get married; they live like the angels in Heaven.
But as for this matter of the dead being raised, haven't you
ever read in the book of Moses, in the passage about the
Bush, how God spoke to him in these words, 'I am the God of
Abraham and the God of Isaac and the God of Jacob'? God
is not a God of the dead, but of the living! That is where you
make your great mistake!"

THE MOST IMPORTANT COMMANDMENTS

12   Then one of the Scribes approached him. He had been
28   listening to the discussion, and noticing how well Jesus had
answered them, he put this question to him,

"What are we to consider the greatest commandment of
all?"

"The first and most important one is this," Jesus replied
—'Hear, O Israel: The Lord our God, The Lord is one: and
thou shalt love the Lord thy God with all thy heart, and with
all thy soul, and with all thy mind, and with all thy strength.'
The second is this, 'Thou shalt love thy neighbour as thyself.'
No other commandment is greater than these."

"I am well answered," replied the Scribe. "You are abso-

lutely right when you say that there is one God and no other
God exists but Him; and to love Him with the whole of our
hearts, the whole of our intelligence and the whole of our
energy, and to love our neighbours as ourselves is infinitely
more important than all these burnt-offerings and sacrifices."

Then Jesus, noting the thoughtfulness of his reply, said
to him,

"You are not far from the Kingdom of God!"

After this nobody felt like asking him any more questions.

JESUS CRITICISES THE SCRIBES' TEACHING
AND BEHAVIOUR

Later while Jesus was teaching in the Temple, he re- 12
marked,   35

"How can the Scribes make out that Christ is David's *son*,
for David himself, inspired by the Holy Spirit, said,

The Lord said unto my *Lord*,
Sit thou on my right hand,
Till I make thine enemies the footstool of thy feet.

David is himself calling Christ 'Lord'—where do they get the
idea that he is his son?"

The vast crowd heard this with great delight, and Jesus
continued in his teaching,

"Be on your guard against these Scribes who love to walk
about in long robes and to be greeted respectfully in public
and to have the front seats in the synagogue and the best
places at dinner-parties! These are the men who live on
widows' property and then put up a screen of lengthy
prayers. They are only adding to their own punishment!"

Then Jesus sat down opposite the Temple almsbox and
watched the people putting their money into it. A great
many rich people put in large sums. Then a poor widow came
up and dropped in two little coins, worth together about a
halfpenny. Jesus called his disciples to his side and said
to them,

"Believe me, this poor widow has put in more than all the
others. For they have all put in what they can easily spare,
but she in her poverty who needs so much, has given away
everything, her whole living!"

JESUS PROPHESIES THE RUIN OF THE TEMPLE

13   Then as Jesus was leaving the Temple, one of his disciples
1 said to him,

"Look, Master, what wonderful stonework, what a size
these buildings are!"

Jesus replied,

"You see these great buildings? Not a single stone will be
left standing on another; it will all be thrown down!"

Then while he was sitting on the slope of the Mount of
Olives facing the Temple, Peter, James, John and Andrew
said to him privately,

"Tell us when will these things happen. What sign will
there be that all these things are going to end?"

So Jesus began to tell them:

"Be very careful that no one deceives you. Many are going
to come in my name and say, 'Here I am,' and will lead many
astray. When you hear of wars and rumours of wars, don't
be alarmed. Such things are bound to happen, but the end
is not yet. Nation will take up arms against nation and
kingdom against kingdom. There will be earthquakes in different places and terrible famines. But this is only the beginning of 'the pains.' You yourselves must keep your wits
about you, for men will hand you over to their councils,
and will beat you in their synagogues. You will have to stand
in front of rulers and kings for my sake to bear your witness
to them—for before the end comes the Gospel must be proclaimed to all nations. But when they are taking you off to
trial, do not worry what you are going to say—simply say
the words you are given when the time comes. For it is not
really you who will speak, but the Holy Spirit.

JESUS FORETELLS UTTER MISERY

13   "A brother is going to betray his own brother to death, and
12 a father his own child. Children will stand up against their
parents and condemn them to death. There will come a time
when the whole world will hate you because you are known
as my followers. Yet the man who holds out to the end will
be saved.

"But when you see 'the abomination of desolation' stand-

ing where it ought not—(let the reader take note of this)—
then those who are in Judaea must fly to the mountains! The
man on his housetop must not go down nor go into his house
to fetch anything out of it, and the man in the field must not
turn back to fetch his cloak. Alas for the women who are
pregnant at that time, and alas for those with babies at their
breasts! Pray God that it may not be winter when that time
comes, for there will be such utter misery in those days as
has never been since the Creation—and never will be again.
Indeed, if the Lord did not shorten those days, no human
being would survive. But for the sake of the people whom
He has chosen He has shortened those days.

HE WARNS AGAINST FALSE CHRISTS,
AND COMMANDS VIGILANCE

"If anyone tells you at that time, 'Look, here is Christ,' or   13
'Look, there he is,' don't believe it! For false Christs and   21
false prophets will arise and will perform signs and wonders,
to deceive, if it be possible, even the men of God's choice.
You must keep your eyes open! I am giving you this warning
before it happens.

"But when that misery is past, the light of the sun will be
darkened and the moon will not give her light; stars will be
falling from the sky and the powers of heaven will rock on
their foundations. Then men shall see the Son of Man coming
in the clouds with great power and glory. And then shall He
send out His angels to summon His Chosen together from
every quarter, from furthest earth to highest heaven. Let
the fig-tree illustrate this for you:—when its branches grow
tender and produce leaves, you know that summer is near.
So when you see these things happening, you may know that
the End is near, at your very doors! I tell you that this
present age will not have passed until all these things have
come true. Heaven and earth will pass away, but what I
have told you will stand. But no one knows the day or the
hour of this Happening, not even the angels in Heaven, no,
not even the Son—only the Father. Keep your eyes open,
keep on the alert, for you do not know when the time will be.
It is as if a man who is travelling abroad had left his house
and handed it over to be managed by his servants. He has

given each one his work to do and has ordered the door-keeper to be on the look-out for his return. Just so must you keep a look-out, for you do not know when the Master of the House will come—it might be late evening, or midnight, or cockcrow, or early morning—otherwise He might come unexpectedly and find you sound asleep. What I am saying to you I am saying to all; keep a good look-out!"

AN ACT OF LOVE

14
1 In two days' time the Festival of the Passover and of Unleavened Bread was due. Consequently, the Chief Priests and the Scribes were trying to think of some trick by which they could get Jesus into their power and have him executed.

"But it must not be on the Festival Day," they said, "or there will be a riot."

Jesus himself was now in Bethany in the house of Simon the leper. As he was sitting at table, a woman approached him with an alabaster flask of very costly spikenard perfume. She broke the neck of the flask and poured the perfume on Jesus' head. Some of those present were highly indignant and muttered,

"What is the point of such wicked waste of perfume? It could have been sold for over thirty dollars and that could have been given to the poor." And there was a murmur of resentment against her. But Jesus said,

"Let her alone, why must you make her feel uncomfortable? She has done a beautiful thing for me. You have the poor with you always and you can do good to them whenever you like, but you will not always have me. She has done all she could—for she has anointed my body for burial before the time. I assure you that wherever the Gospel is preached throughout the whole world, this deed of hers will also be told in memory of her."

JUDAS VOLUNTEERS TO BETRAY JESUS

14
10 Then Judas Iscariot, who was one of the Twelve, went off to the Chief Priests to betray Jesus to them. And when they heard what he had to say, they were delighted and arranged to pay him for it. So he looked out for a convenient opportunity to betray him.

THE PASSOVER-SUPPER PREPARED

On the first day of Unleavened Bread, the day when the   14
Passover was sacrificed, Jesus' disciples said,   12

"Where do you want us to go and make the preparations
for you to eat the Passover?"

Jesus sent off two of them with these instructions,

"Go into the town and you will meet a man carrying a
pitcher of water. Follow him and say to the owner of the
house to which he goes, 'The Master says, where is the room
for me to eat the Passover with my disciples?' And he will
show you a large upstairs room all ready with the furnishings
that we need. That is the place where you are to make our
preparations."

So the disciples left the house and went into the town, and
found everything as he had told them, and prepared for the
Passover.

THE LAST SUPPER TOGETHER: THE
MYSTERIOUS BREAD AND WINE

Late in the evening he arrived with the Twelve. And while   14
they were sitting there, right in the middle of the meal,   17
Jesus remarked,

"Believe me, one of you is going to betray me—someone
who is now having his supper with me."

This shocked and distressed them and they began to say
to him one by one,

"Surely, I'm not the one?"

"It is one of the Twelve," Jesus told them, "a man who is
dipping his hand into the dish with me. It is true that the Son
of Man will follow the road foretold by the Scriptures, but
alas for the man through whom he is betrayed! It would be
better for that man if he had never been born."

And while they were still eating Jesus took a loaf, blessed
it and broke it and gave it to them, with the words,

"Take this, it is my body."

Then he took a cup, and after thanking God, he gave it
to them, and they all drank from it, and he said to them,

"This is my blood which is shed for many in the New
Agreement. I tell you truly I will drink no more wine until
the day comes when I drink it fresh in the Kingdom of God!"

Then they sang a hymn and went out to the Mount of Olives.

"Every one of you will lose your faith because of me," Jesus told them, "as the Scripture says:

I will smite the shepherd,
And the sheep shall be scattered abroad.

Yet after I have risen, I shall go before you into Galilee!"

PETER'S BOLD WORDS—AND JESUS' REPLY

14   Then Peter said to him,
29   "Even if everyone should lose his faith, I never will."

"Believe me, Peter," returned Jesus, "this very night before the cock crows twice, you will disown me three times."

But Peter protested violently,

"Even if it means dying with you, I will never disown you!"

And they all made the same protest.

THE LAST DESPERATE PRAYER IN GETHSEMANE

14   Then they arrived at a place called Gethsemane, and Jesus
32   said to his diciples,

"Sit down here while I pray."

He took with him Peter, James and John, and began to be distraught with horror.

"My heart is in bitter anguish," he told them. "Stay here and keep watch for me."

Then he walked forward a little way and flung himself on the ground, praying that, if it were possible, he might not have to face the ordeal.

"Dear Father," he said, "all things are possible to You, please—let me not have to drink this cup. Yet it is not what I want but what You want."

Then he came and found them fast asleep. He spoke to Peter,

"Are you asleep, Simon? Couldn't you manage to watch for a single hour? Watch and pray, all of you, that you may not have to face temptation. Your spirit is willing, but human nature is weak."

Then he went away again and prayed in the same words, and once more he came and found them asleep. They could

not keep their eyes open and they did not know what to say
for themselves. When he came back for the third time, he
said,

"Are you still going to sleep and take your ease? All right
—the moment has come; now you are going to see the Son of
Man betrayed into the hands of evil men! Wake up, let us
be going! Look, here comes my betrayer!"

JUDAS BETRAYS JESUS

And indeed, while the words were still on his lips, Judas, 14
one of the Twelve, arrived with a mob armed with swords 43
and staves, sent by the Chief Priests and Scribes and elders.
The betrayer had given them a sign; he had said, "The one I
kiss will be the man. Get hold of him and you can take him
away without any trouble." So he walked straight up to
Jesus, cried, "Master!" and kissed him affectionately. And
so they got hold of him and held him. Somebody present drew
his sword and struck at the High Priest's servant, slashing off
his ear. Then Jesus spoke to them,

"So you've come out with your swords and staves to capture me like a bandit, have you? Day after day I was with
you in the Temple teaching, and you never laid a finger on
me. But the Scriptures must be fulfilled."

Then all the disciples deserted him and made their escape.
There happened to be a young man among Jesus' followers
who wore nothing but a linen shirt. They seized him, but he
left the shirt in their hands and took to his heels stark
naked.

JESUS BEFORE THE HIGH PRIEST

So they marched Jesus away to the High Priest in whose 14
presence all the Chief Priests and elders and Scribes had 53
assembled. (Peter followed him at a safe distance, right up
to the High Priest's courtyard. There he sat in the firelight
with the servants, keeping himself warm.) Meanwhile, the
Chief Priests and the whole Council were trying to find some
evidence against Jesus which would warrant the death penalty. But they failed completely. There were plenty of people
ready to give false testimony against him, but their evidence was contradictory. Then some more perjurers stood up
and said,

"We heard him say, 'I will destroy this Temple that was built by human hands and in three days I will build another made without human aid.' "

But even so their evidence conflicted. So the High Priest himself got up and took the centre of the floor.

"Have you no answer to make?" he asked Jesus. "What about all this evidence against you?"

But Jesus remained silent and offered no reply. Again the High Priest asked him,

"Are you Christ, Son of the Blessed One?"

And Jesus said,

"I am! Yes, you will see the Son of Man sitting at the right hand of power, coming in the clouds of heaven."

Then the High Priest tore his robes and cried,

"Why do we still need witnesses? You heard the blasphemy; what is your opinion now?"

And their verdict was that he deserved to die. Then some of them began to spit at him. They blindfolded him and then slapped him, saying,

"Now prophesy who hit you!"

Even the servants who took him away slapped his face.

PETER, IN FEAR, DISOWNS HIS MASTER

14
66 In the meantime, while Peter was in the courtyard below, one of the High Priest's maids came and saw him warming himself. She looked closely at him, and said,

"You were with the Nazarene too—with Jesus!"

But he denied it.

"I don't know him and I don't know what you're talking about."

And he walked out into the gateway, and a cock crew.

Again the maid who had noticed him began to say to the men standing there,

"This is one of them!"

But he denied it again. A few minutes later the bystanders themselves said to Peter,

"You certainly are one of them. Why, you're a Galilean!"

But he started to curse and swear,

"I tell you I don't know the man you're talking about!"

Immediately the cock crew for the second time, and back

into Peter's mind came the words of Jesus, "Before the cock crows twice, you will disown me three times."

And he broke down and wept.

JESUS BEFORE PILATE

As soon as daylight came the Chief Priests called together a committee of elders, Scribes and members of the whole Council, bound Jesus and took him off and handed him over to Pilate. Pilate asked him straight out, 15 1

"Well, you—*are* you the king of the Jews?"

"Yes, I am," he replied.

The Chief Priests brought many accusations. So Pilate questioned him again,

"Have you nothing to say? Listen to all their accusations."

But Jesus made no further answer—to Pilate's astonishment.

Now it was Pilate's custom at festival-time to release a prisoner—anyone they asked for. There was in the prison at the time, with some other rioters, a man called Barabbas who had committed murder in a recent outbreak. The crowd surged forward and began to demand that Pilate should do what he usually did for them. So he spoke to them,

"Do you want me to set free the king of the Jews?"

For he knew perfectly well that the Chief Priests had handed Jesus over to him through sheer malice. But the Chief Priests worked on the crowd to get them to demand Barabbas' release instead. So Pilate addressed them once more,

"Then what am I to do with the man whom you call the king of the Jews?"

They shouted back,

"Crucify him!"

But Pilate replied,

"Why, what crime has he committed?"

But their voices rose to a roar,

"Crucify him!"

And as Pilate wanted to satisfy the crowd, he set Barabbas free for them, and after having Jesus flogged handed him over to be crucified.

Then the soldiers marched him away inside the courtyard of the governor's residence and called their whole company together. They dressed Jesus in a purple robe, and twisting some thorn-twigs into a crown, they put it on his head. Then they began to greet him,

"Hail, Your Majesty—King of the Jews!"

They hit him on the head with a stick and spat at him, and then bowed low before him on bended knee. And when they had finished their fun with him, they took off the purple cloak and dressed him again in his own clothes. Then they led him outside to crucify him. They compelled Simon, a native of Cyrene in Africa (the father of Alexander and Rufus), who was on his way from the fields at the time, to carry Jesus' cross.

THE CRUCIFIXION

15
22
They got him to a place called Golgotha (which means Skull Hill) and they offered him some drugged wine, but he would not take it. Then they crucified him, and shared out his garments, drawing lots to see what each of them would get. It was about nine o'clock in the morning when they nailed him to the cross. Over his head the placard of his crime read, "THE KING OF THE JEWS." They also crucified two bandits at the same time, one on each side of him. And the passers-by jeered at him, shaking their heads in mockery, saying,

"Hi, you! You could destroy the Temple and build it up again in three days, why not come down from the cross and save yourself?"

The Chief Priests also made fun of him among themselves and the Scribes, and said,

"He saved others, he cannot save himself. If only this Christ, the king of Israel, would come down now from the cross, we should see it and believe!"

And even the men who were crucified with him hurled abuse at him.

At midday darkness spread over the whole countryside and lasted until three o'clock in the afternoon, and at three o'clock Jesus cried with a loud voice,

"My God, my God, why did You forsake me?"

Some of the bystanders heard these words which Jesus spoke in Aramaic (*Eli, Eli, lama sabachthani?*), and said,

"Listen, he's calling for Elijah!"

One man ran off and soaked a sponge in vinegar, put it on a stick, and held it up for Jesus to drink, calling out,

"Let him alone! Let's see if Elijah will come and take him down!"

But Jesus let out a great cry, and died. The curtain of the Temple sanctuary was split in two from the top to the bottom. And when the centurion who stood in front of Jesus saw how he died, he said,

"He must indeed have been a son of God!"

There were some women there looking on from a distance, among them Mary of Magdala, Mary the mother of the younger James, Mary the mother of Joses, and Salome. These were the women who used to follow Jesus as he went about in Galilee and minister to his needs. And there were there besides many other women who had come up to Jerusalem with them.

THE BODY OF JESUS IS REVERENTLY
LAID IN A TOMB

When the evening came, because it was the day of Preparation, that is the day before the Sabbath, Joseph from Arimathaea, a distinguished member of the Council, who was himself prepared to accept the Kingdom of God, went boldly into Pilate's presence and asked for the body of Jesus. Pilate was surprised that he was already dead and he sent for the centurion and asked whether he had been dead long. On hearing the centurion's report, he gave Joseph the body of Jesus. So Joseph bought a linen winding-sheet, took Jesus down and wrapped him in it, and then put him in a tomb which had been hewn out of the solid rock, rolling a stone over the entrance to it. Mary of Magdala and Mary the mother of Joses were looking on and saw where he was laid.

15
42

EARLY ON THE FIRST "LORD'S DAY":
THE WOMEN ARE AMAZED

When the Sabbath was over, Mary of Magdala and Mary the mother of James and Salome bought spices so that they could go and anoint him. And very early in the morning on the first day of the week, they came to the tomb, just as the sun was rising.

16
1

"Who is going to roll the stone back from the doorway of the tomb?" they asked each other.

And then as they looked closer, they saw that the stone, which was a very large one, had been rolled back. So they went into the tomb and saw a young man in a white robe sitting on the right-hand side, and they were very frightened. But he said to them,

"There is no need to be startled. You are looking for Jesus of Nazareth Who was crucified. He has risen; He is not here. Look, here is the place where they laid Him. But do not stay here. Go and tell His disciples, and Peter, that He will be in Galilee before you. You will see Him there just as He told you."

And they got out of the tomb and ran away from it. They were trembling with excitement. They did not dare to breathe a word to anyone.

AN ANCIENT APPENDIX

16
9
When Jesus rose early on that first day of the week, He appeared first of all to Mary of Magdala, from whom He had driven out seven evil spirits. And she went and reported this to His sorrowing and weeping followers. They heard her say that He was alive and that she had seen Him, but they did not believe it.

Later, He appeared in a different form to two of them who were out walking, as they were on their way to the country. These two came back and told the others, but they did not believe them either. Still later He appeared to the Eleven themselves as they were sitting at table and reproached them for their lack of faith and reluctance to believe those who had seen Him after He had risen. Then He said to them,

"You must go out to the whole world and proclaim the Gospel to every creature. He who believes it and is baptized will be saved, but he who disbelieves it will be condemned. These signs will follow those who do believe: they will drive out evil spirits in My Name; they will speak with new tongues; they will pick up snakes, and if they drink anything poisonous it will do them no harm; they will lay their hands upon the sick and they will recover."

JESUS, HIS MISSION ACCOMPLISHED, RETURNS TO HEAVEN

After these words to them, the Lord Jesus was taken up 16
into Heaven and was enthroned at the right hand of God. 19
They went out and preached everywhere. The Lord worked
with them, confirming their message by the signs that
followed.

THE GOSPEL OF
LUKE

The author of this Gospel is beyond reasonable doubt Luke, "the beloved physician," companion and fellow-worker of Paul. This work is, of course, only the first of his "two volumes," the second being what we know as the Acts of the Apostles. It is generally recognised that he was not a Jew and that he was a doctor by profession.

This Gospel is thought by many to be the most beautiful of the Four, both because of its style and of the imaginative sympathy with which he paints the portrait of his Master. There is a persistent legend that Luke was an artist, and while this is a matter of uncertainty, we owe to him a definite enrichment and enlargement of the story of Jesus which gives the impression of an artist's sensitivity.

On his own admission Luke has carefully compared and edited existing narratives, but it would seem that he had access to a good deal of additional material, and we can reasonably guess at some of the sources from which he drew it. He would almost certainly know Mark's Gospel; he would be able to draw from the mysterious "Q," which scholars believe to have existed, although there is no trace of it; and he had his own reminiscences and material collected in Caesarea (Acts 24, 27).

Though it is impossible to state accurately how the work was composed, a great many scholars think that there was a first version, possibly written during his travels with Paul, and that later material—the birth stories and the preface, for example—was incorporated later. Luke, like Mark, is writing primarily for the non-Jewish reader. A Gentile centurion, for example, is singled out as having more faith than Jesus had found in Israel; more than once, Samaritans, who were anathema to the Jews, are singled out for praise. Jesus' ancestry is traced back, not to Abraham the father of the Jewish race, but to Adam the father of all mankind.

None of the other evangelists shows so clearly the love and sympathy of Jesus for the sinner, the outcast and the unfortunate. And there is a reverence for women as the story unfolds, which shows the writer, through his understanding of his Master, far ahead of his time. Most scholars consider this Gospel to have been written about 80, that is, some ten years after the fall of Jerusalem. The graphic, but always careful and accurate, style conveys a strong impression of veracity.

PREFATORY NOTE

DEAR THEOPHILUS, *

Since many people have already written an account of the events which have happened among us, basing their work on the evidence of those who we know were eye-witnesses as well as teachers of the Message, I have decided, since I have traced the course of these happenings from the beginning, to set them down for you myself in their proper order, so that you may have reliable information about the matters in which you have already had instruction.

A VISION COMES TO AN OLD PRIEST OF GOD

The story begins, in the days when Herod was King of Judaea, with a priest called Zacharias (who belonged to the Abijah section of the priesthood), whose wife, Elisabeth, was like him, a descendant of Aaron. They were both truly religious people, blamelessly observing all God's commandments and requirements. They were childless through Elisabeth's infertility, and both of them were getting on in years. One day, while Zacharias was performing his priestly functions (it was the turn of his division to be on duty), it fell to him to go into the sanctuary and burn the incense. The crowded congregation outside was praying at the actual time of the incense-burning, when an angel of the Lord appeared on the right side of the incense-altar. When Zacharias saw him, he was terribly agitated and a sense of awe swept over him. But the angel spoke to him,

"Do not be afraid, Zacharias; your prayers have been heard. Elisabeth your wife will bear you a son, and you are

1
5

* *Theophilus:* either a convert from Paganism or a general term, meaning in Greek "Loved by God."

to call him John. This will be joy and delight to you and many more will be glad because he is born. He will be one of God's great men; he will touch neither wine nor strong drink and he will be filled with the Holy Spirit from the moment of his birth. He will turn many of Israel's children to the Lord their God. He will go out before God in the spirit and power of Elijah—to reconcile fathers and children, and bring back the disobedient to the wisdom of good men—and he will make a people fully ready for their Lord."

But Zacharias replied to the angel,

"How can I know that this is true? I am an old man myself and my wife is getting on in years . . ."

"I am Gabriel," the angel answered, "I stand in the presence of God, and I have been sent to speak to you and tell you this good news. Because you do not believe what I have said, you shall live in silence, and you shall be unable to speak a word until the day that it happens. But be sure that everything that I have told you will come true at the proper time."

Meanwhile, the people were waiting for Zacharias, wondering why he stayed so long in the sanctuary. But when he came out and was unable to speak a word to them—for although he kept making signs, not a sound came from his lips—they realised that he had seen a vision in the Temple. Later, when his days of duty were over, he went back home, and soon afterwards his wife Elisabeth became pregnant and kept herself secluded for five months.

"How good the Lord is to me," she would say, "now that He has taken away my disgrace."

A VISION COMES TO A YOUNG WOMAN IN NAZARETH

1
26
Then, six months after Zacharias' vision, the angel Gabriel was sent from God to a Galilean town, Nazareth by name, to a young woman who was engaged to a man called Joseph (a descendant of David). The girl's name was Mary. The angel entered her room and said,

"Greetings to you, Mary. O favoured one!—the Lord be with you!"

Mary was deeply perturbed at these words and wondered what such a greeting could possibly mean. But the angel said to her,

"Do not be afraid, Mary; God loves you dearly. You are

going to be the mother of a son, and you will call him Jesus. He will be great and will be known as the Son of the Most High. The Lord God will give him the throne of his fore-father, David, and he will be King over the people of Jacob for ever. His reign shall never end."

Then Mary spoke to the angel,

"How can this be," she said, "I am not married!"

And then the angel made this reply to her—

"The Holy Spirit will come upon you, the power of the Most High will overshadow you. Your child will therefore be called Holy—the Son of God. Your cousin Elisabeth has also conceived a son, old as she is. Indeed, this is the sixth month for her, a woman who was called barren. For every promise of God is sure to be fulfilled."

"I belong to the Lord, body and soul," replied Mary, "let it happen as you say." And at this the angel left her.

With little delay Mary got ready and hurried off to the hillside town in Judaea where Zacharias and Elisabeth lived. She went into their house and greeted her cousin. When Elisabeth heard her greeting, the unborn child stirred inside her and she herself was filled with the Holy Spirit, and cried out,

"Blessed are you among women, and blessed is your child! What an honour it is to have the mother of my Lord come to see me! Why, as soon as your greeting reached my ears, the child within me jumped for joy! Oh how happy is the woman who believes in God, for He does make His promises to her come true."

Then Mary said, "My heart is overflowing with praise of my Lord, my soul is full of joy in God my Saviour. For He has deigned to notice me, His humble servant and, after this, all the people who ever shall be will call me the happiest of women! The One Who can do all things has done great things for me—oh, Holy is His Name! Truly, His mercy rests on those who fear Him in every generation. He has shown the strength of His arm, He has swept away the high and mighty. He has set kings down from their thrones and lifted up the humble. He has satisfied the hungry with good things and sent the rich away with empty hands. Yes, He has helped Israel, His child: He has remembered the mercy that He promised to our forefathers, to Abraham and his sons for evermore!"

THE OLD WOMAN'S SON, JOHN, IS BORN

1   So Mary stayed with Elisabeth about three months, and
56   then went back to her own home. Then came the time for
Elisabeth's child to be born, and she gave birth to a son.
Her neighbours and relations heard of the great mercy the
Lord had shown her and shared her joy.

When the eighth day came, they were going to circumcise
the child and call him Zacharias, after his father, but his
mother said,

"Oh no! He must be called John."

"But none of your relations is called John," they replied.
And they made signs to his father to see what name he
wanted him to have. He beckoned for a writing-tablet and
wrote the words, "His name is John," which greatly surprised everybody. Then his power of speech quite suddenly
came back, and his first words were to thank God. The neighbours were awe-struck at this, and all these incidents were
reported in the hill-country of Judaea. People turned the
whole matter over in their hearts, and said,

"What is this child's future going to be, for the Lord
plainly has a hand in it?"

Then Zacharias, his father, filled with the Holy Spirit and
speaking like a prophet, said,

"Blessings on the Lord, the God of Israel, because He has
turned His face towards His people and has set them free!
And He has raised up for us a standard of salvation in His
servant David's house! Long, long ago, through the words of
His holy prophets, He promised to do this for us, so that we
should be safe from our enemies and secure from all who hate
us. So does He continue the mercy He showed to our forefathers. So does He remember the holy agreement He made
with them and the oath which He swore to our father
Abraham, to make us this gift: that we, secure from our
enemies, could serve Him unafraid and live before Him in
holiness and righteousness all our days.

"And you, little child, will be called the Prophet of the
Most High, for you will go before the Lord to prepare the
way for His coming. It will be for you to give His people
knowledge of their salvation through the forgiveness of their
sins. Because the heart of our God is full of mercy towards

us, the Light of Heaven shall come to visit us—to shine on those who lie in darkness and under the shadow of death, and to guide our feet into the path of peace."

The little child grew up and became strong in spirit. He lived in lonely places until the day came for him to show himself to Israel.

THE CENSUS BRINGS MARY AND JOSEPH
TO BETHLEHEM

At that time a proclamation was made by Caesar Augustus 2
that all the inhabited world should be registered. This was 1
the first census undertaken while Cyrenius was governor of Syria, and everybody went to the town of his birth to be registered. Joseph went up from the town of Nazareth in Galilee to David's town, Bethlehem, in Judaea, because he was a direct descendant of David, to be registered with his future wife, Mary, now in the later stages of her pregnancy. So it happened that it was while they were there in Bethlehem that she came to the end of her time. She gave birth to her first child, a son. And as there was no place for them inside the inn, she wrapped him up and laid him in a manger.

A VISION COMES TO SHEPHERDS ON
THE HILLSIDE

There were some shepherds living in the same part of the 2
country, keeping guard throughout the night over their flock 8
in the open fields. Suddenly an angel of the Lord stood by their side, the splendour of the Lord blazed around them, and they were terror-stricken. But the angel said to them,

"Do not be afraid! Listen, I bring you glorious news of great joy which is for every man. This very day, in David's town, a Saviour has been born for you. He is Christ, the Lord. Let this prove it to you: you will find a baby, wrapped up and lying in a manger."

And in a flash there appeared with the angel a vast host of the armies of Heaven, praising God, saying,

"Glory to God in the highest Heaven! Peace upon earth to men whom He loves!"

When the angels left them and went back into Heaven, the shepherds said to each other,

"Now let us go straight to Bethlehem and see this event which the Lord has told us about."

So they came as fast as they could and they found Mary and Joseph—and the baby lying in the manger. And when they had seen it, they told everybody what they had been told about the little child. And those who heard them were amazed at what the shepherds said. But Mary treasured all these things and turned them over in her mind. The shepherds went back to work, glorifying and praising God for everything that they had heard and seen, which had happened just as they had been told.

MARY AND JOSEPH BRING THEIR NEWLY-BORN SON TO THE TEMPLE

2
21

At the end of the eight days, the time came for circumcising the child and he was called Jesus, the name given him by the angel before his conception.

When the "purification" time, stipulated by the Law of Moses, was completed, they brought Jesus to Jerusalem to present him to the Lord. This was to fulfil a requirement of the Law—

> Every male that openeth the womb shall be called holy to the Lord.

They also offered the sacrifice prescribed by the Law—

> A pair of turtle-doves, or two young pigeons.

In Jerusalem was a man by the name of Simeon. He was an upright man, devoted to the service of God, living in expectation of the "salvation of Israel." His heart was open to the Holy Spirit, and it had been revealed to him that he would not die before he saw the Lord's Christ. He had been led by the Spirit to go into the Temple, and when Jesus' parents brought the child in to have done to him what the Law required, he took him up in his arms, blessed God and said—

"At last, Lord, You dismiss Your servant in peace, as You promised! For with my own eyes I have seen Your Salvation which You have made ready for every people—a light to show truth to the Gentiles and bring glory to Your people Israel."

Joseph and Jesus' mother were surprised at what Simeon said about the child. And he gave them his blessing and said to Mary, the child's mother,

"This child is destined to make many fall and many rise in Israel and to set up a standard which many will attack—for he will expose the secret thoughts of many hearts. And for you . . . your very soul will be pierced by a sword."

There was also present, Anna, the daughter of Phanuel of the tribe of Asher, who was a prophetess. She was a very old woman, having had seven years married life, and was now a widow of eighty-four. She spent her whole life in the Temple and worshipped God night and day with fastings and prayers. She came up at this very moment, praised God and spoke about Jesus to all those in Jerusalem who were expecting redemption.

When they had completed all the requirements of the Law of the Lord, they returned to Galilee to their own town Nazareth. The child grew up and became strong and full of wisdom. And God's blessing was upon him.

TWELVE YEARS LATER: THE BOY JESUS
GOES WITH HIS PARENTS TO JERUSALEM

Every year at the Passover Festival, Jesus' parents used to go to Jerusalem. When he was twelve years old they went up to the City as usual for the Festival. When it was over they started back home; but, without Joseph and his mother knowing it, the boy Jesus stayed behind in Jerusalem. They went a day's journey assuming that he was somewhere in their company, and then they began to look for him among their relations and acquaintances. They failed to find him, however, and turned back to the City, looking for him as they went. Three days later, they found him—in the Temple, sitting among the teachers, listening to them and asking them questions. All those who heard him were astonished at his powers of comprehension and at the answers that he gave. And when Joseph and Mary saw him, they could hardly believe their eyes, and his mother said to him,

"Why have you treated us like this, my son? Here have your father and I been very worried, looking for you everywhere!"

And Jesus replied,

"But why did you look for me? Did you not know that
I must be in my Father's House?"

But they did not understand this reply. Then he went
home with them to Nazareth and obeyed them. And his
mother treasured all these things in her heart. And as Jesus
grew up in body and mind, he grew also in the love of God
and of those who knew him.

SEVERAL YEARS LATER: JOHN PREPARES
THE WAY OF CHRIST

3
1
In the fifteenth year of the reign of the Emperor Tiberius
(a year when Pontius Pilate was governor of Judaea, Herod
tetrarch of Galilee, Philip, his brother, tetrarch of the territory of Ituraea and Trachonitis, and Lysanias tetrarch of
Abilene, while Annas and Caiaphas were the high-priests),
the word of God came to John, the son of Zacharias, while he
was in the desert. He went into the whole country round
about Jordan proclaiming baptism as a mark of a complete
change of heart and of the forgiveness of sins, as the book of
the prophet Isaiah says—

> The voice of one crying in the wilderness,
> Make ye ready the way of the Lord,
> Make his paths straight.
> Every valley shall be filled,
> And every mountain and hill shall be brought low:
> And the crooked shall become straight,
> And the rough ways smooth:
> And all flesh shall see the salvation of God.

So John used to say to the crowds who came out to be
baptized by him,

"Who warned you, you serpent's brood, to escape from the
wrath to come? See that you do something to show that your
hearts are really changed! Don't go thinking that you can
say to yourselves, 'We are "Abraham's children,"' for I tell
you that God could produce children of Abraham out of
these stones. The axe is already at the root of the tree, and
the tree that fails to produce good fruit is cut down and
thrown into the fire."

Then the crowds would ask him, "Then what shall we do?"

And his answer was, "The man who has two shirts must

share with the man who has none, and the man who has food must do the same."

Some of the tax-collectors came to him also to be baptized and they asked him,

"Master, what are we to do?"

"You must not demand more than the legal amount," he replied.

And the soldiers asked him, "And what are we to do?"

"Don't bully people, don't bring false charges and be content with your pay," he replied.

The people were in a great state of expectation and were inwardly discussing whether John could be Christ or not. But John answered them all in these words,

"It is true that I baptize you with water, but the one who follows me is stronger than I am—indeed I am not good enough to untie his sandals—he will baptize you with the fire of the Holy Spirit. He will come prepared to separate the wheat from the chaff and clear the rubbish from his threshing-floor. The wheat he will collect into his barn and the chaff he will burn with a fire that cannot be put out."

These and many other things John said to the people as he exhorted them and announced the Good News. But the tetrarch Herod, who had been condemned by John in the affair of Herodias, his brother's wife, as well as for the other evil things that he had done, crowned his misdeeds by putting John in prison.

JESUS, THE DESCENDANT OF ADAM,
IS ALSO BAPTIZED, AND
FACES TEMPTATION

When all the people had been baptized, and Jesus was praying after his own baptism, the heavens opened and the Holy Spirit came down upon him in the bodily form of a dove. Then there came a Voice from Heaven, saying, 3
21

"You are my dearly-loved Son, in Whom I am well pleased."

Jesus himself was about thirty years old at this time when he began his work. It was assumed that he was the son of Joseph whose ancestry may be traced through the generations past Abraham, to Adam and back to God.

Jesus returned from the Jordan full of the Holy Spirit and he was led by the Spirit to spend forty days in the desert, where he was tempted by the devil. He ate nothing during that time and afterwards he felt very hungry.

"If you really are the Son of God," the devil said to him, "tell this stone to turn into a loaf."

Jesus answered,

"The Scripture says, '*Man shall not live by bread alone.*'"

Then the devil took him up and showed him all the kingdoms of mankind in a sudden vision, and said to him,

"I will give you all this power and magnificence, for it belongs to me and I can give it to anyone I please. It shall all be yours if you will fall down and worship me."

To this Jesus replied,

"It is written, '*Thou shalt worship the Lord thy God and Him only shalt thou serve.*'"

Then the devil took him to Jerusalem and set him on the highest ledge of the Temple.

"If you really are the Son of God," he said, "throw yourself down from here, for the Scripture says, '*He shall give His angels charge concerning thee, to guard thee,*' and '*On their hands they shall bear thee up, lest haply thou dash thy foot against a stone.*'"

To which Jesus replied,

"It is also said, '*Thou shalt not tempt the Lord thy God.*'"

And when he had exhausted every kind of temptation, the devil withdrew until his next opportunity.

JESUS BEGINS HIS MINISTRY IN GALILEE

4
14   And now Jesus returned to Galilee in the power of the Spirit, and news of him spread through all the surrounding district. He taught in their synagogues, to everyone's great admiration.

Then he came to Nazareth where he had been brought up and, according to his custom, went to the synagogue on the Sabbath day. He stood up to read the Scriptures and the book of the prophet Isaiah was handed to him. He opened the book and found the place where these words are written—

The Spirit of the Lord is upon me,
Because he anointed me to preach good tidings to the poor:
He hath sent me to proclaim release to the captives,

And recovering of sight to the blind,
To set at liberty them that are bruised,
To proclaim the acceptable year of the Lord.

Then he shut the book, handed it back to the attendant and resumed his seat. Every eye in the synagogue was fixed upon him and he began to tell them that "This very day this Scripture has been fulfilled, while you have been listening to it!"

Everybody noticed what he said and was amazed at the beautiful words that came from his lips, and they kept saying, "Isn't this Joseph's son?"

So he said to them,

"I expect you will be saying this proverb to me, 'Cure yourself, doctor!' Let us see you do in your country all that we have heard that you did in Capernaum!" Then he added, "I assure you that no prophet is ever welcomed in his own country. I tell you the plain fact that in Elijah's time, when the heavens were shut up for three and a half years and there was a great famine through the whole country, there were plenty of widows in Israel, but Elijah was not sent to any of them. But he *was* sent to Sarepta, to a widow in the country of Sidon. In the time of Elisha the prophet, there were a great many lepers in Israel, but not one of them was healed —only Naaman, the Syrian."

But when they heard this, everyone in the synagogue was furiously angry. They sprang to their feet and pushed him right out of the town, taking him to the brow of the hill on which it was built, intending to hurl him down bodily. But he walked straight through the whole crowd and went on his way.

JESUS HEALS IN CAPERNAUM

So he came down to Capernaum, a town in Galilee, and taught them on the Sabbath day. They were astonished at his teaching, for what he said had the ring of authority. 4 31

There was a man in the synagogue under the influence of some evil spirit and he yelled at the top of his voice, "Hi! What have you got to do with us, Jesus, you Nazarene—have you come to kill us? I know who you are all right, you're God's Holy One!"

Jesus cut him short and spoke sharply,

"Be quiet! Get out of him!"

And after throwing the man down in front of them, the devils did come out of him without hurting him in the slightest. At this, everybody present was amazed and they kept saying to each other,

"What kind of talk is this? He speaks to these evil spirits with authority and power and out they come."

And his reputation spread over the whole surrounding district.

When Jesus got up and left the synagogue he went into Simon's house. Simon's mother-in-law was suffering from a high fever, and they asked Jesus about her. He stood over her as she lay in bed, brought the fever under control and it left her. At once she got up and began to see to their needs.

Then, as the sun was setting, all those who had friends suffering from all kinds of disease brought them to Jesus and he laid his hands on each one of them separately and healed them. Evil spirits came out of many of these people, shouting, "You are the Son of God!"

But he spoke sharply to them and would not allow them to say any more, for they knew perfectly well that he was Christ.

JESUS ATTEMPTS TO BE ALONE—IN VAIN

4
42   At daybreak, he went off to a deserted place, but the crowds tried to find him and when they did discover him, tried to prevent him from leaving them. But he told them, "I must tell the good news of the Kingdom of God to other towns as well—that is my mission."

And he continued proclaiming his message in the synagogues of Judaea.

SIMON, JAMES, AND JOHN BECOME
JESUS' FOLLOWERS

5
1   One day the people were crowding closely round Jesus to hear God's message, as he stood on the shore of Lake Gennesaret. Jesus noticed two boats drawn up on the beach, for the fishermen had left them there while they were cleaning their nets. He went aboard one of the boats, which belonged to Simon, and asked him to push out a little from the shore.

Then he sat down and continued his teaching of the crowds from the boat.

Then, when he had finished speaking, he said to Simon, "Push out now into deep water and let down your nets for a catch."

Simon replied, "All right, Master! We've worked all night and never caught a thing, but if you say so, I'll let the nets down."

And when they had done this, they caught an enormous shoal of fish—so big that the nets began to tear. So they signalled to their friends in the other boat to come and help them. They came and filled both the boats to sinking point. When Simon Peter saw this, he fell on his knees before Jesus and said,

"Keep away from me, Lord, for I'm only a sinful man!"

For he and his companions (including Zebedee's sons, James and John, Simon's partners) were staggered at the haul of fish that they had made.

Jesus said to Simon, "Don't be afraid, Simon. From now on your catch will be *men*."

So they got the boats ashore, left everything and followed him.

JESUS CURES LEPROSY

In one of the towns, Jesus met a man who was a mass of   5
leprosy. When he saw Jesus, he prostrated himself before   12
him and begged,

"If you want to, Lord, you can make me clean."

Jesus stretched out his hand, placed it on the leper, saying, "Of course I want to. You are clean."

Immediately the leprosy left him and Jesus warned him not to tell anybody, but to go and show himself to the priest and to make the offerings for his recovery that Moses pre-scribed, as evidence to the authorities.

Yet the news about him spread all the more, and enormous crowds collected to hear Jesus and to be healed of their dis-eases. But he slipped quietly away to deserted places for prayer.

JESUS CURES A PARALYTIC IN SOUL AND BODY

One day while Jesus was teaching, some Pharisees and ex-   5
perts in the Law were sitting near him. They had come out of   17

every village in Galilee and Judaea as well as from Jerusalem, and God's power to heal people was with him. In the middle of all this some men arrived carrying a paralytic on a small mat and they tried to get to Jesus, for they wanted to carry the patient in and put him down in front of him. When they failed to find a way of getting him in because of the dense crowd, they went up on to the top of the house and let him down, mat and all, through the tiles, into the middle of the crowd in front of Jesus. When Jesus saw their faith, he said to the man,

"My friend, your sins are forgiven."

The Scribes and the Pharisees began to argue about this, saying, "Who is this man who talks blasphemy? Who can forgive sins? Only God can do that."

Jesus realised what was going on in their minds and spoke straight to them.

"Why must you argue like this in your minds? Which do you suppose is easier—to say, 'Your sins are forgiven' or to say, 'Get up and walk'? But to make you realise that the Son of Man has full authority on earth to forgive sins—I tell *you*," he said to the man who was paralysed, "get up, pick up your mat and go home!"

Instantly, the man sprang to his feet in front of them, picked up the bedding on which he used to lie, and went off home, praising God. Sheer amazement gripped every man present, and they praised God and said in awed voices, "We have seen incredible things today."

JESUS CALLS LEVI TO BE HIS DISCIPLE

5
27   Later on, Jesus went out and looked straight at a tax-collector called Levi, as he sat at his office desk.

"Follow me," he said to him.

And he got to his feet at once, left everything behind and followed him.

Then Levi gave a big reception for Jesus in his own house, and there was a great crowd of tax-collectors and others at table with them. The Pharisees and their companions the Scribes grumbled about this to Jesus' disciples, saying,

"Why do you have your meals with tax-collectors and sinners?"

Jesus answered them,

"It is not the healthy who need the doctor, but those
who are ill. I have not come to invite the 'righteous' but the
'sinners'—to change their ways."

JESUS HINTS AT WHO HE IS

Then they said to him,   5

"Why is it that John's disciples are always fasting and   33
praying, just like the Pharisees' disciples, but yours eat and
drink?"

Jesus answered,

"Can you expect wedding-guests to fast while they have
the bridegroom with them? The day will come when they
will lose the bridegroom; that will be the time for them to fast!"

Then he gave them this illustration.

"Nobody tears a piece from a new garment to patch up an
old one. If he does, he ruins the new one and the new piece
does not match the old.

"Nobody puts new wine into old wine-skins. If he does,
the new wine will burst the skins—the wine will be spilt and
the skins ruined. No, new wine must be put into new wineskins. Of course, nobody who has been drinking old wine will
want the new at once. He is sure to say, 'The old is a good
sound wine.'"

On another Sabbath day, as he happened to be passing
through the wheatfields, his disciples began picking the ears,
rubbing them in their hands, and eating them. Some of the
Pharisees said to them,

"Why are you doing what the Law forbids men to do on
the Sabbath day?"

Jesus answered them and said,

"Have you never read what David and his companions did
when they were hungry? How he went into the House of
God, took the Presentation Loaves, ate some bread himself
and gave some to his companions, even though the Law does
not permit anyone except the priest to eat it?"

Then he added, "The Son of Man is master even of the
Sabbath."

JESUS PROVOKES VIOLENT ANTAGONISM

On yet another Sabbath day when he went into a syna-   6
gogue to teach, there was a man there whose right hand was   6

all wasted away. The Scribes and the Pharisees were watching
Jesus closely to see whether he would heal on the Sabbath
day, which would, of course, give them grounds for an accusation. But he knew exactly what was going on in their minds
and said to the man with the wasted hand,

"Stand up and come out in front."

And he got up and stood there. Then Jesus said to them,

"I am going to ask you a question. Does the Law command us to do good on Sabbath days or do harm—to save
life or destroy it?"

He looked round, meeting all their eyes, and said to the
man,

"Now stretch out your hand."

He did so, and his hand was restored as sound as the other
one. But they were filled with insane fury and kept discussing with each other what they could do to Jesus.

AFTER A NIGHT OF PRAYER JESUS SELECTS
THE TWELVE

6
12   About this time, it happened that he went up into a mountain to pray and spent the whole night in prayer to God.
When daylight came, he summoned his disciples to him and
out of them he chose twelve whom he called Apostles. They
were—

Simon (whom he called Peter),
Andrew, his brother,
James,
John,
Philip,
Bartholomew,
Matthew,
Thomas,
James, the son of Alphaeus,
Simon, called the Patriot,
Judas, the brother of James, and
Judas Iscariot, who later betrayed him.

Then he came down with them and took his stand on a
level piece of ground, surrounded by a large crowd of his disciples and a great number of people from all parts of Judaea
and Jerusalem and the coastal district of Tyre and Sidon

who had come to hear him and to be healed of their diseases.
(And even those who were troubled with evil spirits were
cured.) The whole crowd were trying to touch him with
their hands, for power was going out from him and he was
healing them all.

JESUS DECLARES WHO IS HAPPY AND WHO IS
TO BE PITIED AND DEFINES A NEW
ATTITUDE TOWARDS LIFE

Then Jesus looked steadily at his disciples and said,   6

"How happy are you who own nothing, for the Kingdom   20
of God is yours!

"How happy are you who are hungry now, for you will be
satisfied!

"How happy are you who weep now, for you are going
to laugh!

"How happy you are when men hate you and turn you out
of their company; when they slander you and loathe all that
you stand for because you are loyal to the Son of Man. Be
glad when that happens and jump for joy—your reward in
Heaven is magnificent. For that is exactly how their fathers
treated the prophets.

"But how miserable for you who are rich, for you have had
all your comforts.

"How miserable for you who have all you want, for you
are going to be hungry.

"How miserable for you who are laughing now, for you
will know sorrow and tears.

"How miserable for you when everybody says nice things
about you, for that is exactly how their fathers treated the
false prophets.

"But I say to all of you who will listen to me: love your
enemies, do good to those who hate you, bless those who
curse you, and pray for those who treat you badly.

"As for the man who hits you on one cheek, offer him the
other one as well! And if a man is taking away your coat, do
not stop him from taking your shirt as well. Give to everyone
who asks you and when a man has taken what belongs to you,
don't demand it back.

"Treat men exactly as you would like them to treat you.
If you love those who love you, what credit is that to you?

Even sinners love those who love them! And if you do good
to those who do good to you, what credit is that to you?
Even sinners do that. And if you lend to those from whom
you hope to get your money back, what credit is that to you?
Even sinners lend to sinners and get their money back. No,
you are to love your *enemies* and do good and lend without
expecting to get anything back. Your reward will be wonderful and you will be sons of the Most High. For He is good to
the ungrateful and the wicked!

"You must be kind, as your Father in Heaven is kind. Don't
judge other people and you will not be judged yourselves.
Don't condemn and you will not be condemned. Make allowances for others and they will make allowances for you. Give
and men will give to you—yes, good measure, pressed down,
shaken together and running over will they pour into your
lap. For whatever measure you use with other people, they
will use in their dealings with you."

THE NEED FOR THOROUGH-GOING SINCERITY

6   Then he gave them an illustration—
39   "Can one blind man be guide to another blind man? Surely
they will both fall into the ditch together. A disciple is not
above his teacher, but when he is fully trained he will be like
his teacher.

"Why do you look at the speck of sawdust in your
brother's eye and fail to notice the plank in your own? How
can you say to your brother, 'Let me take the speck out of
your eye,' when you cannot see the plank in your own? You
fraud, take the plank out of your own eye first and then you
can see clearly enough to remove your brother's speck.

"It is impossible for a good tree to produce bad fruit—as
impossible as it is for a bad tree to produce good fruit. Do
not men know what a tree is by its fruit? You cannot pick
figs from briars, or gather a bunch of grapes from a black-
berry bush! A good man produces good from the good things
stored up in his heart, and a bad man produces evil from his
own stores of evil. For his words will certainly show what is
treasured in his heart.

"And what is the point of calling me 'Lord, Lord,' without
doing what I tell you to do? Let me show you what the man
who comes to me, hears what I have to say, and puts it into

practice, is really like. He is like a man building a house, who dug down to rock-bottom and made the foundation of his house on the rock. Then when the flood came and the flood-water swept down upon that house, it could not shift it because it was properly built. But the man who hears me and does nothing about it is like a man who builds his house with a foundation upon soft earth. When the flood-water sweeps down upon it, it collapses and the whole house crashes down in ruins."

A ROMAN CENTURION'S EXTRAORDINARY FAITH IN JESUS

When Jesus had finished these talks to the people, he came to Capernaum, where it happened that there was a man very seriously ill and in fact at the point of death. He was the slave of a centurion who thought very highly of him. When the centurion heard about Jesus, he sent some Jewish elders to him with the request that he would come and save his servant's life. When they came to Jesus, they urged him strongly to grant this request, saying that the centurion deserved to have this done for him. "He loves our nation and has built us a synagogue out of his own pocket," they said.

So Jesus went with them, but as he approached the house, the centurion sent some of his personal friends with the message,

"Don't trouble yourself, sir! I'm not important enough for you to come into my house—I didn't think I was fit to come to you in person. Just give the order, please, and make my slave well. I am used to working under orders, and I have soldiers under me. I can say to one, 'Go,' and he goes, or I can say to another, 'Come here,' and he comes; or I can say to my servant, 'Do this job,' and he does it."

These words amazed Jesus and he turned to the crowd who were following behind him, and said,

"I have never found faith like this anywhere in Israel!"

Then those who had been sent by the centurion returned to the house and found the slave perfectly well.

JESUS BRINGS A DEAD YOUTH BACK TO LIFE

Not long afterwards, Jesus went into a town called Nain, accompanied by his disciples and a large crowd of people. As

7
1

7
11

they approached the city gate, it happened that some people
were carrying out a dead man, the only son of his widowed
mother. The usual crowd of fellow-townsmen was with her.
When the Lord saw her, his heart went out to her and he said,

"Don't cry."

Then he walked up and put his hand on the bier while the
bearers stood still. Then he said,

"Young man, *wake up!*"

And the dead man sat up and began to talk, and Jesus
handed him to his mother. Everybody present was awe-
struck and they praised God, saying,

"A great prophet has arisen among us and God has turned
His face towards His people."

And his reputation spread through the whole of Judaea
and the surrounding countryside.

JESUS SENDS JOHN A PERSONAL MESSAGE

7
18
John's disciples reported all these happenings to him. Then
he summoned two of them and sent them to the Lord with
this message,

"Are you the One Who was to come, or are we to look for
someone else?"

When the men came to Jesus, they said,

"John the Baptist has sent us to you with this message,
'Are you the One Who was to come, or are we to look for
someone else?' "

At that very time Jesus was healing many people of their
diseases and ailments and evil spirits, and he restored the gift
of sight to many who were blind. Then he answered them,

"Go and tell John what you have seen and heard. The
blind are recovering their sight, cripples are walking again,
lepers being healed, the deaf hearing, dead men are being
brought to life again, and the Good News is going to those in
need. *And happy is the man who never loses his faith in me.*"

JESUS EMPHASISES THE GREATNESS OF JOHN—
AND THE GREATER IMPORTANCE OF
THE KINGDOM OF GOD

7
24
When these messengers had gone back, Jesus began to talk
to the crowd about John.

"What did you go out into the desert to look at? Was it

a reed waving in the breeze? Well, *what* was it you went out
to see? A man dressed in fine clothes? But the men who wear
fine clothes live in palaces. But what *did* you really go to see?
A prophet? Yes, I tell you, a prophet and even more than a
prophet! This is the man of whom the Scripture says,

Behold, I send my messenger before thy face,
Who shall prepare thy way before thee.

Believe me, no one greater than John has ever been born
and yet a humble member of the Kingdom of God is greater
than he.

"All the people, yes, even the tax-collectors, when they
heard John, acknowledged God and were baptized by his baptism. But the Pharisees and the experts in the Law spoiled
God's purpose for them, for they refused John's baptism.

"What can I say that the men of this generation are like—
what sort of men are they? They are like children sitting in
the market-place and calling out to each other, 'We played
at weddings for you, but you wouldn't dance, and we played
at funerals for you, and you wouldn't cry!' For John the
Baptist came in the strictest austerity and you say he is crazy.
Then the Son of Man came, enjoying life, and you say, 'Look,
a drunkard and a glutton, a bosom-friend of the tax-collector
and the outsider!' Ah well, Wisdom stands or falls by the way
her whole family behaves."

JESUS CONTRASTS UNLOVING RIGHTEOUSNESS
WITH LOVING PENITENCE

Then one of the Pharisees asked Jesus to a meal with him.   7
When Jesus came into the house, he took his place at the   36
table and a woman, known in the town as a bad woman,
found out that Jesus was there and brought an alabaster flask
of perfume and stood behind him crying, letting her tears fall
on his feet and then drying them with her hair. Then she
kissed them and anointed them with the perfume. When
the Pharisee who had invited him saw this, he said to himself, "If this man were really a prophet, he would know who
this woman is and what sort of a person is touching him.
He would have realised that she is a bad woman." Then
Jesus spoke to him,

"Simon, there is something I want to say to you."

"Very well, Master," he returned, "say it."

"Once upon a time, there were two men in debt to the same money-lender. One owed him fifty dollars and the other five. And since they were both unable to pay, he generously cancelled both their debts. Now, which one of them do you suppose will love him more?"

"Well," returned Simon, "I suppose it will be the one who has been more generously treated."

"Exactly," replied Jesus, and then turning to the woman, he said to Simon,

"You can see this woman? I came into your house but you provided no water to wash my feet. But she has washed my feet with her tears and dried them with her hair. There was no warmth in your greeting, but she, from the moment I came in, has not stopped covering my feet with kisses. You gave me no oil for my head, but she has put perfume on my feet. That is why I tell you, Simon, that her sins, many as they are, are forgiven; for she has shown me so much love. But the man who is forgiven only a little will love only a little."

Then he said to her,

"Your sins are forgiven."

And the men at table with him began to say to themselves, "And who is this man, who even forgives sins?"

But Jesus said to the woman,

"It is your faith that has saved you. Go in peace."

Not long after this incident, Jesus went through every town and village preaching and telling the people the good news of the Kingdom of God. He was accompanied by the Twelve and some women who had been cured of evil spirits and illnesses—Mary, known as "the woman from Magdala" (who had once been possessed by seven evil spirits), Joanna the wife of Chuza, Herod's agent, Susanna, and many others who used to look after his comfort from their own resources.

JESUS' PARABLE OF THE MIXED RECEPTION
GIVEN TO THE TRUTH

8
4   When a large crowd had collected and people were coming to him from one town after another, he spoke to them and gave them this parable:

"A sower went out to sow his seed, and while he was sow-

ing, some of the seed fell by the roadside and was trodden
down and the birds gobbled it up. Some fell on the rock, and
when it sprouted it withered for lack of moisture. Some fell
among briars which grew up with the seeds and choked the
life out of them. But some seed fell on good soil and grew and
produced a crop—a hundred times what had been sown."

And when he had said this, he called out,

"Let the man who has ears to hear use them!"

Then his disciples asked him the meaning of the parable.
To which Jesus replied,

"You have been given the chance to understand the secrets
of the Kingdom of God, but the others are given parables so
that they go through life with their eyes open and see nothing,
and with their ears open, but understanding nothing of what
they hear.

"This is what the parable means. The seed is the message
of God. The seed sown by the roadside represents those who
hear the message, and then the devil comes and takes it away
from their hearts so that they cannot believe it and be saved.
That sown on the rock represents those who accept the message when they hear it with great delight, but have no real
root. They believe for a little while but when the time of
temptation comes, they lose faith. And the seed sown among
the briars represents the people who hear the message and go
on their way, and what with worries and riches and pleasures
of living, the life is choked out of them, and they produce no
'crop.' But the seed sown on good soil means the men who
hear the message and accept it in a good and honest heart,
and go on steadily producing a good crop.

TRUTH IS NOT A SECRET TO BE HIDDEN
BUT A GIFT TO BE USED

"Nobody lights a lamp and covers it with a basin or puts   8
it under the bed. No, a man puts his lamp on a lamp-stand   16
so that those who come in can see the light. For there is nothing hidden now which will not become perfectly plain and
there are no secrets now which will not become as clear as
daylight. So take care how you listen—more will be given to
the man who has something already, but the man who has
nothing will lose even what he thinks he has."

Then his mother and his brothers arrived to see him, but

could not get near him because of the crowd. So a message
was passed to him,

"Your mother and your brothers are standing outside
wanting to see you."

To which he replied,

"My mother and my brothers? That means those who
listen to God's message and obey it."

JESUS' MASTERY OF WIND AND WATER

8   It happened on one of those days that he embarked on a
22 boat with his disciples and said to them,

"Let us cross over to the other side of the lake."

So they launched the boat, and when they were under
way he dropped off to sleep. Then a squall of wind swept
down upon the lake and they were being swamped and were
in grave danger. Coming forward, they woke him up, saying,

"Master, Master, we're drowning!"

Then he got up and reprimanded the wind and the stormy
waters, and they died down, and everything was still. Then
he said to them,

"What has happened to your faith?"

But they were frightened and bewildered and kept saying
to each other,

"Who ever can this be? He gives orders to the wind and
water and *they obey him.*"

JESUS ENCOUNTERS AND HEALS
A DANGEROUS LUNATIC

8   They sailed on to the country of the Gerasenes which is
26 on the opposite side of the lake to Galilee. And as Jesus disembarked, a man from the town who was possessed by evil
spirits met him. He had worn no clothes for a long time and
did not live inside a house, but among the tombs. When
he saw Jesus, he let out a howl and fell down in front of
him, yelling,

"What have you got to do with me, you Jesus, Son of the
Most High God? Please, please, don't torment me."

For Jesus was commanding the evil spirit to come out of
the man. Again and again the evil spirit had taken control
of him, and though he was bound with chains and fetters and

closely watched, he would snap his bonds and go off into the
desert with the devil at his heels. Then Jesus asked him,

"What is your name?"

"Legion!" he replied. For many evil spirits had gone into
him, and were now begging Jesus not to order them off to the
bottomless pit. It happened that there was a large herd of
pigs feeding on the mountain-side, so they implored him to
allow them to go into the pigs, and he let them go. And when
the evil spirits came out of the man and went into the pigs,
the whole herd rushed down the cliff into the lake and were
drowned. When the swineherds saw what had happened,
they took to their heels, pouring out the story to the people
in the town and countryside. These people came out to see
what had happened, and approached Jesus. They found the
man, whom the evil spirits had left, sitting down at Jesus'
feet, properly dressed and quite composed, and this frightened
them. Those who had seen it told the others how the man
with the evil spirits had been cured. And the whole crowd of
people from the district surrounding the Gerasenes' country
begged Jesus to go away from them, for they were thoroughly scared. Then he re-embarked on the boat and turned
back. The man who had had the evil spirits kept begging that
he might go with Jesus, but he sent him away with the words,

"Go back home and tell them all what wonderful things
God has done for you."

So the man went away and told the marvellous story of
what Jesus had done for him, all over the town.

On Jesus' return, the crowd welcomed him back, for they
had all been looking for him.

JESUS HEALS IN RESPONSE TO FAITH

Then up came Jairus (he was president of the synagogue),   8
and fell at Jesus' feet, begging him to come into his house, for 41
his daughter, an only child about twelve years old, was dying.

But as he went, the crowds nearly suffocated him. Among
them was a woman who had had a haemorrhage for twelve
years and who had derived no benefit from any treatment.
She came up behind Jesus and touched the edge of his cloak,
with the result that her haemorrhage stopped at once.

"Who was that who touched me?" said Jesus.

And when everybody denied it, Peter remonstrated,

"Master, the crowds are all round you and are pressing you on all sides. . . ."

But Jesus said,

"Somebody touched me, for I felt that power went out from me."

Then the woman realised that she had not escaped notice and she came forward trembling, and fell at his feet and admitted before everybody why she had had to touch him, and how she had been instantaneously cured.

"Daughter," said Jesus, "it is your faith that has healed you —go in peace."

While he was still speaking, somebody came from the synagogue president's house to say,

"Your daughter is dead—there is no need to trouble the Master any further."

But when Jesus heard this, he said to him,

"Now don't be afraid, go on believing and she will be all right."

Then when he came to the house, he would not allow anyone to go in with him except Peter and John and James, and the child's parents. All those already there were weeping and wailing over her, but he said,

"Stop crying! She is not dead, she is fast asleep."

This drew a scornful laugh from them, for they had seen her die. But he turned them all out, took the little girl's hand and called out to her,

"Wake up, my child!"

And her spirit came back and she got to her feet at once, and Jesus ordered food to be given to her. Her parents were nearly out of their minds with joy, but Jesus told them not to tell anyone what had happened.

JESUS COMMISSIONS THE TWELVE TO
PREACH AND HEAL

9 Then he called the Twelve together and gave them power
1 and authority over all evil spirits and the ability to heal disease. He sent them out to preach the Kingdom of God and to heal the sick, with these words,

"Take nothing for your journey—neither a stick nor a purse nor food nor money, nor even extra clothes! When you come to stay at a house, remain there until you go on your

way again. And where they will not welcome you, leave that
town, and shake the dust off your feet as a protest against
them!"

So they set out, and went from village to village preaching
the Gospel and healing people everywhere.

HEROD'S UNEASY CONSCIENCE AFTER HIS
EXECUTION OF JOHN

All these things came to the ears of Herod the tetrarch and
caused him acute anxiety, because some people were saying
that John had risen from the dead, some maintaining that
the prophet Elijah had appeared, and others that one of the
old-time prophets had come back.

"I beheaded John," said Herod. "Who can this man be
that I hear all these things about?"

And he tried to find a way of seeing Jesus.

THE TWELVE RETURN AND TELL THEIR STORY

Then the Apostles returned, and when they had made their
report to Jesus of what they had done, he took them with him
and retired into a town called Bethsaida.

JESUS WELCOMES THE CROWDS, TEACHES,
HEALS AND FEEDS THEM

But the crowds observed this and followed him. And he
welcomed them and talked to them about the Kingdom of
God, and cured those who were in need of healing. Then the
day drew to its close and the Twelve came to him and said,

"Please dismiss the crowd now so that they can go to the
villages and country round about and find some food and
shelter, for we're quite in the wilds here."

"You give them something to eat!" returned Jesus.

"But we've nothing here," they replied, "except five loaves
and two fish, unless you want us to go and buy food for all
this crowd?" (There were approximately five thousand men
there.)

Then Jesus said to the disciples,

"Get them to sit down in groups of about fifty."

This they did, making them all sit down. Then he took
the five loaves and the two fish and looked up to Heaven,
blessed them, broke them into pieces and passed them to his

disciples to serve to the crowd. Everybody ate and was satisfied. Afterwards they collected twelve baskets full of broken
pieces which were left over.

JESUS ASKS A QUESTION AND RECEIVES
PETER'S MOMENTOUS ANSWER

9   Then came this incident. While Jesus was praying by him-
18 self the disciples approached him, and he asked them this
question:

"Who are the crowd saying that I am?"

"Some say that you are John the Baptist," they replied.
"Others that you are Elijah, and others think that one of the
old-time prophets has come to life again."

Then he said,

"And who do you say that I am?"

"*God's Christ!*" said Peter.

JESUS FORETELLS HIS OWN SUFFERING: THE
PARADOX OF LOSING LIFE TO FIND IT

9   But Jesus expressly told them not to say a word to any-
21 body, at the same time warning them of the inevitability of
the Son of Man's great suffering, of his repudiation by the
elders, Chief Priests and Scribes, and of his death and rising
again on the third day. Then he spoke to them all,

"If anyone wants to follow in my footsteps, he must give
up all right to himself, carry his cross every day and keep
close behind me. For the man who wants to save his life will
lose it, but the man who loses his life for my sake will save it.
For what is the use of a man gaining the whole world if he
loses or forfeits his own soul? If anyone is ashamed of me and
my words, the Son of Man will be ashamed of him, when he
comes in his glory and the glory of the Father and the holy
angels. I tell you the simple truth—there are men standing
here today who will not taste death until they have seen the
Kingdom of God!"

PETER, JOHN AND JAMES ARE ALLOWED TO
SEE THE GLORY OF JESUS

9   About eight days after these sayings, Jesus took Peter and
28 James and John and went off with them to the mountain to

pray. And then, while he was praying, the whole appearance
of his face changed and his clothes became white and dazzling. And there were two men talking with Jesus who were
Moses and Elijah—revealed in heavenly splendour and their
talk was about the way he must take and the end he must
fulfil in Jerusalem. But Peter and his companions had been
overcome by sleep and it was as they struggled into wakeful-
ness that they saw the glory of Jesus and the two men standing with him. Just as they were parting from him, Peter said
to Jesus,

"Master, it is wonderful for us to be here! Let us make
three shelters,—one for you, one for Moses and one for
Elijah." But he did not know what he was saying. While he
was still talking, a cloud overshadowed them and awe swept
over them as it enveloped them. A Voice came out of the
cloud, saying,

"This is My Son, My Chosen! See that you listen to Him!"

And while the Voice was speaking, they found there was
no one there at all but Jesus. The disciples were reduced to
silence, and in those days never breathed a word to anyone
of what they had seen.

JESUS HEALS AN EPILEPTIC BOY

Then on the following day, on their descent from the   9
mountain, a great crowd met him. And now we have a man   37
from the crowd shouting out,

"Master, please come and look at my son! He's my only
child, and without any warnings some spirit gets hold of him
and he calls out suddenly. Then it convulses him until he
foams at the mouth, and only after a fearful struggle does
it go away and leaves him bruised all over. I begged your
disciples to get rid of it, but they couldn't."

"You really are an unbelieving and difficult people," replied Jesus. "How long am I going to be with you and how
long must I put up with you? Bring him here to me."

But even while the young man was on his way, the spirit
hurled him to the ground in a dreadful convulsion. Then Jesus
reprimanded the evil spirit, healed the lad and handed him
back to his father. And everybody present was amazed at
this demonstration of the power of God.

THE REALISM OF JESUS IN THE MIDST
OF ENTHUSIASM

9   And while everybody was amazed at all the things they
43*b* saw him do, Jesus said to the disciples,

"Listen very carefully to what they are saying now, for the
Son of Man is going to be handed over to the power of men."

But they made no sense of this saying—something made it
impossible for them to understand it, and they were afraid to
ask him what he meant.

JESUS AND "GREATNESS"

9   Then an argument arose among them as to who should be
46 the greatest. But Jesus, knowing what they were arguing
about, took a little child and made him stand by his side.
And then he said to them,

"Anyone who accepts a little child in my name is really
accepting me, and the man who accepts me is really accepting
the One Who sent me. It is the humblest among you all who
is really the greatest."

Then John broke in,

"Master, we saw a man driving out evil spirits in your
name, but we stopped him, for he is not one of us who follow
you."

But Jesus told him,

"You must not stop him. The man who is not against you
is on your side."

HE SETS OFF FOR JERUSALEM TO MEET
INEVITABLE DEATH

9   Now as the days before he should be taken back into
51 Heaven were running out, he resolved to go to Jerusalem, and
sent messengers in front of him. They set out and entered
a Samaritan village to make preparations for him. But the
people there refused to welcome him because he was obviously intending to go to Jerusalem. When the disciples James
and John saw this, they said,

"Master, do you want us to call down fire from heaven
and burn them all up?"

But Jesus turned and reproved them, and they all went on
to another village.

As the little company made its way along the road, a man said to him,

"I'm going to follow you wherever you go."

And Jesus replied,

"Foxes have earths, birds have nests, but the Son of Man has nowhere to lay his head."

But he said to another man,

"Follow me."

And he replied,

"Let me first go and bury my father."

But Jesus told him,

"Leave the dead to bury their own dead. You must come away and preach the Kingdom of God."

Another man said to him,

"I am going to follow you, Lord, but first let me settle my affairs at home."

But Jesus told him,

"Anyone who puts his hand to the plough and then looks behind him is useless for the Kingdom of God."

JESUS NOW DESPATCHES THIRTY-FIVE COUPLES
TO PREACH AND HEAL THE SICK

Later on the Lord commissioned seventy other disciples, and sent them off in two's as advance-parties into every town and district where he intended to go.

"There is a great harvest," he told them, "but only a few are working in it—which means you must pray to the Lord of the harvest that he will send out more reapers.

"Now go on your way. I am sending you out like lambs among wolves. Don't carry a purse or a bag or a pair of shoes, and don't stop to pass the time of day with anyone you meet on the road. When you go into a house, say first of all, 'Peace be to this household!' If there is a lover of peace there, he will accept your words of blessing, and if not, they will come back to you. Stay in the same house and eat and drink whatever they put before you—a workman deserves his wages. But don't move from one house to another.

"Whatever town you go into and the people welcome you, eat the meals they give you and heal the people who are ill there. Tell them, 'The Kingdom of God has now come to you.' But whenever you come into a town and they will not welcome you, you must go into the streets and say, 'We brush off even the dust of your town from our feet as a protest against you. But it is still true that the Kingdom of God has arrived!' I assure you it will be better for Sodom in 'that Day' than for that town.

"Alas for you, Chorazin, and alas for you, Bethsaida! For if Tyre and Sidon had seen the demonstrations of God's power that you have seen, they would have repented long ago and sat in sackcloth and ashes. It will be better for Tyre and Sidon in the Judgment than for you! As for you, Capernaum, are you on your way up to heaven? I tell you you will go crashing down to hell!"

Then he added to the Seventy,

"Whoever listens to you is listening to me, and the man who has no use for you has no use for me either. And the man who has no use for me has no use for the One Who sent me!"

JESUS TELLS THE RETURNED MISSIONERS NOT TO BE ENTHUSIASTIC OVER MERE POWER

10
17 Later the Seventy came back full of joy. "Lord," they said, "even evil spirits obey us when we use your name!"

"Yes," returned Jesus, "I was watching and saw Satan fall from heaven like a flash of lightning! It is true that I have given you the power to tread on snakes and scorpions and to overcome all the enemy's power—there is nothing at all that can do you any harm. Yet it is not your power over evil spirits which should give you such joy, but the fact that your names are written in Heaven."

JESUS PRAYS ALOUD TO HIS FATHER

10
21 At that moment Jesus himself was inspired with joy, and exclaimed,

"O Father, Lord of Heaven and earth, I thank You for hiding these things from the clever and intelligent and for showing them to mere children! Yes, I thank You, Father, that this was Your Will." Then he went on,

"Everything has been put in my hands by my Father; and nobody knows who the Son really is except the Father. Nobody knows Who the Father really is except the Son—and the man to whom the Son decides to reveal Him!"

Then he turned to his disciples and said to them quietly,

"How fortunate you are to see what you are seeing! I tell you that many prophets and kings have wanted to see what you are seeing but they never saw it, and to hear what you are hearing but they never heard it."

JESUS SHOWS THE RELEVANCE OF THE LAW
TO ACTUAL LIVING

Then one of the experts in the Law stood up to test him and said,

"Master, what must I do to be sure of eternal life?"

"What does the Law say and what has your reading taught you?" said Jesus.

"The Law says, 'Thou shalt love the Lord thy God with all thy heart and with all thy soul and with all thy strength and with all thy mind—and thy neighbour as thyself,' " he replied.

"Quite right," said Jesus. "Do that and you will live."

But the man, wanting to justify himself, continued,

"But who is my 'neighbour'?"

And Jesus gave him the following reply:

"A man was once on his way down from Jerusalem to Jericho. He fell into the hands of bandits who stripped off his clothes, beat him up, and left him half dead. It so happened that a priest was going down that road, and when he saw him, he passed by on the other side. A Levite also came on the scene and when he saw him, he too passed by on the other side. But then a Samaritan traveller came along to the place where the man was lying, and at the sight of him he was touched with pity. He went across to him and bandaged his wounds, pouring on oil and wine. Then he put him on his own mule, brought him to an inn and did what he could for him. Next day he took out two dollars and gave it to the inn-keeper with the words, 'Look after him, will you? I will pay you back anything more than this that you spend, when I come through here on my return.' Which of these three seems to you to have been a neighbour to the bandits' victim?"

10
25

"The man who gave him practical sympathy," he replied.

"Then you go and give the same," returned Jesus.

YET EMPHASISES THE NEED FOR QUIET
LISTENING TO HIS WORDS

10 As they continued their journey, Jesus came to a village
38 and a woman called Martha welcomed him to her house. She
had a sister by the name of Mary who settled down at the
Lord's feet and was listening to what he said. But Martha
was very worried about her elaborate preparations and she
burst in, saying,

"Lord, don't you *mind* that my sister has left me to do
everything all by myself? Tell her to get up and help me!"

But the Lord answered her,

"Martha, my dear, you are worried and bothered about a
great many things. Only a few things are really needed, perhaps
only one. Mary has chosen the most important thing
and you must not tear her away from it!"

JESUS GIVES A MODEL PRAYER

11 One day it happened that Jesus was praying and after he
1 had finished, one of his disciples said,

"Lord, teach us how to pray, as John used to teach his
disciples."

"When you pray," returned Jesus, "you should say,
'Father, may Your Name be honoured—may Your Kingdom
come! Give us each day the bread we need, and forgive
us our sins, for we forgive anyone who owes anything to us;
and keep us clear of temptation.' "

THE WILLINGNESS OF THE FATHER TO
ANSWER PRAYER

11 Then he added,
5 "If any of you has a friend, and you go to him in the middle
of the night and say, 'Lend me three loaves, my dear fellow,
for a friend of mine has just arrived after a journey and I
have no food to put in front of him.' Then he answers from
inside the house, 'Don't bother me with your troubles. The
front door is locked and my children and I have gone to bed.
I simply cannot get up now and give you anything!' Yet, I

tell you, that even if he won't get up and give him what he wants simply because he is his friend, yet if he persists, he will rouse himself and give him everything he needs. And so I tell you, ask and it will be given you, search and you will find, knock and the door will be opened to you. The one who asks will always get; the one who is searching will always find, and the door is opened to the man who knocks. Some of you are fathers, and if your son asks you for some fish, would you give him a snake instead, or if he asks you for an egg, would you make him a present of a scorpion? So, if you, for all your evil, know how to give good things to your children, how much more likely is it that your Heavenly Father will give the Holy Spirit to those who ask!"

JESUS SHOWS THE ABSURDITY OF "HIS BEING IN LEAGUE WITH THE DEVIL"

Another time, Jesus was expelling an evil spirit which was preventing a man from speaking, and as soon as the evil spirit left him, the dumb man found his speech, to the amazement of the crowds.

But some of them said,

"He expels these spirits because he is in league with Beelzebub, the chief of the evil spirits."

Others among them, to test him, tried to get a sign from Heaven out of him. But he knew what they were thinking and told them,

"Any kingdom divided against itself is doomed and a disunited household will collapse. And if Satan disagrees with Satan, how does his kingdom continue?—for I know you are saying that I expelled evil spirits because I am in league with Beelzebub. But if I do expel devils because I am an ally of Beelzebub, who is your own sons' ally when they do the same thing? They can settle that question for you. But if it is by the finger of God that I am expelling evil spirits, *then the Kingdom of God has swept over you unawares!*

"When a strong man armed to the teeth guards his own house, his property is in peace. But when a stronger man comes and conquers him, he removes all the arms on which he pinned his faith and divides the spoil among his friends.

"Anyone who is not with me is against me, and the man who does not gather with me is really scattering.

THE DANGER OF A SPIRITUAL VACUUM
IN A MAN'S SOUL

11   "When the evil spirit comes out of a man, it wanders
24   through waterless places looking for rest, and when it fails
to find any, it says, 'I will go back to my house where I came
from.' When it arrives, it finds it clean and all in order.
Then it goes and collects seven other spirits more evil than
itself to keep it company, and they all go in and make themselves at home. The last state of that man is worse than the first."

JESUS BRINGS SENTIMENTALITY DOWN
TO EARTH

11   And while he was still saying this, a woman in the crowd
27   called out and said,
"Oh, what a blessing for a woman to have brought you
into the world and nursed you!"
But Jesus replied,
"Yes, but a far greater blessing to hear the word of God
and obey it."

HIS SCATHING JUDGMENT ON HIS
CONTEMPORARY GENERATION

11   Then as the people crowded closely around him, he con-
29   tinued,
"This is an evil generation! It looks for a sign and it will
be given no sign except that of Jonah. Just as Jonah was a
sign to the people of Nineveh, so will the Son of Man be
a sign to this generation. When the Judgment comes, the
Queen of the South will rise up with the men of this generation and she will condemn them. For she came from the ends
of the earth to listen to the wisdom of Solomon, and you
have something greater than the wisdom of Solomon with
you now! The men of Nineveh will stand up at the Judgment with this generation and will condemn it. For they did
repent when Jonah preached to them, and you have something greater than Jonah with you now!

THE NEED FOR COMPLETE SINCERITY

11   "No one takes a lamp and puts it in a cupboard or under
33   a bucket, but it is put on a lamp-stand so that those who

come in can see the light. The lamp of your body is your
eye. When your eye is sound, your whole body is full of
light, but when your eye is evil, your whole body is full of
darkness. So be very careful that your light never becomes
darkness. For if your whole body is full of light, with no part
of it in shadow, it will all be radiant, like the light you get
from a brightly-burning lamp."

While he was talking, a Pharisee invited him to dinner.
So he went into his house and sat down at table. When the
Pharisee noticed this, he was surprised that he did not wash
before the meal. But the Lord said to him,

"You Pharisees are fond of cleaning the outside of your
cups and dishes, but inside yourselves you are full of greed
and wickedness! Have you no sense? Don't you realise that
the One Who made the outside is the Maker of the inside as
well? Far better to make the inside clean by doing good and
you will find the outside things become clean as a matter of
course. But alas for you Pharisees, for you pay out your
tithe of mint and rue and every little herb, and lose sight
of the justice and the love of God. Yet these are the things
you ought to have been concerned with—it need not mean
leaving the lesser duties undone. Yes, alas for you Pharisees,
who love the front seats in the synagogues and having men
bow down to you in public! Alas for you Pharisees, play-
actors that you are, for you are like unmarked graves—
men walk over your corruption without ever knowing it is
there."

JESUS DENOUNCES THE LEARNED FOR
OBSCURING THE TRUTH

Then one of the experts in the Law said to him,   11

"Master, when you say things like this, you are insulting   45
us as well."

And he returned,

"Yes, and I do blame you experts in the Law! For you pile
up back-breaking burdens for men to bear, but you yourselves will not lift a finger to shift them. Alas for you, for
you build memorial tombs for the prophets—the very men
whom your fathers murdered. You show clearly enough how
you approve your fathers' actions. They did the actual killing and you put up a memorial to it. That is why the Wis-

dom of God has said, 'I will send them prophets and apostles, some they will kill and some they will persecute!' So that the blood of all the prophets shed from the foundation of the earth, from Abel to Zachariah who died between the altar and the sanctuary, shall be charged to this generation!

"Alas for you experts in the Law, for you have taken away the key of knowledge. You have never gone in yourselves and you have stopped everyone else who was at the door!"

And when he left the house, the Scribes and the Pharisees began to regard him with bitter animosity and tried to draw him out on a great many subjects, waiting to pounce on some incriminating remark.

Meanwhile, the crowds had gathered in thousands, so that they were actually treading on each other's toes, and Jesus, speaking primarily to his disciples, said,

"Be on your guard against yeast—I mean the yeast of the Pharisees, which is sheer pretence. For there is nothing covered up which is not going to be exposed, nor anything private which is not going to be made public. Whatever you may say in the dark will be heard in daylight, and whatever you whisper within four walls will be shouted from the housetops.

MAN NEED ONLY FEAR GOD

12 "I tell you that, as friends of mine, you need not be afraid
 4 of those who can kill the body, but afterwards cannot do anything more. I will show you the only One you need to fear—the One Who, after He has killed, has power to throw you into destruction! Yes, I tell you, it is right to stand in awe of Him. The market-price of five sparrows is two cents, isn't it? Yet not one of them is forgotten in God's sight. Why, the very hairs of your heads are all numbered! Don't be afraid, then, you are worth far more than sparrows! I tell you that every man who publicly acknowledges me, I will acknowledge in the presence of the angels of God. But the man who publicly disowns me will find himself disowned before the angels of God!

"Anyone who speaks against the Son of Man will be forgiven, but there is no forgiveness for the man who speaks evil against the Holy Spirit. And when they bring you before the synagogues and magistrates and authorities, don't worry as

to what defence you are going to put up or what words you
are going to use. The Holy Spirit will tell you at the time
what is the right thing for you to say."

JESUS GIVES A WARNING ABOUT THE LOVE
OF MATERIAL SECURITY

Then someone out of the crowd said to him,   12
"Master, tell my brother to share his legacy with me."   13
But Jesus replied,

"My dear man, who appointed me a judge or arbitrator in
your affairs?"

And then, turning to the disciples, he said to them,

"Notice that, and be on your guard against covetousness
in any shape or form. For a man's real life is nothing to do
with how much he possesses."

Then he gave them a parable in these words,

"Once upon a time, a rich man's farmland produced heavy
crops. So he said to himself, 'What shall I do, for I have no
room to store this harvest?' Then he said, 'I know what I'll
do. I'll pull down my barns and build bigger ones where I can
store all my grain and my goods and I can say to my soul,
Soul, you have plenty stored up there for years to come.
Relax! Eat, drink and have a good time!' But God said to
him, 'You fool, this very night you will be asked for *your
soul*! Then, who is going to have all that you have prepared?'
That is what happens to the man who hoards things for himself and is not rich where God is concerned."

And then he added to the disciples,

"That is why I tell you, don't worry about life, wondering
what you are going to eat. And stop bothering about what
clothes you will need. Life is much more important than
food, and the body more important than clothes. Think of
the ravens. They neither sow nor reap, and they have neither
store nor barn, but God feeds them. And how much more
valuable do you think you are than birds? Can any of you
make himself an inch taller however much he worries about
it? And if you can't manage a little thing like this, why do
you worry about anything else? Think of the wild flowers,
and how they neither work nor weave. Yet I tell you that
Solomon in all his glory was never arrayed like one of these.
If God so clothes the grass, which flowers in the field today

and is burnt in the stove tomorrow, is He not much more likely to clothe you, you little-faiths? You must not worry about getting food or drink, or live in a state of anxiety. The whole heathen world is busy about getting food and drink, and your Father knows well enough that you need such things. No, set your heart on His Kingdom, and your food and drink will come as a matter of course. Don't be afraid, you tiny flock! Your Father plans to give you the Kingdom. Sell your possessions and give the money away. Get yourselves purses that never grow old, inexhaustible treasure in Heaven, where no thief can ever get at it, or moth ruin it. For your heart is sure to be in the same place as your treasure.

JESUS' DISCIPLES MUST BE ON THE ALERT

12 "You must be ready dressed and have your lamps alight,
35 like men who wait to welcome their lord and master on his return from the wedding-feast, so that when he comes and knocks at the door, they may open for him at once. Happy are the servants whom their lord finds on the alert when he arrives. I assure you that then he will himself get dressed, make them sit down to dinner, and come and wait on them. And if he should come just after midnight or in the very early morning and find them still on the alert, their happiness is assured. But be certain of this, that if the householder had known the time when the burglar would come, he would not have left his house to be broken into. So you must be on the alert, for the Son of Man is coming at a time you may not expect."

Then Peter said to him.

"Lord, do you mean this parable for us or for everybody?"

But the Lord continued,

"Well, who will be the faithful, sensible steward whom his master will put in charge of his household to give them their supplies at the proper time? Happy is the servant if his master finds him doing so when he returns. I tell you he will promote him to look after all his property. But suppose the servant says to himself, 'My master takes his time about returning,' and then begins to beat the men and women servants and to eat and drink and get drunk, that servant's lord and master will return suddenly and unexpectedly, and

he will utterly expose him and send him to join all the other
hypocrites. The slave who knows his master's plan but does
not get ready or act upon it will be severely punished, but
the servant who did not know the plan, though he has done
wrong, will be let off lightly. Much will be expected from the
one who has been given much, and the more a man is trusted,
the more people will expect of him.

"It is fire that I have come to bring upon the earth—how
I could wish it were already ablaze! There is a baptism that I must undergo and how strained I am until it is
over!

JESUS DECLARES THAT HIS COMING IS
BOUND TO BRING DIVISION

"Do you think I have come to bring peace on the earth?   12
No, I tell you, not peace, but division. For from now on,   51
there will be five people divided against each other in one
house, three against two, and two against three. It is going
to be father against son, and son against father, and mother
against daughter, and daughter against mother; mother-in-
law against daughter-in-law, and daughter-in-law against
mother-in-law!"

INTELLIGENCE SHOULD BE USED NOT ONLY
ABOUT THE WEATHER BUT ABOUT THE
TIMES IN WHICH MEN LIVE

Then he said to the crowds,   12
"When you see a cloud appear in the west, you say at once   54
that it is going to rain, and so it does. And when you feel the
south wind blowing, you say that it is going to be hot, and so
it is. You frauds! You know how to interpret the look of the
earth and the sky. Why can't you interpret the meaning of
the times in which you live?

"And why can't you decide for yourselves what is right?
For instance, when you are going before the magistrate with
your opponent, do your best to come to terms with him while
you have the chance, or he may rush you off to the judge,
and the judge hand you over to the police-officer, and the
police-officer throw you into prison. I tell you you will
never get out again until you have paid out your last
cent."

JESUS IS ASKED ABOUT THE SUPPOSED
SIGNIFICANCE OF DISASTERS

13 It was just at this moment that some people came up to
1   tell him the story of the Galileans whose blood Pilate had
mixed with that of their own sacrifices. Jesus made this
reply to them:

"Are you thinking that these Galileans were worse than
any other men of Galilee because this happened to them? I
assure you that is not so. You will die just as miserable a
death unless your hearts are changed. You remember those
eighteen people who were killed at Siloam when the tower
collapsed upon them? Are you imagining that they were
worse than any of the other people who lived in Jerusalem?
I assure you they were not. You will all die just as tragically
unless your whole outlook is changed."

AND HINTS AT GOD'S PATIENCE WITH
THE JEWISH NATION

13 Then he gave them a parable:
6   "Once upon a time a man had a fig-tree growing in his
garden, and when he came to look for the figs, he found none
at all. So he said to his gardener, 'Look, I have come expecting fruit on this fig-tree for three years running and never
found any. Better cut it down. It's using up valuable space.'
And the gardener replied, 'Master, don't touch it this year
till I have had a chance to dig round it and give it a bit of
manure. Then, if it bears after that, it will be all right. But
if it doesn't, then you can cut it down.'"

JESUS REDUCES THE SABBATARIANS
TO SILENCE

13 It happened that he was teaching in one of the syna-
10 gogues on the Sabbath day. In the congregation was a
woman who for eighteen years had been enfeebled from some
psychological cause. She was bent double and was quite unable to straighten herself up. When Jesus noticed her, he
called her to him and said,

"You are set free from your illness!"

And he put his hands upon her, and at once she stood
upright and praised God. But the president of the syna-

gogue, in his annoyance at Jesus' healing on the Sabbath, announced to the congregation,

"There are six days in which men may work. Come on one of them and be healed, and not on the Sabbath day!"

But the Lord replied,

"You hypocrites, every single one of you unties his ox or his ass from the stall on the Sabbath day and leads him away to water! This woman, a daughter of Abraham, whom you all know Satan has kept bound for eighteen years—surely she should be released from her bonds on the Sabbath day!"

These words reduced his opponents to shame, but the crowd was thrilled at all the glorious things he did.

Then he went on,

"What is the Kingdom of God like? What illustration can I use to make it plain to you? It is like a grain of mustard seed which a man took and dropped in his own garden. It grew and became a tree and the birds came and nested in its branches."

Then again he said,

"What can I say the Kingdom of God is like? It is like the yeast which a woman took and covered up in three basins full of flour until the whole lot had risen."

THE KINGDOM IS NOT ENTERED BY DRIFTING
BUT BY DECISION

So he went on his way through towns and villages, teach-   13
ing as he went and making his way towards Jerusalem.   22
Someone remarked,

"Lord, are only a few men to be saved?"

And Jesus told them,

"You must do your utmost to get in through the narrow door, for many, I assure you, will try to do so and will not succeed, once the master of the house has got up and shut the door. Then you may find yourselves standing outside and knocking at the door crying, 'Lord, please open the door for us.' He will reply to you, 'I don't know who you are or where you come from.' 'But . . .' you will protest, 'we have had meals with you, and you taught in our streets!' Yet he will say to you, 'I tell you I do not know where you have come from. Be off, you scoundrels!' At that time there will be tears and gnashing of teeth—to see Abraham and Isaac and Jacob and all the prophets inside the Kingdom of God,

and you yourselves shut out! Yes, and people will come from
the east and the west, and from the north and the south, and
take their seats in the Kingdom of God. There are some at
the back now who will be in front then, and there are some
in front now who will then be far behind."

THE PHARISEES WARN JESUS OF HEROD;
HE REPLIES

13 Just then some Pharisees arrived to tell him,
31 "You must get right away from here, for Herod intends
to kill you."

"Go and tell that fox," returned Jesus, "today and tomorrow I am expelling evil spirits and continuing my work
of healing, and on the third day my work will be finished.
But I must journey on today, tomorrow and the next day,
for it would never do for a prophet to meet his death outside
Jerusalem!

"Oh Jerusalem, Jerusalem, you murder the prophets and
stone the messengers that are sent to you! How often have I
longed to gather your children round me like a bird gathering
her brood together under her wings, but you would never
have it. Now, all you have left is your house—deserted.
For I tell you that you will never see me again till the day when
you cry, 'Blessed is He Who comes in the Name of the Lord!'"

STRICT SABBATARIANISM IS AGAIN REBUKED

14 One Sabbath day he went into the house of one of the lead-
1   ing Pharisees for a meal, and they all watched him closely.
Right in front of him was a man afflicted with dropsy. So
Jesus spoke to the Scribes and Pharisees and said,
"Well, is it right to heal on the Sabbath day or not?"
And there was no reply. So Jesus took the man and healed
him and let him go. Then he said to them,
"If an ass or a cow belonging to one of you fell into a well,
wouldn't you rescue him without the slightest hesitation
even though it were the Sabbath?"
And this again left them quite unable to reply.

A LESSON IN HUMILITY

14 Then he gave a little word of advice to the guests when
7   he noticed how they chose the best seats.

"When you are invited to a wedding reception, don't sit down in the best seat. It might happen that a more distinguished man than you has also been invited. Then your host might say, 'I am afraid you must give up your seat for this man.' And then, with considerable embarrassment, you will have to sit in the humblest place. No, when you are invited, go and take your seat in an inconspicuous place, so that when your host comes in he may say to you, 'Come on, my dear fellow, we've got a much better seat than this for you.' That is the way to get the admiration of your fellow guests! For everyone who makes himself important will become insignificant, while the man who makes himself insignificant will find himself important."

Then, addressing his host, Jesus said,

"When you give a dinner or supper party, don't invite your friends or your brothers or relations or wealthy neighbours, for the chances are they will invite you back, and you will be fully repaid. No, when you give a party, invite the poor, the lame, the crippled and the blind. That way lies real happiness for you. They have no means of repaying you, but you will be repaid when good men are rewarded—at the Resurrection."

Then, one of the guests, hearing these remarks of Jesus, said,

"What happiness for a man to be present at the feast in the Kingdom of God!"

MEN WHO ARE "TOO BUSY" FOR THE
KINGDOM OF GOD

But Jesus said to him,   14

"Once upon a time, a man planned a big supper party and   15
invited a great many people. At supper-time, he sent his servant out to tell those who were invited, 'Please come, everything is ready now.' But they all, as one man, made their excuses. The first said, 'I have bought some land. I must go and look at it. Please excuse me.' Another one said, 'I have bought five yoke of oxen and am on my way to try them out. Please accept my excuses.' And another one said, 'I have just got married and I am sure you will understand I cannot come.' So the servant returned and told all this to his master. The master of the house was extremely annoyed

and said to his servant, 'Hurry out now into the streets and
alleys of the town, and bring here the poor and crippled and
blind and lame.' Then the servant said, 'I have done what
you told me, sir, and there are still empty places.' Then the
master replied, 'Now go out to the roads and hedgerows and
make them come inside, so that my house may be full up.
For I tell you that not one of the men I invited shall have
a taste of my supper.' "

Now as Jesus proceeded on his journey, great crowds
accompanied him, and he turned and spoke to them,

"If anyone comes to me without 'hating' his father and
mother and wife and children and brothers and sisters, and
even his own life, he cannot be a disciple of mine. The man
who will not take up his cross and follow in my footsteps
cannot be my disciple.

"If any of you wanted to build a tower, wouldn't he first
sit down and work out the cost of it, to see if he can afford
to finish it? Otherwise, when he has laid the foundation and
found himself unable to complete the building, everyone who
sees it will begin to jeer at him, saying, 'This is the man who
started to build but couldn't finish it off.' Or, suppose there
is a king who is going to war with another king, doesn't he
sit down first and consider whether he can engage the 20,000
of the other king with his own 10,000? And if he decides he
can't, then, while the other king is still a long way off, he
sends messengers to him to ask for conditions of peace. So it
is with you; only the man who says goodbye to all his
possessions can be my disciples.

"Salt is a very good thing, but if salt loses its flavour, what
can you use to restore it? It is no good for the ground and no
good as manure. People just throw it away. Every man who
has ears should use them!"

JESUS SPEAKS OF THE LOVE OF GOD
FOR THE "LOST"

15   Now all the tax-collectors and "outsiders" came up to hear
1   what he had to say. The Pharisees and the Scribes complained
of this, remarking that,

"This man accepts sinners and even eats his meals with
them."

So Jesus spoke to them, using this parable:

"Wouldn't any man among you who owned a hundred sheep, and lost one of them, leave the ninety-nine to themselves in the field and go after the one which is lost until he finds it? And when he has found it, he will put it on his shoulders with great joy, and as soon as he gets home, he will call his friends and neighbours together. 'Come and celebrate with me,' he will say, 'for I have found that sheep of mine which was lost.' I tell you that it is the same in Heaven—there is more joy over one sinner whose heart is changed than over ninety-nine righteous people who have no need for repentance.

"Or if there is a woman who has ten coins, if she should lose one, won't she take a lamp and search the house from top to bottom until she finds it? And when she has found it, she calls her friends and neighbours together. 'Come and celebrate with me,' she says, 'for I have found that coin I lost.' I tell you, it is the same in Heaven—there is rejoicing among the angels of God over one sinner whose heart is changed."

Then he continued,

"Once there was a man who had two sons. The younger one said to his father, 'Father, give me the share of the property that will come to me.' So he divided up his property between the two of them. Before very long, the younger son collected all his belongings and went off to a foreign land, where he squandered his wealth in the wildest extravagance. And when he had run through all his money, a terrible famine arose in that country, and he began to feel the pinch. Then he went and hired himself out to one of the citizens of that country who sent him out into the fields to feed the pigs. He got to the point of longing to stuff himself with the food the pigs were eating, and not a soul gave him anything. Then he came to his senses and cried aloud, 'Why, dozens of my father's hired men have got more food than they can eat and here am I dying of hunger! I will get up and go back to my father, and I will say to him, "Father, I have done wrong in the sight of Heaven and in your eyes. I don't deserve to be called your son any more. Please take me on as one of your hired men." ' So he got up and went to his father. But while he was still some distance off, his father saw him and his heart went out to him, and he ran and fell

on his neck and kissed him. But his son said, 'Father, I have
done wrong in the sight of Heaven and in your eyes. I don't
deserve to be called your son any more. . . .' 'Hurry!' called
out his father to the servants, 'fetch the best clothes and put
them on him! Put a ring on his finger and sandals on his feet,
and get that calf we've fattened and kill it, and we will have
a feast and a celebration. For this is my son—I thought he
was dead, and he's alive again. I thought I had lost him, and
he's found!' And they began to get the festivities going.

"But the elder brother was out in the fields, and as he
came near the house, he heard music and dancing. So he
called one of the servants across to him and enquired what
was the meaning of it all. 'Your brother has arrived, and
your father has killed the calf we fattened because he has got
him home again safe and sound,' was the reply. But he was
furious and refused to go inside the house. So his father came
outside and called him. Then he burst out, 'Look, how many
years have I slaved for you and never disobeyed a single
order of yours, and yet you have never given me so much as
a young goat, so that I could give my friends a dinner? But
when that son of yours arrives, who has spent all your money
on prostitutes, for *him* you kill the calf we've fattened!' But
the father replied, 'My son, you have been with me all the
time and everything I have is yours. But we *had* to celebrate
and show our joy. For this is your brother; I thought he
was dead—and he's alive. I thought he was lost—and he
is found!' "

A CLEVER ROGUE, AND THE RIGHT USE
OF MONEY *

16
1
   Then there is this story he told his disciples:
   "Once there was a rich man whose agent was reported to
him to be mismanaging his property. So he summoned him
and said, 'What's this that I hear about you? Give me an
account of your stewardship—you're not fit to manage my
household any longer.' At this the agent said to himself,
'What am I going to do now that my employer is taking
away the stewardship from me? I am not strong enough to
dig and I can't sink to begging. Ah, I know what I'll do so

* See Appendix, Note 3.

that when I lose my job people will welcome me into their homes!' So he sent for each one of his master's debtors. 'How much do you owe to my master?' he said to the first. 'A hundred gallons of oil,' he replied. 'Here,' replied the agent, 'take your bill, sit down, hurry up and write in fifty.' Then he said to another, 'And what's the size of your debt?' 'A thousand bushels of wheat,' he replied. 'Take your bill,' said the agent, 'and write in eight hundred.' Now the master praised this rascally steward because he had been so careful for his own future. For the children of this world are considerably more shrewd in their own way than the children of light. Now my advice to you is to use 'Money,' tainted as it is, to make yourselves friends, so that when it comes to an end, they may welcome you into eternal habitations.

"The man who is faithful in the little things will be faithful in the big things, and the man who cheats in the little things will cheat in the big things too. So that if you are not fit to be trusted to deal with the wicked wealth of this world, who will trust you with the true riches? And if you are not trustworthy with someone else's property, who will give you property of your own? No servant can serve two masters. He is bound to hate one and love the other, or give his loyalty to one and despise the other. You cannot serve God and worship money at the same time."

Now the Pharisees, who were very fond of money, heard all this with a sneer. But he said to them,

"You are the people who advertise your goodness before men, but God knows your hearts. Remember, there are things men consider perfectly splendid which are detestable in the sight of God!

JESUS STATES THAT THE KINGDOM OF GOD HAS SUPERSEDED "THE LAW AND THE PROPHETS"

"The Law and the Prophets were in force until John's day. From then on the Good News of the Kingdom of God has been proclaimed and men are pressing into it.

"Yet it would be easier for Heaven and earth to disappear than for a single point of the Law to become a dead letter.

"Any man who divorces his wife and marries another
woman commits adultery. And so does any man who marries
the woman who was divorced from her husband.

JESUS SHOWS THE FEARFUL CONSEQUENCE
OF SOCIAL INJUSTICE

16
19
"There was once a rich man who used to dress in purple
and fine linen and lead a life of luxury. And there was a
poor man called Lazarus who was put down at his gate. He
was covered with sores. He used to long to be fed with the
scraps from the rich man's table. Yes, and the dogs used
to come and lick his sores. Well, it happened that the poor
man died, and was carried by the angels into Abraham's
bosom. The rich man also died and was buried. And from
Hell he looked up and saw Abraham a long way away, and
Lazarus in his arms. 'Father Abraham!' he cried out, 'please
pity me. Send Lazarus to dip the tip of his finger in water
and cool my tongue, for I am in agony in these flames.' But
Abraham replied, 'Remember, my son, that you used to get
the good things in your lifetime, while Lazarus got the bad.
Now, in this place, he is being comforted, while you are in
agony. And besides this, a great chasm has been set between you and us, so that those who want to go to you from
this side cannot do so, and people cannot come to us from
your side.' At this he said, 'Then I beg you to send him to
my father's house, for I have five brothers. He could tell
them about all this and at least stop them from coming to
this place of torture.' But Abraham said, 'They have Moses
and the prophets: they can listen to them.' 'Ah no, father
Abraham,' he said, 'if only someone went to them from the
dead, they would change completely.' But Abraham told
him, 'If they will not listen to Moses and the prophets, they
would not be convinced even if somebody rose from the
dead.' "

JESUS WARNS HIS DISCIPLES ABOUT SPOILING
THE SPIRIT OF THE NEW KINGDOM

17
1
Then Jesus said to his disciples,
"It is inevitable that there should be pitfalls, but alas for
the man who is responsible for them! It would be better for
that man to have a millstone hung round his neck and be

thrown into the sea, than that he should trip up these little
ones. So be careful how you live. If your brother offends
you, take him to task about it, and if he is sorry, forgive him.
Yes, if he wrongs you seven times in one day and turns to you
and says, 'I am sorry' seven times, you must forgive him."

And the apostles said to the Lord,

"Give us more faith."

And he replied,

"If your faith were as big as a grain of mustard-seed, you
could say to this fig-tree, 'Pull yourself up by the roots and
plant yourself in the sea,' and it would do what you
said!"

FOR THE DISCIPLE TO WORK IN THE KINGDOM
MUST BE TAKEN AS A MATTER OF COURSE

"If any of you has a servant ploughing or looking after the 17
sheep, are you likely to say to him when he comes in from the 7
fields, 'Come straight in and sit down to your meal'? Aren't
you more likely to say, 'Get my supper ready: change your
clothes, and wait while I eat and drink: and then, when I've
finished, you can have your meal'? Do you feel particularly
grateful to your servant for doing what you tell him? I don't
think so. It is the same with yourselves—when you have
done everything that you are told to do, you can say, 'We
are not much good as servants, for we have only done what
we ought to do.' "

JESUS HEALS TEN MEN OF LEPROSY: ONLY
ONE SHOWS HIS GRATITUDE

In the course of his journey to Jerusalem, Jesus crossed 17
the boundary between Samaria and Galilee, and as he was 11
approaching a village, ten lepers met him. They kept their
distance but shouted out,

"Jesus, Master, have pity on us!"

When Jesus saw them, he said,

"Go and show yourselves to the priests."

And it happened that as they went on their way, they were
cured. And one of their number, when he saw that he was
cured, turned round and thanked God at the top of his voice,
and then fell on his face before Jesus and thanked him. This
man was a Samaritan. And at this Jesus remarked,

"Weren't there ten men healed? Where are the other
nine? Is nobody going to turn and praise God for what has
been done, except this stranger?"

And he said to the man,

"Stand up now, and go on your way. It is your faith that
has made you well."

JESUS TELLS THE PHARISEES THAT THE
KINGDOM IS HERE AND NOW

17 Later, there was an occasion when he was asked by the
20 Pharisees when the Kingdom of God would come, and he
gave them this reply:

"The Kingdom of God never comes by watching for
it. Men cannot say, 'Look, here it is,' or 'there it is,' for the
Kingdom of God is inside you."

JESUS TELLS HIS DISCIPLES ABOUT
THE FUTURE

17 Then he said to the disciples,
22 "The time will come when you will long to see again a
single day of the Son of Man, but it will not be possible.
People will say to you, 'Look, there he is,' or 'Look, here he
is.' Stay where you are and don't go off looking for him!
For the Day of the Son of Man will be like lightning flashing
from one end of the sky to the other. But before that
happens, he must go through much suffering and be utterly
repudiated by this generation. In the time of the coming of
the Son of Man, life will be as it was in the days of Noah.
People ate and drank, married and got married, right up to
the day when Noah entered the Ark—and then came the
Flood and destroyed them all. It will be just the same as it was
in the days of Lot. People ate and drank, bought and sold,
planted and built, but on the day that Lot left Sodom, it
rained fire and brimstone from heaven, and destroyed them
all. That is how it will be on the day when the Son of Man is
revealed. When that Day comes, the man who is on the top
of his house, with his goods inside it, must not come down to
get them. And the man out in the fields must not turn back.
Remember what happened to Lot's wife. Whoever tries to
preserve his life will lose it, and the man who is prepared to
lose his life will preserve it. I tell you, that night there will be

two men in one bed; one man will be taken and the other
will be left. Two women will be turning the grinding-mill
together; one will be taken and the other left."

"But where will this happen, Lord?" they asked him.

" 'Wherever there is a dead body, there the vultures will
flock,' " he replied.

JESUS URGES HIS DISCIPLES TO PERSIST
IN PRAYER

Then he gave them an illustration to show that they must
always pray and never lose heart.

"Once upon a time," he said, "there was a magistrate in a
town who had no fear of God and no respect for his fellow
men. There was a widow in the town who kept coming to
him, saying, 'Please protect me from the man who is trying
to ruin me.' And for a long time he refused. But later he
said to himself, 'Although I don't fear God and have no
respect for men, yet this woman is such a nuisance that I shall
give judgment in her favour, or else her continual visits will
be the death of me!' "

Then the Lord said,

"Notice how this dishonest magistrate behaved. Do you
suppose God, patient as He is, will not see justice done for his
chosen who appeal to him day and night? I assure you He
will not delay in seeing justice done.

"Yet, when the Son of Man comes, will he find men on
earth who believe in him?"

JESUS TELLS A STORY AGAINST THE
SELF-RIGHTEOUS

Then he gave this illustration to certain people who
were confident of their own goodness and looked down on
others:

"Two men went up to the Temple to pray, one was a
Pharisee, the other was a tax-collector. The Pharisee stood
and prayed like this with himself, 'O God, I do thank Thee
that I am not like the rest of mankind, greedy, dishonest,
impure, or even like that tax-collector over there. I fast
twice every week; I give away a tenth-part of all my income.'
But the tax-collector stood in a distant corner, scarcely
daring to look up to Heaven, and with a gesture of despair,

said, 'God, have mercy on a sinner like me.' I assure you
that he was the man who went home justified in God's sight,
rather than the other one. For everyone who sets himself up
as somebody will become a nobody, and the man who makes
himself nobody will become somebody."

JESUS WELCOMES BABIES

18
15 Then people began to bring babies to him for him to put
his hands on them. But when the disciples noticed it, they
frowned on them. But Jesus called out for them to be
brought to him, and said,

"You must let little children come to me, and you must
never stop them coming. The Kingdom of Heaven is made
of little children like these. I tell you, the man who will not
accept the Kingdom of God like a little child will never get
into it at all."

JESUS AND RICHES

18
18 Then one of the Jewish rulers put this question to him,
"Master, I know that you are good; tell me, please, what
must I do to be sure of eternal life?"

"I wonder why you call me good?" returned Jesus. "No
one is good—only God. You know the Commandments—

"Thou shalt not commit adultery.

"Thou shalt not commit murder.

"Thou shalt not steal.

"Thou shalt not bear false witness.

"Honour thy father and thy mother."

"All these," he replied, "I have carefully kept since I was
quite young."

And when Jesus heard that, he said to him,

"There is still one thing you have missed. Sell everything
you have and give the money away to the poor, and you will
have riches in Heaven. And then come and follow me."

But when he heard this, he was greatly distressed for he
was very rich.

And when Jesus saw how his face fell, he remarked,

"How difficult it is for those who have great possessions to
enter the Kingdom of God! A camel could squeeze through
the eye of a needle more easily than a rich man could get into
the Kingdom of God."

Those who heard Jesus say this, exclaimed,

"Then who can possibly be saved?"

Jesus replied,

"Humanly speaking it is impossible, but with God everything is possible."

"Well," rejoined Peter, "we have left all that we ever had
and followed you."

And Jesus told them,

"Believe me, nobody has left his home or wife, or brothers
or parents or children for the sake of the Kingdom of God,
without receiving very much more in this present life, as
well as gaining eternal life in the world to come."

JESUS FORETELLS HIS DEATH AND
RESURRECTION

Then Jesus took the Twelve on one side and spoke to them,   18

"Listen to me. We are now going up to Jerusalem and   31
everything that has been written by the prophets about the
Son of Man will come true. For he will be handed over to
the heathen, and he is going to be jeered at and insulted
and spat upon, and then they will flog him and kill him. But
he will rise again on the third day."

But they did not understand any of this. His words were
quite obscure to them and they had no idea of what he
meant.

ON THE WAY TO JERICHO HE HEALS A
BLIND BEGGAR

Then, as he was approaching Jericho, it happened that   18
there was a blind man sitting by the roadside, begging. He   35
heard the crowd passing and enquired what it was all about.
And they told him, Jesus the man from Nazareth is going
past you. So he shouted out,

"Jesus, Son of David, have pity on me!"

Those who were in front tried to hush his cries. But that
made him call out all the more,

"Son of David, have pity on me!"

So Jesus stood quite still and ordered the man to be
brought to him. And when he was quite close, he said to
him,

"What do you want me to do for you?"

"Lord, make me see again," he cried.

"You can see again. Your faith has cured you," returned Jesus.

And his sight was restored at once, and he followed Jesus, praising God. And all the people who saw it thanked God too.

THE CHIEF TAX-COLLECTOR IS CONVERTED
TO FAITH IN JESUS

19
1 Then he went into Jericho and was making his way through it. And here we find a man called Zacchaeus, a chief collector of taxes and wealthy, wanting to see what sort of person Jesus was. But the crowd prevented him from seeing him, for he was very short. So he ran ahead and climbed up into a sycamore tree to get a view of him as he was heading that way. When Jesus reached the spot, he looked up and saw the man and said,

"Zacchaeus, hurry up and come down. I am going to be your guest today."

So Zacchaeus hurriedly climbed down and gladly welcomed him. But the bystanders muttered their disapproval saying,

"Now he has gone to stay with a sinner."

But Zacchaeus himself stopped and said to the Lord,

"Look, sir, I will give half my property to the poor. And if I have swindled anybody out of anything I will pay him back four times as much."

Jesus said to him,

"Salvation has come to this house today."

Then he added to the people,

"Zacchaeus is a descendant of Abraham as much as you are, and it was the lost that the Son of Man came to seek— and to save."

LIFE REQUIRES COURAGE, AND IS HARD ON
THOSE WHO DARE NOT USE THEIR GIFTS

19
11 Then as the crowd still listened attentively, Jesus went on to give them this parable. For the fact that he was nearing Jerusalem made them imagine that the Kingdom of God was on the point of appearing.

"Once upon a time a man of good family went abroad to

accept a kingdom and then to return. He summoned ten of
his servants and gave them each ten dollars, with the words,
'Use this money to trade with until I come back.' But the
citizens detested him and they sent a delegation after him, to
say, 'We will not have this man to be our king.' Then later,
when he had received his kingdom, he returned and gave
orders for the servants to whom he had given the money to be
called to him, so that he could find out what profits they had
made. The first came into his presence, and said, 'Sire, your
ten dollars have made a hundred dollars more.' 'Splendid,
my good fellow,' he said, 'since you have proved trustworthy
over this small amount, I am going to put you in charge of ten
towns.' The second came in and said, 'Sire, your ten dollars
have made fifty dollars.' And he said to him, 'Good, you're
appointed governor of five towns.' When the last came, he
said, 'Sire, here are your ten dollars, which I have been keeping wrapped up in a handkerchief. I have been scared—I
know you're a hard man, getting something for nothing and
reaping where you never sowed.' To which he replied, 'You
scoundrel, your own words condemn you! You knew perfectly well, did you, that I am a hard man who gets something
for nothing and reaps where he never sowed? Then why
didn't you put my money into the bank, and then when I
returned I could have had it back with the interest? Then he
said to those who were standing by, 'Take his ten dollars and
give it to the fellow who has a hundred.'

" 'But, Sire, he has a hundred dollars already,' they said
to him. 'Yes,' he replied, 'and I tell you that the man who
has got something will get more given to him. But as for
the man who has nothing, even his "nothing" will be taken
away. And as for these enemies of mine who objected to
my being their king, bring them here and execute them in
my presence.' "

After these words, Jesus walked on ahead of them on the
road to Jerusalem.

JESUS ARRANGES HIS OWN ENTRANCE
INTO JERUSALEM

Then as he was approaching Bethphage and Bethany, near 19
the hill called the Mount of Olives, he sent off two of his   29
disciples, telling them,

"Go into the village just ahead of you, and there you will
find a colt tied on which no one has ever yet ridden. Untie
it and bring it here. And if anybody asks you, 'Why are you
untying it?' just say, 'The Lord needs it.'"

So the messengers went off and found things just as he had
told them. In fact, as they were untying the colt, the owners
did say, "Why are you untying it?" and they replied, "The
Lord needs it." So they brought it to Jesus and, throwing
their cloaks upon it, mounted Jesus on its back. Then as he
rode along, people spread out their garments in the roadway.
And as he approached the City, where the road slopes down
from the Mount of Olives, the whole crowd of his disciples
joyfully shouted praises to God for all the marvellous things
that they had seen him do.

"God bless the King Who comes in the Name of the
Lord!" they cried. "There is peace in Heaven and glory on
high!"

There were some Pharisees in the crowd who said to Jesus,
"Master, restrain your disciples!"

To which he replied,

"I tell you that if they kept quiet, the stones in the road
would burst into cheers."

THE SIGHT OF THE CITY MOVES HIM TO TEARS

19
41

And as he came still nearer to the City, he caught sight of
it and wept over it, saying,

"Ah, if you only knew, even at this eleventh hour, on what
your peace depends—but you cannot see it. The time is
coming when your enemies will encircle you with ramparts,
surrounding you and hemming you in on every side. And
they will hurl you and all your children to the ground—yes,
they will not leave one stone standing upon another—all because you did not know when God Himself was visiting you."

Then he went into the Temple, and proceeded to throw
out the traders there.

"It is written," he told them, " '*My house shall be a house
of prayer*,' but you have turned it into a thieves' kitchen!"

JESUS TEACHES DAILY IN THE TEMPLE

19
47

Then day after day he was teaching inside the Temple.
The Chief Priests, the Scribes and the national leaders were

all the time trying to get rid of him, but they could not find any way to do it since all the people hung upon his words.

Then one day as he was teaching the people in the Temple, and preaching the gospel to them, the Chief Priests, the Scribes and elders confronted him in a body and asked him this direct question,

"Tell us by whose authority you act as you do—who gave you such authority?"

"I have a question for you, too," replied Jesus. "John's baptism, now—tell me, did it come from Heaven or was it purely human?"

At this they began arguing with each other.

"If we say, 'from Heaven,' he will say to us, 'Then why didn't you believe in him?' but if we say it was purely human, this mob will stone us to death, for they are convinced that John was a prophet." So they replied that they did not know where it came from.

"Then," returned Jesus, "neither will I tell you by what authority I do what I am doing."

HE TELLS THE PEOPLE A POINTED STORY

Then he turned to the people and told them this parable: 20
"There was once a man who planted a vineyard, let it out 9
to farm-workers, and went abroad for some time. Then, when the season arrived, he sent a servant to the farm-workers so that they could give him the proceeds of the vineyard. But the farm-workers beat him up and sent him back empty-handed. So he sent another servant, and they beat him up as well, manhandling him disgracefully, and sent him back empty-handed. Then he sent a third servant, but after wounding him severely they threw him out. Then the owner of the vineyard said, 'What shall I do now? I will send them my son who is so dear to me. Perhaps they will respect *him*.' But when the farm-workers saw him, they talked the matter over with each other and said, 'This man is the heir—come on, let's kill him, and we shall get everything that would have gone to him.' And they threw him outside the vineyard and killed him. What then, do you suppose the owner will do to them? He will come and destroy the men who were working his property, and hand it over to others."

When they heard this, they said,
"God forbid!"
But he looked them straight in the eyes and said,
"Then what is the meaning of this Scripture—

The stone which the builders rejected,
The same was made the head of the corner?

The man who falls on that stone will be broken, and the man
on whom it falls will be crushed to powder."

THE AUTHORITIES RESORT TO TRICKERY

20
19 The Scribes and Chief Priests longed to get their hands on
him at that moment, but they were afraid of the people.
They knew well enough that his parable referred to them.
They watched him, however, and sent some spies into the
crowd, pretending to be honest men, to fasten on something that he might say which could be used to hand him
over to the authority and power of the governor.

These men asked him,
"Master, we know that what you say and teach is right,
and that you teach the way of God truly without fear or
favour. Now, *is it right for us to pay taxes to Caesar or not?*"
But Jesus saw through their trickery and said to them,
"Show me one of the coins. Whose face is this, and whose
name is in the inscription?"
"Caesar's," they said.
"Then give to Caesar," he replied, "what belongs to Caesar,
and to God what belongs to God."
So his answer gave them no sort of handle that they could
use against him publicly. And in fact they were so taken
aback by his answer that they had nothing more to say.

JESUS EXPOSES THE IGNORANCE OF
THE SADDUCEES

20
27 Then up came some of the Sadducees (who deny that there
is any resurrection) and they asked him,
"Master, Moses told us in the Scripture, 'If a married man
should die without any children, his brother should marry
his widow and raise up a family for him.' Now, there were
once seven brothers. The first got married and died childless,
and the second and the third married the woman, and in fact

all the seven married her and died without leaving any children. Lastly, the woman herself died. Now, in this 'resurrection' whose wife is she of these seven men, for she belonged to all of them?"

"People in this world," Jesus replied, "marry and get married. But those who are reckoned worthy of reaching that world, which means rising from the dead, neither marry nor get married. They cannot die any more but live like the angels; for being children of the resurrection, they are the sons of God. And for the matter of the dead being raised, Moses showed this to be true in the story of the Bush, when he talks of the Lord being the God of Abraham, the God of Isaac and the God of Jacob. For God is not a God of the dead, but of the living. For all men are alive to Him."

To this some of the Scribes replied,

"Master, that was a good answer."

And indeed nobody had the courage to ask him any more questions. But Jesus went on to say,

"How can they say that Christ is David's *son*? For David himself says in the book of Psalms—

The Lord said unto my *Lord*,
Sit thou on my right hand,
Till I make thine enemies the footstool of thy feet.

David is plainly calling him 'Lord.' How then can he be his *son*?"

JESUS WARNS HIS DISCIPLES AGAINST
RELIGIOUS PRETENTIOUSNESS

Then while everybody was listening, Jesus remarked to his disciples, 20
45

"Be on your guard against the Scribes who enjoy walking round in long robes and love having men bow to them in public, getting front seats in the synagogue, and the best places at dinner parties—while all the time they are battening on widows' property and covering it up with long prayers. These are the men who are heading for the deepest damnation."

Then he looked up and saw the rich people dropping their gifts into the treasury, and he noticed a poor widow drop in two coppers, and he commented,

"I assure you that this poor widow has put in more than all of them, for they have all put in what they can easily spare, but she in her poverty has given away her whole living."

JESUS FORETELLS THE DESTRUCTION
OF THE TEMPLE

21
5   Then when some of them were talking about the Temple and pointing out the beauty of its lovely stonework and the various ornaments that people had given, he said,

"Yes, you can gaze on all this today, but the time is coming when not a single stone will be left upon another, without being torn down."

So they asked him,

"Master, when will this happen, and what sign will there be that these things are going to take place?"

"Be careful that you are not deceived," he replied. "There will be many coming in my name, saying 'I am He' and 'The Time is very near now.' Never follow men like that. And when you hear about wars and disturbances, don't be alarmed. These things must happen first, but the end will not come just yet."

AND PROPHESIES WORLD-WIDE
SUFFERING

21
10   Then he continued,

"Nation will rise up against nation, and kingdom against kingdom; there will be great earthquakes and famines and plagues in this place or that. There will be dreadful sights, and great signs from heaven. But before all this happens, men will arrest you and persecute you, handing you over to synagogue or prison, or bringing you before kings and governors, for my name's sake. This will be your chance to witness for me. So make up your minds not to think out your defence beforehand. I will give you such eloquence and wisdom that none of your opponents will be able to resist or contradict it. But you will be betrayed, even by parents and brothers and kinsfolk and friends, and there will be some of you who will be killed and you will be hated everywhere for my name's sake. Yet, not a hair of your head will perish. Hold on, and you will win your souls!

"But when you see Jerusalem surrounded by armed forces, then you will know that the time of her devastation has arrived. Then is the time for those who are in Judaea to fly to the hills. And those who are in the city itself must get out of it, and those who are already in the country must not try to get into the city. For these are the days of vengeance, when all that the Scriptures have said will come true. Alas for those who are pregnant and those who have tiny babies in those days! For there will be bitter misery in the land and punishment for this people. They will die by the sword. They will be taken off as prisoners into all nations. Jerusalem will be trampled under foot by the heathen until the heathen's day is over. There will be signs in the sun and moon and stars, and on the earth there will be dismay among the nations and bewilderment at the roar of the surging sea. Men's courage will fail completely as they realise what is threatening the world, for the powers of heaven will rock on their foundations. Then men will see the Son of Man coming in a cloud with great power and splendour! But when these things begin to happen, look up, hold your heads high, for you will soon be free."

VIGILANCE IS ESSENTIAL

Then he gave them a parable.   21

"Look at a fig-tree, or indeed any tree, when it begins to   29
burst its buds, and you realise without anybody telling you that summer is nearly here. So, when you see these things happening, you can be equally sure that the Kingdom of God has nearly come. Believe me, this generation will not disappear until all this has taken place. Earth and heaven will pass away, but my words will never pass away.

"Be on your guard—see to it that your minds are never clouded by dissipation or drunkenness or the worries of this life, or else that Day may catch you like the springing of a trap—for it will come upon every inhabitant of the whole earth.

"You must be vigilant at all times, praying that you may be strong enough to come safely through all that is going to happen, and stand in the presence of the Son of Man."

And every day he went on teaching in the Temple, and

every evening he went off and spent the night on the hill
which is called the Mount of Olives. And the people used
to come early in the morning to listen to him in the Temple.

22   JUDAS ISCARIOT BECOMES THE TOOL OF
I   THE AUTHORITIES

Now as the Feast of Unleavened Bread, called the Passover, was approaching, fear of the people made the Chief
Priests and Scribes try desperately to find a way of getting
rid of Jesus. Then a diabolical plan came into the mind of
Judas Iscariot, who was one of the Twelve. He went and
discussed with the Chief Priests and officers a method of
getting Jesus into their hands. They were delighted and
arranged to pay him for it. He agreed, and began to look
for a suitable opportunity for betrayal when there was no
crowd present.

           JESUS MAKES ARRANGEMENTS FOR HIS LAST
               PASSOVER WITH HIS DISCIPLES

22   Then the day of Unleavened Bread arrived, on which the
7   Passover Lamb had to be sacrificed, and Jesus sent off Peter
and John with the words, "Go and make all the preparations
for us to eat the Passover."
     "Where would you like us to do this?" they asked.
     And he replied,
     "Listen, just as you're going into the city you will meet a
man carrying a jug of water. Follow him to the house he is
making for. Then say to the owner of the house, 'The Master
has this message for you—which is the room where my disciples and I may eat the Passover?' And he will take you
upstairs and show you a large room with all the furniture we
need. Make all your preparations there."
     So they went off and found everything exactly as he had
told them it would be, and they made the Passover preparations.
     Then, later on, he came and took his seat at table with the
Apostles, and spoke to them,
     "You do not know how I have longed to eat this Passover
with you before the time comes for me to suffer. Believe me,
I shall not eat the Passover again until all that it means is
fulfilled in the Kingdom of God."

Then taking a cup from them, he thanked God and said, "Take this and share it amongst you, for I tell you that I shall drink no more wine until the Kingdom of God comes."

THE MYSTERIOUS WORDS WHICH WERE
REMEMBERED LATER

Then he took a loaf and after thanking God he broke it 22 and gave it to them, with these words, 19

"This is my body which is given for you: do this in remembrance of me."

So too, he gave them a cup after supper with the words,

"This cup is the New Agreement made in my own blood which is shed for you, though the hand of the man who is betraying me lies with mine at this moment on the table. The Son of Man goes on his appointed way: yet alas for the man who betrays him!"

JESUS AGAIN TEACHES HUMILITY

And at this they began to argue among themselves as to 22 which of them was going to do such a thing. 23

And then a quarrel arose among them as to who should be considered the most important.

But Jesus said to them,

"Among the heathen it is their kings who lord it over them, and their rulers are given the title of 'benefactors.' But it must not be so with you! *Your* greatest man must become like a junior and your leader must be a servant. Who is the greater, the man who sits down to dinner or the man who serves him? Obviously, the man who sits down to dinner— yet *I* am the one who is the servant among you. But you are the men who have stood by me in all that I have gone through, and as surely as my Father has given me my King- dom, so I give you the right to eat and drink at my table in that Kingdom. Yes, you will sit on thrones and rule the twelve tribes of Israel!

THE PERSONAL WARNING TO SIMON

"Oh Simon, Simon, Satan has asked to have you all to sift 22 like wheat—but I have prayed for *you* that you may not 31 lose your faith. Yes, when you have turned back to me, you must strengthen these brothers of yours."

Peter said to him,

"Lord, I am ready to go to prison, or even to die with
you!"

"I tell you, Peter," returned Jesus, "you will disown me
three times before the cock crows!"

JESUS TELLS HIS DISCIPLES THAT THE
CRISIS HAS ARRIVED

22   Then he continued to them all,
35   "That time when I sent you out without any purse or
wallet or shoes—did you find you needed anything?"

"No, not a thing," they replied.

"But now," Jesus continued, "if you have a purse or wallet,
take it with you, and if you have no sword, sell your coat
and buy one! For I tell you that this Scripture must be fulfilled in me—

And he was reckoned with transgressors.

So comes the end of all that they wrote about me."

Then the disciples said,

"Lord, look, here are two swords."

And Jesus returned,

"That is enough."

Then he went out of the city and went up the Mount of
Olives, as he had often done before, with the disciples following him. And when he reached his usual place, he said to
them,

"Pray that you may not have to face temptation!"

Then he went off by himself, about a stone's throw away,
and falling on his knees, prayed in these words—

"Father, if You are willing, take this cup away from me—
but it is not my will, but Yours, that must be done."

And an angel from Heaven appeared strengthening him.
He was in agony and prayed even more intensely so that he
sweated great drops like blood falling to the ground. Then
he got to his feet from his prayer and walking back to the
disciples, he found they had fallen asleep because they could
not bear their grief.

"Why are you sleeping?" he said to them. "You must get
up and go on praying that you may not have to face temptation."

THE MOB ARRIVES AND JUDAS BETRAYS

While he was still speaking a crowd of people arrived, led   22
by the man called Judas, one of the Twelve. He stepped up   47
to Jesus to kiss him.

"Judas, are you going to betray the Son of Man with a
kiss?" said Jesus to him.

And the disciples, seeing what was going to happen, cried,
"Lord, shall we use our swords?"

And one of them did slash at the High Priest's servant, cutting off his right ear. But Jesus retorted,

"Enough of that!"

And he touched his ear and healed him. Then he spoke to
the Chief Priests, Temple officers and elders who were there
to arrest him,

"So you have come out with your swords and staves as if
I were a bandit. Day after day I was with you in the Temple
and you never laid a finger on me—but this is your hour and
all the power of darkness is yours!"

JESUS IS ARRESTED: PETER FOLLOWS BUT
DENIES HIS MASTER THREE TIMES

Then they arrested him and marched him off to the High   22
Priest's house. Peter followed at a distance, and sat down   54
among some people who had lighted a fire in the middle of
the courtyard and were sitting round it. A servant-maid saw
him sitting there in the firelight, peered into his face and said,

"This man was with him too."

But he denied it and said,

"I don't know him, girl!"

A few minutes later someone else noticed Peter, and said,
"You're one of these men too."

But Peter said,

"Man, I am not!"

Then about an hour later someone else insisted,

"I am convinced this fellow was with him. Why he is a
Galilean!"

"Man," returned Peter, "I don't know what you're talking
about."

And immediately, just as he was speaking, the cock crew.
And the Lord turned his head and looked straight at Peter,

and into his mind flashed the words that the Lord had said
to him . . . "You will disown me three times before the cock
crows today." And he went outside and wept bitterly.

Then the men who held Jesus made a great game of knocking him about. And they blindfolded him and asked him,
"Now, prophet, guess who hit you that time?"

And that was only the beginning of the way they insulted
him.

IN THE EARLY MORNING JESUS IS
FORMALLY INTERROGATED

22
66
Then when daylight came, the assembly of the elders of
the people, which included both Chief Priests and Scribes,
met and marched him off into their own Council. There they
asked him,

"If you really are Christ, tell us!"

"If I tell you, you will not believe me, and if I ask you a
question, you will not answer me. But from now on the Son
of Man will take his seat at the right hand of Almighty God."

Then they all said,

"So you are the Son of God then?"

"You are right; I am," answered Jesus.

Then they said,

"Why do we need to call any more witnesses, for we ourselves have heard him say this thing?"

JESUS IS TAKEN BEFORE PILATE

23
1
Then they rose up in a body and took him off to Pilate,
and began their accusation in these words,

"Here is this man whom we have found corrupting our
people, and telling them that it is wrong to pay taxes to
Caesar, claiming that he himself is Christ, a king."

But Pilate addressed his question to Jesus,

"Are you the king of the Jews?"

"Yes, I am," he replied.

Then Pilate spoke to the Chief Priests and the crowd,

"I find nothing criminal about this man."

But they pressed their charge, saying,

"He's a trouble-maker among the people. He teaches
through the whole of Judaea, all the way from Galilee to this
place."

When Pilate heard this, he enquired whether the man were a Galilean, and when he discovered that he came under Herod's jurisdiction, he passed him on to Herod who happened to be in Jerusalem at that time. When Herod saw Jesus, he was delighted, for he had been wanting to see him for a long time. He had heard a lot about Jesus and was hoping to see him perform a miracle. He questioned him very thoroughly, but Jesus gave him absolutely no reply, though the Chief Priests and Scribes stood there making the most violent accusations. So Herod joined his own soldiers in scoffing and jeering at Jesus. Finally, they dressed him up in a gorgeous cloak, and sent him back to Pilate. On that day Herod and Pilate became firm friends, though previously they had been at daggers drawn.

PILATE DECLARES JESUS' INNOCENCE

Then Pilate summoned the Chief Priests, the officials and the people, and addressed them in these words,

23
13

"You have brought this man to me as a mischief-maker among the people, and I want you all to realise that, after examining him in your presence, I have found nothing criminal about him, in spite of all your accusations. And neither has Herod, for he has sent him back to us. Obviously then, he has done nothing to deserve the death penalty. I propose, therefore, to teach him a sharp lesson and let him go."

But they all yelled as one man,

"Take this man away! We want Barabbas set free!"

(Barabbas was a man who had been put in prison for causing a riot in the city and for murder.) But Pilate wanted to set Jesus free and he called out to them again, but they shouted back at him,

"Crucify, crucify him!"

Then he spoke to them, for the third time,

"What is his crime, then? I have found nothing in him that deserves execution; I am going to teach him his lesson and let him go."

But they shouted him down, yelling their demand that he should be crucified.

Their shouting won the day, for Pilate pronounced the official decision that what they wanted should be done. He released the man for whom they asked, the man who had been imprisoned for rioting and murder, and surrendered Jesus to their wishes.

And as they marched him away, they caught hold of Simon, a native of Cyrene in Africa, who was on his way home from the fields, and put the cross on his back for him to carry behind Jesus.

ON THE WAY TO THE CROSS

23
27 A huge crowd of people followed him, including women who wrung their hands and wept for him. But Jesus turned to them and said,

"Women of Jerusalem, don't shed your tears for me, but for yourselves and your children! For the days are coming when men will say, 'Lucky are the women who cannot have children—the bodies which have never borne them, and the breasts which have never sucked them.' Then men will begin to say to the mountains, 'Fall upon us!' and will say to the hills, 'Cover us up!' For if this is what men do when the wood is green, what will they do when it is seasoned?"

JESUS IS CRUCIFIED WITH TWO CRIMINALS

23
32 Two criminals were also led out with him for execution, and when they came to the place called The Skull, they crucified him with the criminals one on each side of him. But Jesus himself was saying,

"Father, forgive them; they do not know what they are doing."

Then they shared his clothes out among them by casting lots for them.

The people stood and stared while their rulers jeered, "He saved other people, let's see him save himself, if he is really God's Christ and His Chosen!"

The soldiers also made a joke out of it by coming up and presenting sour wine to him, saying,

"If you are the King of the Jews, why not save yourself?"

There was a placard over his head which read,

"THIS IS THE KING OF THE JEWS."

One of the criminals hanging there covered him with abuse.

"Aren't you Christ? Why don't you save yourself—and us?"

But the other one checked him with the words,

"Aren't you afraid of God even when you're getting the same punishment as he is? And it's fair enough for us, for we've only got what we deserve, but this man never did anything wrong in his life."

Then he said,

"Jesus, don't forget me when you come into your kingdom."

And Jesus answered,

"I tell you truly, this very day you will be with me in Paradise."

THE DARKNESS, AND THE DEATH OF JESUS

It was now about mid-day, but darkness came over the whole countryside until three in the afternoon, for the sun was eclipsed. The veil in the Temple sanctuary was split in two, and Jesus gave a great cry. Then he said, **23 44**

"Father, I commend my spirit into Your hands."

And with these words, he died.

When the centurion saw what had happened, he exclaimed reverently,

"That was indeed a good man!"

And the whole crowd that had collected for the spectacle, when they saw what had happened, went home in bitter grief. And those who had known him, as well as the women who had followed him from Galilee, remained standing at a distance and saw all this happen.

JOSEPH FROM ARIMATHAEA LAYS THE
BODY OF JESUS IN A TOMB

Now there was a man called Joseph, a member of the Jewish Council. He was a good and just man, and had neither agreed with their plan nor voted for their decision. He came from the Jewish city of Arimathaea and was awaiting the Kingdom of God. He went to Pilate and asked for Jesus' body. He took it down and wrapped it in linen and placed it in a rock-hewn tomb which had not been used before. **23 50**

It was now the day of the Preparation and the Sabbath was just approaching, so the women who had accompanied

Jesus from Galilee followed Joseph, noted the tomb and the position of the body, and then went home to prepare spices and perfumes. On the Sabbath they rested, in obedience to the commandment.

THE FIRST DAY OF THE WEEK:
THE EMPTY TOMB

24
1   But at the first signs of dawn on the first day of the week, they went to the tomb, taking with them the aromatic spices they had got ready. They discovered that the stone had been rolled away from the tomb, but on going inside, the body of the Lord Jesus was not to be found. While they were still puzzling over this, two men suddenly stood at their elbow, dressed in dazzling light. The women were terribly frightened, and turned their eyes away and looked at the ground. But the two men spoke to them,

"Why do you look for the Living among the dead? He is not here: He has risen! Remember that He said to you, while He was still in Galilee—that the Son of Man must be betrayed into the hands of sinful men, and must be crucified, and must rise again on the third day."

Then they did remember what he had said, and they turned their backs on the tomb and went and told all this to the Eleven and the others who were with them.

It was Mary of Magdala, Joanna, Mary, the mother of James, and their companions who made this report to the Apostles. But it struck them as sheer imagination, and they did not believe the women. Only Peter got up and ran to the tomb. He stooped down and saw the linen clothes lying there all by themselves, and he went home wondering at the thing that had happened.

THE WALK TO EMMAUS

24
13   Then on the same day we find two of them going off to Emmaus, a village about seven miles from Jerusalem. As they went they were deep in conversation about everything that had happened. While they were absorbed in their serious talk and discussion, Jesus Himself approached and walked along with them, but something prevented them from recognising Him. Then He spoke to them,

"What is all this discussion that you are having on your walk?"

They stopped, their faces drawn with misery, and the one called Cleopas replied,

"You must be the only stranger in Jerusalem who hasn't heard all the things that have happened there recently!"

"What things?" asked Jesus.

"Oh, all about Jesus, from Nazareth. There was a man— a prophet strong in what he did and what he said, in God's eyes as well as the people's. Haven't you heard how our Chief Priests and rulers handed him over for execution, and had him crucified? But we were hoping he was the one who was to come and set Israel free. . . .

"Yes, and as if that were not enough, it's getting on for three days since all this happened; and some of our women-folk have shocked us deeply. They went to the tomb at dawn, and then when they couldn't find his body they said that they had had a vision of angels who said that he was alive. Some of our people went straight off to the tomb and found things just as the women had described them—but they didn't see *him*!"

Then He Himself spoke to them,

"Aren't you being stupid, and slow to believe in all the things the prophets have said? Was it not inevitable that Christ should suffer like that and so find His glory?"

Then, beginning with Moses and all the prophets, He explained to them everything in the Scriptures that referred to Himself.

They were by now approaching the village to which they were going. He gave the impression that He meant to go on further, but they stopped Him with the words,

"Do stay with us. It is nearly evening and soon the day will be over."

So He went indoors to stay with them. *Then it happened!* While He was sitting at table with them He took the loaf, gave thanks, broke it and passed it to them. Their eyes opened wide and *they knew Him*! But He vanished even while they stared at Him. Then they said to each other,

"Wasn't your heart glowing while He was with us on the road, and when He made the Scriptures so plain to us?"

And they got to their feet without delay and turned back
to Jerusalem. There they found the Eleven and their friends
all together full of the news—

"The Lord is really risen—He has appeared to Simon
now!"

Then they told the story of their walk, and how they
recognised Him when He broke the loaf.

JESUS SUDDENLY APPEARS TO THE
DISCIPLES

24
36 And while they were still talking about these things, Jesus
Himself stood among them and said,

"Peace be to you all!"

But they shrank back in terror for they thought they were
seeing a ghost.

"Why are you so worried?" said Jesus, "and why are these
doubts springing up in your minds? Look at My hands and
My feet—it is really I Myself! Feel Me and see; ghosts have
no flesh or bones as you can see that I have."

And while they still could not believe that anything so
glorious could be true and were quite bewildered, Jesus said,

"Have you anything here to eat?"

They gave Him some fish and a piece of honeycomb, which
He took and ate in front of them. Then He said,

"Here and now are fulfilled the words that I told you
when I was with you: that everything written about Me in
the Law of Moses and in the prophets and psalms must come
true."

Then He made them able to understand the Scriptures,
and added,

"That is how it was written, and that is why it was inevitable that Christ should suffer and rise from the dead on
the third day. And so must the change of heart and the forgiveness of sins be proclaimed in His Name to all nations,
beginning at Jerusalem.

JESUS COMMISSIONS THEM WITH THE
NEW MESSAGE

24
48 "You are eye-witnesses of these things. Now I hand over
to you the Message of the Father. Stay in the city, then,
until you are clothed with power from on high."

Then He led them outside as far as Bethany, where He blessed them with uplifted hands. While He was in the act of blessing them he was parted from them and was carried up to Heaven.

And they worshipped Him and turned back to Jerusalem with great joy, and spent their days in the Temple, praising and blessing God.

THE GOSPEL OF
JOHN

It is quite plain that in this Gospel we are breathing a very
different atmosphere from that of Matthew, Mark and Luke.
The story itself shows great differences, almost the whole of
the "action" taking place in Jerusalem; while a large amount
of both the teaching and the healing ministries described by
Mark, for example, find no place in "John" at all. There is
also the remarkable difference that in this Gospel Jesus is
recognised as the Messiah in the very first chapter by John,
Andrew and Philip. Consequently John's version lacks the
note of mounting tension which is very strong in the other
three. The discourses of Jesus differ remarkably from those
in the other three Gospels, where they consist for the most part
of parables or short memorable rules of the way in which life
is meant to be lived. In John's Gospel the discourses are long
and different in style; they deal almost entirely with the
great themes of Life, Light, Love, Truth and Christ's rela-
tionship with the Father. There are many similes and meta-
phors but no parables at all.

Naturally, this and many other sharp differences have given
rise to an enormous amount of study and research. There is
a vast body of literature commenting on the situation, and
offering widely different explanations. To mention but one
basic problem: in view of the difference of style between this
and the other three Gospels, are we to suppose that Jesus
spoke in different styles on different occasions, or are we to
suppose that John is rewriting in his own style of Greek what
Jesus spoke in Aramaic? The subject is obviously much too
large to be more than introduced here, and the reader in
search of further information is referred to the List of Recommended Books at the end of the Preface.

Whether this Gospel was written as a conscious supplement
(or even a deliberate corrective) to the other three, we simply
do not know. But the majority of Christian scholars, for all

*their disagreements, would not deny the enormous spiritual
value of this document. It seems probable that the author
knew Jesus personally, and although modern scholarship is
mostly against considering him to be the apostle John, there
can be no doubt that the author had close spiritual acquaint-
ance with Christ, and had reflected long and deeply on the
nature of the divine Word. Here he gives to the world the
results of his thoughts, prayers and meditations about the Life
which is the Light of men.*

*Modern scholarship has gradually set the probable date of
the Gospel earlier and earlier, and it is now fairly generally
agreed that it was written at Ephesus between 90 and 110.*

PROLOGUE

A T THE beginning God expressed Himself. That Personal
Expression was with God and was God, and He existed
with God from the beginning. All creation took place
through Him, and none took place without Him. In Him
appeared Life and this Life was the Light of mankind. The
Light still shines in the darkness, and the darkness has never
put it out.

THE GOSPEL'S BEGINNING ON EARTH

A man called John was sent by God as a witness to the   1
Light, so that any man who heard his testimony might be-   6
lieve in the Light. This man was not himself the Light: he
was sent simply as a personal witness to that Light.

The true Light which shines on every man was coming into
the world. He came into the World—the World He had
created—and the World failed to recognise Him. He came
into His own creation, and His own people would not accept
Him. Yet wherever men did accept Him He gave them the
power to become sons of God. These were the men who
really believed in Him, and their birth depended not on the
course of nature nor on any impulse or plan of man, but on
God.

So the Expression of God became a human being and lived
among us. We saw His splendour (the splendour, as of the
Father's only Son), full of grace and truth. And it was about
Him that John stood up and testified, exclaiming: "Here is

the One I was speaking about when I said that although He
would come after me He would always be in front of me; for
He existed before I was born!" Indeed, every one of us has
shared in His riches—there is a grace in our lives because of
His love. For while the Law was given by Moses, Love and
Truth came through Jesus Christ. It is true that no one has
ever seen God at any time. Yet the divine and only Son, Who
lives in the closest intimacy with the Father, has made Him
known.

JOHN'S WITNESS

1   This then is the testimony of John, when the Jews sent
19   priests and Levites to ask him who he was. He admitted
with complete candour, "I am not Christ."

So they asked him, "Who are you then? Are you Elijah?"

"No, I am not," he replied.

"Are you the Prophet?"

"No," he replied.

"Well then," they asked again, "who are you? We want
to give an answer to the people who sent us. What would
you call yourself?"

"I am a Voice shouting in the desert," he replied, " '*Make
straight the way of the Lord!*' as Isaiah the prophet said."

Among those who had been sent to John were some from
the Pharisees and they questioned him, "What is the reason,
then, for your baptizing people if you are not Christ and not
Elijah and not the Prophet?"

To which John returned, "I do baptize—with water. But
somewhere among you stands a Man you do not know.
He comes after me, it is true, but I am not fit to undo His
sandals!" (All this happened in Bethany on the far side of
Jordan where the baptisms of John took place.)

On the following day, John saw Jesus coming towards him
and said, "Look, there is the Lamb of God Who will take
away the sin of the world! This is the Man I meant when
I said 'A Man comes after me Who is always in front of me,
for He existed before I was born!' It is true I have not known
Him, yet it was to make Him known to the people of Israel
that I came and baptized people with water."

Then John gave this testimony, "I have seen the Spirit
come down like a dove from Heaven and rest upon Him.

Indeed, it is true that I did not recognise Him by myself, but the One Who sent me to baptize with water told me this: 'The One on Whom you will see the Spirit coming down and resting is the Man Who baptizes with the Holy Spirit!' Now I have seen this happen and I declare publicly before you all that *He is the Son of God!*"

MEN BEGIN TO FOLLOW JESUS

On the following day it happened that John was again standing with two of his disciples. He looked full at Jesus as He walked along and said, "There is the Lamb of God!" The two disciples heard what he said and followed Jesus. Then Jesus turned round and when He saw them following Him, spoke to them. "What do you want?" He said.

"Master, where are you staying?" they replied.

"Come and see," returned Jesus.

So they went and saw where He was staying and remained with Him the rest of that day. (It was then about four o'clock in the afternoon.) One of the two men who had heard what John said and had followed Jesus was Andrew, Simon Peter's brother. He went straight off and found his own brother, Simon, and told him, "We have found the Messiah!" (meaning, of course, Christ). And he brought him to Jesus.

Jesus looked steadily at him and said, "You are Simon, the son of John. From now on your name is Cephas"—(that is, Peter, meaning "a rock").

The following day Jesus decided to go into Galilee. He found Philip and said to him, "Follow me!" Philip was a man from Bethsaida, the town that Andrew and Peter came from. Now Philip found Nathanael and told him, "We have discovered the Man Whom Moses wrote about in the Law and Whom the Prophets wrote about too. He is Jesus, the son of Joseph and comes from Nazareth."

"Can anything good come out of Nazareth?" retorted Nathanael.

"You come and see," replied Philip.

Jesus saw Nathanael coming towards Him and remarked, "Now here is a true man of Israel; there is no deceit in him!"

"How can you know me?" returned Nathanael.

"When you were underneath that fig-tree," replied Jesus, "before Philip called you, I saw you."

At which Nathanael exclaimed, "Master, You are the Son of God, You are the King of Israel!"

"Do you believe in Me," replied Jesus, "because I said I had seen you underneath that fig-tree? You are going to see something greater than that! Believe Me," He added, "I tell you all that you will see Heaven wide open and God's angels ascending and descending around the Son of Man!"

THE SON OF GOD AND A VILLAGE WEDDING

2
1 Two days later there was a wedding in the Galilean village of Cana. Jesus' mother was there and He and His disciples were invited to the festivities. Then it happened that the supply of wine gave out, and Jesus' mother told Him, "They have no more wine."

"Is that your concern, or Mine?" replied Jesus. "My time has not come yet."

So His mother said to the servants, "Mind you do whatever He tells you."

In the room six very large stone water-jars stood on the floor (actually for the Jewish ceremonial cleansing), each holding about twenty gallons. Jesus gave instructions for these jars to be filled with water, and the servants filled them to the brim. Then He said to them, "Now draw some out and take it to the Master of Ceremonies," which they did. When this man tasted the water, which had now become wine, without knowing where it came from (though naturally the servants who had drawn the water knew), he called out to the bridegroom and said to him, "Everybody I know puts his good wine on first and then when men have had plenty to drink, he brings out the poor stuff. But you have kept back your good wine till now!" Jesus gave this, the first of His Signs, at Cana in Galilee. He demonstrated His power and His disciples believed in Him.

JESUS IN THE TEMPLE

2
12 After this incident, Jesus, accompanied by His mother, His brothers and His disciples, went down to Capernaum and stayed there a few days. The Jewish Passover was approaching and Jesus made the journey up to Jerusalem. In the Temple He discovered cattle and sheep dealers and pigeon-sellers, as well as money-changers sitting at their tables. So

He made a rough whip out of rope and drove the whole
lot of them, sheep and cattle as well, out of the Temple. He
sent the coins of the money-changers flying and turned their
tables upside down. Then He said to the pigeon-dealers,
"Take those things out of here. Don't you dare turn My
Father's house into a shop!" His disciples remembered the
scripture—

The zeal of thine house shall eat me up.

As a result of this, the Jews said to Him, "What sign can
you give us to justify what you are doing?"

"Destroy this temple," Jesus retorted, "and I will rebuild
it in three days!"

To which the Jews replied, "This Temple took forty-six
years to build, and are you going to rebuild it in three days?"

He was, in fact, speaking about the temple of His own
body, and when He was raised from the dead the disciples
remembered what He had said to them and that made them
believe both in the Scripture and what Jesus had said.

While He was in Jerusalem at Passover-time, at the height
of the festivities many believed in Him as they saw the Signs
that He gave. But Jesus, on His side, did not trust Himself to
them—for He knew them all. He did not need anyone to tell
Him what people were like: He understood human nature.

JESUS AND A RELIGIOUS LEADER

One night Nicodemus, a leading Jew and a Pharisee, came
to see Jesus.

"Master," he began, "we realize that you are a teacher who
has come from God. Obviously no one could show the Signs
that you show unless God were with him."

"Believe Me," returned Jesus, "a man cannot even see the
Kingdom of God without being born over again."

"And how can a man who's getting old possibly be born?"
replied Nicodemus. "How can he go back into his mother's
womb a second time and be born?"

"I assure you," said Jesus, "that unless a man is born from
water and from spirit he cannot get into the Kingdom of God.
Flesh gives birth to flesh and spirit gives birth to spirit: you
must not be surprised that I told you that men must be born
again. The wind blows where it likes, you can hear the sound

of it but you have no idea where it comes from and where it goes. Nor can you tell how a man is born by the wind of the Spirit."

"How on earth can things like this happen?" replied Nicodemus.

"So you are one of Israel's teachers," said Jesus, "and you do not know about this sort of thing? Believe Me, we are talking about something we really know and we are witnessing to something we have actually observed, yet men like you will not accept our evidence. Yet if I have spoken to you about things which happen to you on this earth and you will not believe Me, what chance is there that you will believe Me if I tell you about what happens in Heaven? No one has ever been up to Heaven except the Son of Man Who came down from Heaven. The Son of Man must be lifted above the heads of men—as Moses lifted up that serpent in the desert —so that any man who believes in Him may have eternal life. For God loved the world so much that He gave His only Son, so that everyone who believes in Him should not be lost, but should have eternal life. You must understand that God has not sent His Son into the world to pass sentence upon it, but to save it—through Him. Any man who believes in Him is not judged at all. It is the one who will not believe who stands already condemned, because he will not believe in the character of God's only Son. This *is* the judgment—that light has entered the world and men have preferred darkness to light because their deeds are evil. Anybody who does wrong hates the light and keeps away from it, for fear his deeds may be exposed. But anybody who is living by the truth will come to the light to make it perfectly plain that all he has done has been done through God."

JESUS AND JOHN AGAIN

3
22
After this Jesus went into the country of Judaea with His disciples and stayed there with them while the work of baptism was being carried on. John, too, was in Aenon near Salim, baptizing people because there was plenty of water in that district and they came to him for baptism. (John, of course, had not yet been thrown into prison.)

This led to a question arising between John's disciples and some of the Jews about the whole matter of being cleansed.

They approached John and said to him, "Master, look, the
man who was with you on the other side of Jordan, the one
you spoke about, is now baptizing and everybody is coming
to him!"

"A man can receive nothing at all," replied John, "unless
it is given him from Heaven. You yourselves can witness
that I said, 'I am not Christ but I am the man sent in front
of Him.' It is the bridegroom who possesses the bride, yet the
bridegroom's friend who merely stands and listens to him can
be really glad to hear the bridegroom's voice. That is why
my happiness is now complete. He must grow greater and
greater and I less and less.

"The One Who comes from above is naturally above everybody. The one who arises from the earth belongs to the earth
and speaks from the earth. The One Who comes from Heaven
is above all others and He bears witness to what He has seen
and heard—yet no one accepts His testimony. Yet if a man
does accept it, he finds himself thereby acknowledging the
fact that God is true. For the One Whom God sent speaks
the authentic words of God—and there can be no measuring
of the Spirit given to *Him*! The Father loves the Son and has
put everything into His hand. The man who believes in the
Son has eternal life. The man who refuses to believe in the
Son will not see life; he lives under the anger of God."

JESUS MEETS A SAMARITAN WOMAN

Now, when the Lord found out that the Pharisees had
heard that "Jesus is making and baptizing more disciples
than John"—although, in fact, it was not Jesus who did the
baptizing but His disciples—He left Judaea and went off
again to Galilee, which meant His passing through Samaria.
There He came to a little town called Sychar, which is near
the historic plot of land that Jacob gave to his son, Joseph,
and "Jacob's Spring" was there. Jesus, tired with the journey,
sat down beside it. The time was about midday. Presently, a
Samaritan woman arrived to draw some water.

"Please give Me a drink," Jesus said to her, for His disciples had all gone away to the town to buy food. The
Samaritan woman said to Him, "How can you, a Jew, ask
for a drink from me, a Samaritan woman?" (For Jews have
nothing to do with Samaritans.)

4

1

"If you knew what God can give," Jesus replied, "and if
you knew Who it is that said to you, 'Give Me a drink,' I
think you would have asked Him, and He would have given
you living water!"

"Sir," said the woman, "you have nothing to draw water
with and this well is deep—where can you get your living
water? Are you a greater man than our ancestor, Jacob, who
gave us this well, and drank here himself with his family, and
his cattle?"

Jesus said to her, "Everyone who drinks this water will be
thirsty again. But whoever drinks the water I will give him
will never be thirsty again. For My gift will become a spring
in the man himself, welling up into eternal life."

The woman said, "Sir, give me this water, so that I may
stop being thirsty—and not have to come here to draw water
any more!"

"Go and call your husband and then come back here," said
Jesus to her.

"I haven't got a husband!" the woman replied.

"Yes, you are quite right in saying, 'I haven't got a husband,' " replied Jesus, "for you have had five husbands and
the man you have now is not your husband at all. Yes, you
spoke the simple truth when you said that."

"Sir," said the woman again, "I can see that you are a
prophet! Now our ancestors worshipped on this mountain,
but you Jews say that Jerusalem is the place where men
ought to worship——"

"Believe Me," returned Jesus, "the time is coming when
worshipping the Father will not be a matter of 'on this
mountain' or 'in Jerusalem.' Nowadays you are worshipping
with your eyes shut. We Jews are worshipping with our eyes
open, for the salvation of mankind is to come from our race.
Yet the time is coming, yes, and has already come, when true
worshippers will worship the Father in spirit and in reality.
Indeed, the Father looks for men who will worship Him like
that. God is Spirit, and those who worship Him can only
worship in spirit and in reality."

"Of course I know that Messiah is coming," returned the
woman, "you know, the One Who is called Christ. When He
comes He will make everything plain to us."

"I am Christ, speaking to you now," said Jesus.

At this point the disciples arrived, and were very surprised
to find Him talking to a woman, but none of them asked,
"What do You want?" or "What are You talking to her
about?" So the woman left her water-pot behind and went
into the town and began to say to the people, "Come out and
see the man who told me everything I've ever done! Can this
be 'Christ'?" So they left the town and started to come to
Jesus.

Meanwhile the disciples were begging Him, "Master, do eat
something."

To which Jesus replied, "I have food to eat that you know
nothing about."

This, of course, made the disciples ask each other, "Do you
think anyone has brought Him any food?"

Jesus said to them, "My food is doing the Will of Him Who
sent Me and finishing the work He has given Me. Don't you
say, 'Four months more and then comes the harvest?' But
I tell you to open your eyes and look at the fields—they are
gleaming white already for the harvest! The reaper is already
being rewarded and getting in a harvest for eternal life, so
that the sower and the reaper may be glad together. For in
this harvest the old saying comes true, 'One man sows and
another man reaps.' I have sent you to reap a harvest for
which you never laboured; other men have worked hard and
you have reaped the result of their labours."

Many of the Samaritans who came out of that town believed in Him through the woman's testimony, "He told me
everything I've ever done." And when they arrived they
begged Him to stay with them. He did stay there two days
and far more believed in Him because of what He Himself
said. As they told the woman, "We don't believe any longer
now because of what you said. We have heard Him with our
own ears. We know now that this is really the Man Who will
save the world!"

JESUS, IN CANA AGAIN, HEALS IN RESPONSE TO FAITH

After the two days were over, Jesus left and went away to   4
Galilee. (For Jesus Himself testified that a prophet enjoys no   43
honour in his own country.) And on His arrival the people
received Him with open arms. For they had seen all that He
had done in Jerusalem during the Festival since they had

themselves been present. So Jesus came again to Cana in Galilee, the place where He made the water into wine. At Capernaum there was an official whose son was very ill. When he heard that Jesus had left Judaea and had arrived in Galilee, he went off to see Him and begged Him to come down and heal his son, who was by this time nearly dying.

Jesus said to him, "I suppose you will never believe unless you see signs and wonders."

"Sir," returned the official, "please come down before my boy dies!"

"You can go home," returned Jesus, "your son is alive and well."

And the man believed what Jesus had said to him and went away home.

On the journey back his servants met him with the report: "Your son is alive and well." So he asked them at what time he had begun to recover, and they replied that "the fever left him yesterday at one o'clock in the afternoon." Then the father knew that this must have happened at the very moment when Jesus had said to him, "Your son is alive and well." And he and his whole household believed in Jesus. This, then, was the second Sign that Jesus gave on His return from Judaea to Galilee.

JESUS HEALS IN JERUSALEM

5 Some time later came one of the Jewish feast-days and
1 Jesus went up to Jerusalem. There is in Jerusalem near the sheep-gate a pool surrounded by five arches, which has the Hebrew name of Bethzatha. Under these arches a great many sick people were in the habit of lying; some of them were blind, some lame, and some had withered limbs. They used to wait there for the "moving of the water," for at certain times an angel used to come down into the pool and disturb the water, and then the first person who stepped into the water after the disturbance would be healed of whatever he was suffering from. One particular man had been there ill for thirty-eight years. When Jesus saw him lying there on his back—knowing that he had been like that for a long time, He said to him, "Do you want to get well again?"

"Sir," replied the sick man, "I just haven't got anybody to put me into the pool when the water is all stirred up. What happens is that while I'm trying to get there somebody else gets down into it first."

"Get up," said Jesus, "pick up your mat and walk!"

At once the man recovered, picked up his mat and walked.

This happened on a Sabbath day, which made the Jews keep on telling the man who had been healed, "It's the Sabbath, you know; it's not right for you to carry your bed."

"The man who made me well," he replied, "was the one who told me, 'Pick up your mat and walk.' "

Then they asked him, "And who is the man who told you to do that?"

But the one who had been healed had no idea who it was, for Jesus had slipped away in the dense crowd. Later Jesus found him in the Temple and said to him, "Look: you are a fit man now. Do not sin again or something worse might happen to you!"

Then the man went off and informed the Jews that the One Who had made him well was Jesus. It was because Jesus did such things on the Sabbath day that the Jews persecuted Him. But Jesus' answer to them was this, "My Father is still at work and therefore I work as well."

This remark made the Jews all the more determined to kill Him, because not only did He break the Sabbath but He referred to God as His own Father, so putting Himself on equal terms with God.

JESUS MAKES HIS TREMENDOUS CLAIM

Jesus said to them, "I assure you that the Son can do nothing of His own accord, but only what He sees the Father doing. What the Son does is always modelled on what the Father does, for the Father loves the Son and shows Him everything that He does Himself. Yes, and He will show Him even greater things than these to fill you with wonder. For just as the Father raises the dead and makes them live, so does the Son give life to any man He chooses. The Father is no man's judge: He has put judgment entirely into the Son's hands so that all men may honour the Son equally with the Father. The man who does not honour the Son does not honour the Father Who sent Him. I solemnly assure you that the man who hears what I have to say and believes in the One Who has sent Me has eternal life. He does not have to face judgment; he has already passed from death into life. Yes, I assure you that a time is coming, in fact has already come, when the dead will hear the voice of the Son of God and when they have heard it *they will live!* For just as the Father has Life in Himself, so by the Father's gift, the Son has Life in Himself as well. And He has given Him authority to judge because He is Son of Man. No, do not be surprised —the time is coming when all those who are dead and buried will hear His voice and out they will come—those who have done right will rise again to Life, but those who have done wrong will rise to face judgment!

"By Myself I can do nothing. As I hear, I judge, and My judgment is true because I do not live to please Myself but to do the will of the Father Who sent Me. You may say that I am bearing witness about Myself, that therefore what I say about Myself has no value, but I would remind you that there is One Who witnesses about Me and I know that His witness about Me is absolutely true. You sent to John, and he testified to the truth. Not that it is man's testimony that I accept—I only tell you this to help you to be saved. John certainly was a lamp that burned and shone and for a time you were willing to enjoy the light that he gave. But I have a higher testimony than John's. The work that the Father gave Me to complete, yes, these very actions which I do are My witness that the Father has sent Me. This is how the Father Who sent Me has given His own personal testimony to Me.

"Now you have never at any time heard what He says or seen what He is like. Nor do you really believe His Word in your hearts, for you refuse to believe the Man Whom He has sent. You pore over the Scriptures for you imagine that you will find eternal life in them. And all the time they give their testimony to Me! But you are not willing to come to Me to have real life! Men's approval or disapproval means nothing to Me, but I can tell that you have none of the love of God in your hearts. I have come in the Name of My Father and you will not accept Me. Yet if another man comes simply in his own name, you will accept him. How on earth can you believe while you are for ever looking for each other's approval and not for the glory that comes from the one God? There is no need for you to think that I have come to accuse

you before the Father. You already have an accuser—Moses,
in whom you put all your confidence! For if you really believed Moses, you would be bound to believe Me; for it was
about Me that he wrote. But if you do not believe what he
wrote, how can you believe what I say?"

JESUS SHOWS HIS POWER OVER MATERIAL THINGS

After this, Jesus crossed the lake of Galilee (or Tiberias), **6**
and a great crowd followed Him because they had seen the **1**
Signs which He gave in His dealings with the sick. But Jesus
went up the mountain-side and sat down there with His disciples. The Passover, the Jewish festival, was near. So Jesus,
raising His eyes and seeing a great crowd on their way towards Him, said to Philip, "Where can we buy food for these
people to eat?" (He said this to test Philip, for He Himself
knew what He was going to do.)

"Ten dollars' worth of bread would not be enough for
them," Philip replied, "even if they had only a little each."

Then Andrew, Simon Peter's brother, another disciple, put
in, "There is a boy here who's got five little barley loaves
and a couple of fish, but what's the good of that for such a
crowd?"

Then Jesus said, "Get the people to sit down."

There was plenty of grass there, and the men, some five
thousand of them, sat down. Then Jesus took the loaves,
gave thanks for them and distributed them to the disciples
and the disciples passed them on to the people sitting on the
grass. They distributed the fish in the same way, giving them
as much as they wanted. When they had eaten enough, Jesus
said to His disciples, "Collect the pieces that are left over so
that nothing is wasted."

So they did as He suggested and filled twelve baskets with
the broken pieces of the five barley loaves which were left
over after the people had eaten! When the men saw this Sign
of Jesus' power, they kept saying, "This certainly is the
Prophet who was to come into the world!"

Then Jesus, realising that they were going to carry Him off
and make Him their king, retired once more to the mountain
quite alone.

In the evening, His disciples went down to the lake, embarked on the boat and made their way across the lake to

Capernaum. Darkness had already fallen and Jesus had not returned to them. A strong wind sprang up and the water grew very rough. When they had rowed about three or four miles, they saw Jesus walking on the water and coming towards the boat, and they were terrified. But He spoke to them, "Don't be afraid: it is I Myself."

So they gladly took Him aboard, and at once the boat reached the shore they were making for.

JESUS TEACHES ABOUT THE TRUE BREAD

6
22 The following day, the crowd who had sat on the other side of the lake noticed that only one boat had been there, and that Jesus had not embarked on it with His disciples, but that they had in fact gone off by themselves. Some other small boats from Tiberias were beached quite near the place where they had eaten the food and the Lord had given thanks. When the crowd realised that neither Jesus nor the disciples were there any longer, they themselves got into the boats and went off to Capernaum to look for Jesus. When they had found Him on the other side of the lake, they said to Him, "Master, when did you come here?"

"Believe Me," replied Jesus, "you are looking for Me now not because you saw My Signs but because you ate that food and had all you wanted. You should not work for the food which does not last but for that food which lasts on into eternal life. This is the food the Son of Man will give you, and He is the One Who bears the stamp of God the Father."

This made them ask Him, "What must we do to carry out the work of God?"

"The true work of God," replied Jesus, "is that you believe in the One that He has sent to you."

Then they asked Him, "Then what sign can you give us that will make us believe in you? What work are you doing? Our forefathers ate manna in the desert just as the Scripture says,

He gave them bread out of heaven to eat."

To which Jesus replied, "Yes, but you must believe Me that what matters is not that Moses *gave you* bread from Heaven but that My Father *is giving you* the true bread from Heaven. For the bread of God which comes down from Heaven gives life to the world."

This made them say to Him, "Lord, please give us this bread, always!"

Then Jesus said to them, "I Myself am the bread of life. The man who comes to Me will never be hungry and the man who believes in Me will never again be thirsty. Yet I have told you that you have seen Me and do not believe. Everything that My Father gives Me will come to Me and I will never refuse anyone who comes to Me. For I have come down from Heaven, not to do what I want, but to do the Will of Him Who sent Me. The Will of Him Who sent Me is that I should not lose anything of what He has given Me, but should raise it up when the Last Day comes. And this is the Will of the One Who sent Me, that everyone who sees the Son and trusts Him should have eternal life, and I will raise him up when the Last Day comes."

At this, the Jews began grumbling at Him because He said, "I am the bread which came down from Heaven," remarking, "Is not this Jesus, the son of Joseph, whose parents we know? How can he say that 'I have come down from Heaven'?"

So Jesus answered them, "Do not grumble among yourselves. Nobody comes to Me unless he is drawn to Me by the Father Who sent Me, and I will raise him up when the Last Day comes. In the Prophets it is written—

And they shall all be taught of God,

and this means that everybody who has heard the Father's Voice and learned from Him will come to Me. Not that anyone has ever seen the Father except the One Who comes from God—He has seen the Father. I assure you that the man who trusts in Him has eternal life already. I Myself am the bread of life. Your forefathers ate manna in the desert, *and they died*. This is bread that comes down from Heaven, so that a man may eat it and not die. I Myself am the living bread which came down from Heaven, and if anyone eats this bread he will live for ever. The bread which I will give is My body and I shall give it for the life of the world."

This led to a fierce argument among the Jews, some of them saying, "How can this man give us his body to eat?"

So Jesus said to them, "Unless you do eat the body of the Son of Man and drink His blood, you are not really living at all. The man who eats My flesh and drinks My blood has eternal life and I will raise him up when the Last Day comes. For My body is really food and My blood is really drink. The man who eats My body and drinks My blood shares My life and I share his. Just as the living Father sent Me and I am alive because of the Father, so the man who lives on Me will live because of Me. *This* is the Bread which came down from Heaven! It is not like the manna which your forefathers used to eat, *and died*. The man who eats this Bread will live for ever."

Jesus said all these things while teaching in the synagogue at Capernaum. Many of His disciples heard Him say these things, and commented, "That was a hard thing for Him to say; who could accept that?"

Then Jesus knowing intuitively that His disciples were complaining about what He had just said went on, "Is this too much for you? Then what would happen if you were to see the Son of Man going up to the place where He was before? It is the Spirit which gives life. The flesh will not help you here. The things that I have told you are spiritual and are Life. But some of you will not believe Me."

For Jesus knew from the beginning which of His followers did not trust Him and who was the man who would betray Him. Then He added, "This is why I said to you, 'No one can come to Me unless My Father puts it into his heart to come.' "

As a consequence of this, many of His disciples withdrew and no longer followed Him. So Jesus said to the Twelve, "And are you too wanting to go away?"

"Lord," answered Simon Peter, "who else should we go to? *Your words have the ring of eternal life!* And we believe and are convinced that You are the Holy One of God."

Jesus replied, "Did I not choose you Twelve—and one of you has the devil in his heart?"

He was speaking of Judas, the son of Simon Iscariot, one of the Twelve, who was planning to betray Him.

JESUS DELAYS HIS ARRIVAL AT THE FESTIVAL

7   After this, Jesus moved about in Galilee but decided not to
1   do so in Judaea since the Jews were planning to take His life. A Jewish festival, "The Feast of the Tabernacles," was approaching and his brothers said to Him, "You ought to leave

here and go to Judaea so that your disciples can see what you
are doing, for nobody works in secret if he wants to be known
publicly. If you are going to do things like this, let the world
see what you are doing." For not even his brothers had any
faith in him. Jesus replied by saying, "It is not yet the right
time for Me to act, but any time is suitable for you. You see,
it is impossible for you to arouse the world's hatred, but I
provoke hatred because I show the world how evil its deeds
really are. No, you go up to the Festival; I shall not go up
now, for it is not yet time for Me to go." And after these
remarks He remained where He was in Galilee.

After His brothers had gone up to the City, He went up
later Himself, not openly but as though He did not want to
be seen. Consequently, the Jews kept looking for Him at the
Festival and asking, "Where is that man?" And there was
an undercurrent of discussion about Him among the crowds.
Some would say, "He is a good man," others maintained that
he was not, but that he was "misleading the people." Nobody, however, spoke openly about him for fear of the Jews.

But at the very height of the Festival, Jesus went up to the
Temple and began teaching. The Jews were amazed and remarked, "How does this man know all this—he has never
been taught?"

Jesus replied to them, "My teaching is not really Mine but
comes from the One Who sent Me. If anyone wants to do
God's will, he will know whether My teaching is from God or
whether I merely speak on My own authority. A man who
speaks on his own authority has an eye for his own reputation. But the man who is considering the glory of God Who
sent him is a true man. There can be no dishonesty about
him.

"Did not Moses give you the Law? Yet not a single one
of you obeys the Law. *Why are you trying to kill Me?*"

The crowd answered, "You must be mad! Who is trying
to kill you?"

Jesus answered them, "I have done one thing and you are
all amazed at it. Moses gave you circumcision (not that it
came from Moses originally but from your forefathers), and
you will circumcise a man even on the Sabbath. If a man
receives the cutting of circumcision on the Sabbath to avoid
breaking the Law of Moses, why should you be angry with

Me because I have made a man's body perfectly whole on the Sabbath? You must not judge by the appearance of things but by the reality!"

Some of the people of Jerusalem, hearing Him talk like this, remarked, "Isn't this the man that they are trying to kill? It's amazing—he talks quite openly and they haven't a word to say to him. Surely our rulers haven't decided that this really is Christ! But then, we know this man and where he comes from—when Christ comes, no one will know where He comes from."

Then Jesus, in the middle of His teaching, called out in the Temple, "So you know Me and know where I have come from? But I have not come of My own accord; I am sent by One Who is true and you do not know Him! I do know Him, because I come from Him and He has sent Me here."

Then they attempted to arrest Him, but actually no one laid a finger on Him because the right moment had not yet arrived. Many of the crowd believed in Him and kept on saying, "When Christ comes, is He going to show greater signs than this man has done?"

The Pharisees heard the crowd whispering these things about Him and they and the Chief Priests sent officers to arrest Him. Then Jesus said, "I shall be with you only a little while longer and then I am going to Him Who sent Me. You will look for Me then but you will never find Me. You cannot come where I shall be."

This made the Jews say to each other, "Where is he going to hide himself so that we cannot find him? Surely, he's not going to our refugees among the Greeks to teach Greeks? What does he mean when he says 'You will look for me and you will not find me' and 'You cannot come where I shall be'?"

Then, on the last day, the climax of the Festival, Jesus stood up and cried out, "If any man is thirsty, he can come to Me and drink! The man who believes in Me, as the Scripture said, will have rivers of living water flowing from his inmost heart." (Here he was speaking about the Spirit which those who believe in Him would receive. The Holy Spirit had not yet been given because Jesus had not yet been glorified.) When they heard these words, some of the people were saying, "This really is the Prophet." Others said, "This is

Christ!" But some said, "And is Christ going to come from Galilee? Don't the Scriptures say that Christ is to be descended from David, and is to come from Bethlehem, the village where David lived?"

So the people were in two minds about Him—some of them wanted to arrest Him, but so far no one laid hands on Him.

Then the officers returned to the Pharisees and Chief Priests who said to them, "Why haven't you brought him?"

"Nobody ever spoke like that!" they replied.

"Has he pulled the wool over your eyes, too?" retorted the Pharisees. "Have any of the authorities or any of the Pharisees believed in him? But this crowd, who know nothing about the Law, is damned anyway!"

One of their number, Nicodemus (the one who had previously been to see Jesus) remarked to them, "But surely our Law does not condemn the accused without hearing what he has to say, and finding out what he has done?"

"Are you a Galilean, too?" they answered him. "Search as you like—you won't find that any prophet comes out of Galilee!"

So they broke up their meeting and went home, while Jesus went off to the Mount of Olives.

Early next morning He returned to the Temple and the entire crowd came to Him. So He sat down and began to teach them. But the Scribes and Pharisees brought in to Him a woman who had been caught in adultery. They put her right in front of the crowd and said to Him, "Now, Master, this woman has been caught in adultery, in the very act. According to the Law, Moses commanded people like her to be stoned to death. Now, what do you say about her?" *

They said this to test Him, so that they might have some good grounds for an accusation. But Jesus stooped down and began to write with His finger in the dust on the ground. But as they continued their questioning, He straightened Himself up and said to them, "Let the one of you who has not sinned throw the first stone." Then He stooped down again and continued writing with His finger. And when they heard what He said, they were convicted by their own consciences and went out, one by one, beginning with the eldest until they had all gone.

* See Appendix, Note 4.

Jesus was left alone, with the woman still standing where they had put her. So He stood up and said to her, "Where are they all—did no one condemn you?"

And she said, "No one, sir."

"Neither do I condemn you," said Jesus to her. "Go home and do not sin again."

JESUS' BOLD CLAIMS—ABOUT HIMSELF— AND HIS FATHER

8
12 Later, Jesus spoke to the people again and said, "I am the Light of the world. The man who follows Me will not walk in the dark but will live his life in the light."

This made the Pharisees say to Him, "You are merely testifying to yourself—your evidence is worthless."

Jesus answered, "Even if I am testifying to Myself, My evidence is reliable, for I know where I have come from and I know where I am going, but you have no idea where I come from or where I am going. You are judging by human standards, but I am not judging anyone. Yet, if I should judge, My judgment would be true, for I am not alone—the Father Who sent Me is always with Me. In your Law, it is stated that the witness of two persons is valid. I am one testifying to Myself and the second witness to Me is the Father Who sent Me."

"And where is this father of yours?" they replied.

"You do not know My Father," returned Jesus, "any more than you know Me: if you had known Me, you would have known Him."

Jesus made these statements while He was teaching in the Temple treasury. Yet no one arrested Him, for the right time had not yet come.

Later, Jesus spoke to them again and said, "I am going away and you will try to find Me, but you will die in your sin. You cannot come where I am going."

This made the Jews say, "Is he going to kill himself, then? Is *that* why he says, 'You cannot come where I am going'?"

"The difference between us," Jesus said to them, "is that you come from below and I am from above. You belong to this world but I do not. That is why I told you you will die in your sins. For if you cannot believe that I am what I am, you cannot avoid dying in your sins."

Then they said, "*Who are you?*"

"I am what I have told you I was from the beginning,"
replied Jesus. "There is much in you that I could speak
about and condemn. But He Who sent Me is true and I am
only speaking to this world what I Myself have heard from
Him."

They did not realise that He was talking to them about the
Father. So Jesus resumed, "When you have lifted up the
Son of Man, then you will realise that I am what I say I am,
and that I do nothing on My own authority but I speak
simply as My Father has taught Me. The One Who sent Me
is with Me now: the Father has never left Me alone for I
always do what pleases Him." And even while He said these
words, many people believed in Him.

So Jesus said to the Jews who believed in Him, "If you are
faithful to what I have said, you are truly My disciples. And
you will know the truth and the truth will set you free!"

"But we are descendants of Abraham," they replied, "and
we have never in our lives been any man's slaves. How can
you say to us, 'You will be set free'?"

Jesus returned, "Believe Me when I tell you that every
man who commits sin is a slave. Now a slave is no permanent
part of a household, but a son is. If the Son, then, makes you
free men, you really are free. I know that you are descended
from Abraham, but some of you are looking for a way to kill
Me because you can't bear My words. I am telling you what
I have seen in the presence of My Father, and you are doing
what you have seen in the presence of your father."

"Our father is Abraham!" they retorted.

"If you were the children of Abraham, you would do the
sort of things Abraham did. But in fact, at this moment, you
are looking for a way to kill Me, simply because I am a man
who has told you the truth that I have heard from God.
Abraham would never have done that. No, you are doing
your father's work."

"We were not born in sin!" they retorted. "We have one
Father—God."

"If God were really your Father," replied Jesus, "you
would have loved Me. For I came from God and I am with
you now as One sent from God. I did not come of My own
accord—He sent Me. The reason why you do not recognise

My words is that you cannot bear to hear what I have to say. No, your father is the devil, and what you are wanting to do is what your father longs to do. He always was a murderer, and has never dealt with the truth, since the truth will have nothing to do with him. Whenever he tells a lie, he speaks in his true character for he is a liar and the father of lies. And it is because I speak the truth that you will not believe Me. Which of you can prove Me guilty of sin? If I am speaking the truth, why is it, yes, why is it, you will not believe Me? The man who is born of God can hear the words of God and the reason why you cannot hear the words of God is simply this, that you are not the sons of God."

"How right we are," retorted the Jews, "in calling you a Samaritan, and mad at that!"

"No," replied Jesus, "I am not mad. I am honouring My Father and you are trying to discredit Me. But I am not concerned with My own glory: there is One Whose concern it is, and He is the true Judge. Believe Me when I tell you that if anybody accepts My words, he will never experience death at all."

"Now we know that you're mad," replied the Jews. "Why, Abraham died and the prophets, too, and yet you say, 'If a man accepts my words, he will never know what death is!' Are you greater than our father, Abraham? He died, and so did the prophets—who are you making yourself out to be?"

"If I were trying to glorify Myself," returned Jesus, "such glory would be worthless. But it is the Father Who glorifies Me, the very One Who you say is your God—though you have never known Him. But I know Him, and if I said I did not know Him, I should be as much a liar as you are! But I do know Him and I am faithful to what He says. As for your father, Abraham, his great joy was that he would see My coming. Now he has seen it and he is over-joyed."

"Look," said the Jews to Him, "you are not fifty yet—and have you seen Abraham?"

"I tell you in solemn truth," returned Jesus, "before there was an Abraham, I AM!"

At this, they picked up stones to hurl at Him, but Jesus disappeared and made His way out of the Temple.

JESUS AND BLINDNESS, PHYSICAL AND
SPIRITUAL

Later as Jesus walked along He saw a man who had been
blind from birth.

"Master, whose sin caused this man's blindness," asked the
disciples, "his own or his parents'?"

"He was not born blind because of his own sin or that
of his parents," returned Jesus, "but to provide an opportunity to show the power of God. We must carry on the
work of Him Who sent Me while the daylight lasts. Night is
coming, when no one can work. I am the world's light as long
as I am in it."

Saying this, He spat on the ground and made a sort of
paste with the saliva. This He applied to the man's eyes and
said, "Go and wash in the pool of Siloam." (Siloam means
"one who has been sent.") So the man went off and washed
and came home with his sight restored.

His neighbours and the people who had often seen him
before as a beggar remarked, "Isn't this the man who used
to sit and beg?"

"Yes, that's the one," said some.

Others said, "No, but he's very like him."

But he himself said, "I'm the man all right!"

"Then how was your blindness cured?" they asked.

"The man called Jesus made some paste and smeared it on
my eyes," he replied, "and then he said, 'Go to Siloam and
wash.' So off I went and washed—and that's how I got my
sight!"

"Where is he now?" they asked.

"I don't know," he returned.

So they brought the man who had once been blind before
the Pharisees. (It should be noted that Jesus made the paste
and restored his sight on a Sabbath day.) The Pharisees asked
the question all over again as to how he had become able
to see.

"He put a paste on my eyes; I washed it off; now I can see
—that's all," he replied.

Some of the Pharisees commented, "This man cannot be
from God since he does not observe the Sabbath."

"But how can a sinner give such wonderful signs as these?"

others demurred. And they were in two minds about Him. Finally, they asked the blind man again, "And what do *you* say about him? You're the one whose sight was restored."

"I believe he is a prophet," he replied.

The Jews did not really believe that the man had been blind and then had become able to see, at all, until they had summoned his parents and asked them, "Is this your son who you say was born blind? How does it happen that he can now see?"

"We know that this is our son, and we know that he was born blind," returned his parents, "but how he can see now, or who made him able to see, we have no idea. Why don't you ask him? He is a grown-up man; he can answer for himself."

His parents said this because they were afraid of the Jews who had already agreed that anybody who admitted that Christ had done this thing should be excommunicated. It was this fear that made the parents say, "Ask him, he is a grown-up man."

So, once again they summoned the man who had been born blind and said to him, "You should give God the glory for what has happened to you. We know that this man is a sinner."

"Whether he is a sinner or not, I couldn't tell, but one thing I am sure of," the man replied, "I used to be blind, now I can see!"

"But what did he *do* to you—how did he make you see?" they continued.

"I've told you before," he replied. "Weren't you listening? Why do you want to hear it all over again? Are you wanting to be his disciples too?"

At this, they turned on him furiously.

"You're the one who is his disciple! We are disciples of Moses. We know that God spoke to Moses, but as for this man, we don't even know where he came from."

"Now here's the extraordinary thing," he retorted, "you don't know where he came from and yet he gave me the gift of sight. Everybody knows that God does not listen to sinners. It is the man who has a proper respect for God and does what God wants him to do—he's the one God listens to. Why, since the world began, nobody's ever heard of a man who was born blind being given his sight. If this man did not come from God, he couldn't do such a thing!"

"You misbegotten wretch!" they flung back at him. "Are you trying to teach *us*?" And they threw him out.

Jesus heard that they had expelled him and when He had found him, He said, "Do you believe in the Son of Man?"

"And who is he, sir?" the man replied. "Tell me, so that I can believe in him."

"You have seen Him," replied Jesus. "It is the One Who is talking to you now."

"Lord, I do believe," he said, and worshipped Him.

Then Jesus said, "I have come into the world to find that I judged it—those who cannot see have their eyes opened and those who think they can see become blind."

Some of the Pharisees near Him overheard this and said, "So we're blind, too, are we?"

"If you were blind," returned Jesus, "nobody could blame you, but, as you insist 'We can see,' your guilt remains."

JESUS DECLARES HIMSELF THE TRUE
SHEPHERD OF MEN

Then Jesus said, "Believe Me when I tell you that anyone 10 who enters into the sheepfold by any other way than the door 1 is a thief and a rogue. It is the shepherd of the flock who goes in by the door. It is to him the door-keeper opens the door and it is his voice that the sheep recognise. He calls his own sheep by name and leads them out of the fold and when he has driven all his own flock outside, he goes in front of them himself, and the sheep follow him because they know his voice. They will never follow a stranger—indeed, they will run away from him, for they do not recognise strange voices."

Jesus gave them this illustration but they did not grasp the point of what He was saying to them. So Jesus said to them once more, "I do assure you that I Myself am the 'door' for the sheep. All who have gone before Me are like thieves and rogues, but the sheep did not listen to them. I am the 'door.' If a man goes in through Me, he will be safe and sound; he can come in and out and find his food. The thief comes with the sole intention of stealing and killing and destroying, but I came to bring them life, and far more life than before. I am the good shepherd. The good shepherd gives his life for the sake of his sheep. But the hired man, who is not the shepherd, and does not own the sheep, sees the wolf coming, deserts the sheep and runs away. And the wolf will attack the flock and send them flying. The hired man runs away because he is only a hired man and has no interest in the sheep. I am the good shepherd, and I know those that are Mine and My sheep know Me, just as the Father knows Me and I know the Father. And I am giving My life for the sake of the sheep.

"And I have other sheep who do not belong to this fold. These also I must lead, and they will hear My voice. So there will be one flock and one Shepherd. This is the reason why the Father loves Me—that I lay down My life, and I lay it down to take it up again! No one is taking it from Me, but I lay it down of My own free will. I have the power to lay it down and I have the power to take it up again. This is an order that I have received from My Father."

JESUS PLAINLY DECLARES WHO HE IS

10   Once again, the Jews were in two minds about Him be-
19   cause of these words, many of them remarking, "The devil's in him and he's insane. Why do you listen to him?"

But others were saying, "This is not the sort of thing a devil-possessed man would say! Can a devil make a blind man see?"

Then came the Dedication Festival at Jerusalem. It was winter-time and Jesus was walking about inside the Temple in Solomon's Cloisters. So the Jews closed in on Him and said, "How much longer are you going to keep us in suspense? If you really are Christ, tell us so straight out!"

"I have told you," replied Jesus, "and you do not believe it. What I have done in My Father's name is sufficient to prove my claim, but you do not believe because you are not My sheep. My sheep recognise My voice and I know who they are. They follow Me and I give them eternal life. They will never die and no one can snatch them out of My hand. My Father, Who has given them to Me, is greater than all. And no one can tear anything out of the Father's hand. I and the Father are One."

Again the Jews reached for stones to stone Him to death, but Jesus answered them, "I have shown you many good things from the Father, for which of these do you intend to stone Me?"

"We're not going to stone you for any good things," replied the Jews, "but for blasphemy: because you, who are only a man, are making yourself out to be God."

"Is it not written in your own Law," replied Jesus, " 'I have said ye are gods'? and if he called those men 'gods' to whom the Word of God came (and the Scripture cannot be broken), can you say to the One Whom the Father has consecrated and sent into the world 'You are blaspheming' because I said 'I am the Son of God'? If I fail to do what My Father does, then do not believe Me. But if I so do, even though you have no faith in Me personally, then believe in the things that I do. Then you may come to know and realise that the Father is in Me and I am in the Father."

And again they tried to arrest Him, but He moved out of their reach.

Then Jesus went off again across the Jordan to the place where John had first baptized and there He stayed. A great many people came to Him, and said, "John never gave us any sign but all he said about this man was true."

And in that place many believed in Him.

JESUS SHOWS HIS POWER OVER DEATH

Then it happened that a man by the name of Lazarus became seriously ill. He lived in Bethany, the village where Mary and her sister Martha lived. (Lazarus was the brother of the Mary who poured perfume upon the Lord and wiped His feet with her hair.) So the sisters sent word to Jesus: "Lord, Your friend is very ill." 11

1

When Jesus received the message, He said, "This illness is not meant to end in death; it is going to bring glory to God—for it will show the glory of the Son of God."

Now Jesus loved Martha and her sister and Lazarus. So when He heard of Lazarus' illness He stayed where He was two days longer. Only then did He say to His disciples, "Let us go back into Judaea."

"Master!" returned the disciples, "only a few days ago, the Jews were trying to stone You to death—are You going there again?"

"There are twelve hours of daylight every day, are there

not?" replied Jesus. "If a man walks in the daytime, he does
not stumble, for he has the light to see by. It is only if he
walks at night that he stumbles because he cannot see where
he is going."

Jesus made these remarks; then after a pause He said to
them, "Our friend Lazarus has fallen asleep, but I am going
to wake him up."

At this, His disciples said, "Lord, if he has fallen asleep,
he will be all right."

Actually Jesus had spoken about his death, but they thought
that He was speaking about falling into natural sleep. This
made Jesus tell them quite plainly, "Lazarus has died, and
I am glad that I was not there—for your sakes, that you may
learn to believe. And now, let us go to him."

Thomas (known as the Twin) then said to his fellow disciples, "Come on, then, let us all go and die with Him!"

When Jesus arrived, He found that Lazarus had been already in the grave four days. Now Bethany is quite near
Jerusalem, rather less than two miles away, and a good many
of the Jews had come out to see Martha and Mary to offer
them sympathy over their brother's death. When Martha
heard that Jesus was on His way, she went out and met Him,
while Mary stayed in the house.

"If only You had been here, Lord," said Martha, "my
brother would never have died. And I know that, even now,
God will give You whatever You ask from Him."

"Your brother will rise again," Jesus replied to her.

"I know," said Martha, "that he will rise again in the
resurrection at the last day."

"I Myself am the Resurrection and the Life," Jesus told
her. "The man who believes in Me will live even though he
dies, and anyone who is alive and believes in Me will never
die at all. Can you believe that?"

"Yes, Lord," replied Martha. "I have always believed that
You are Christ, the Son of God, the One Who was to come
into the world." Saying this, she went away and called Mary
her sister, quietly, "The Master's here and is asking for you,"
she said. When Mary heard this she sprang to her feet and
went to Him. Now Jesus had not yet arrived at the village
itself, but was still where Martha had met Him. So when the
Jews who had been condoling with Mary in the house saw her

get up quickly, they followed her, imagining that she was going off to the grave to weep there.

When Mary met Jesus, she looked at Him and then fell down at His feet. "If only You had been here, Lord," she said, "my brother would never have died."

When Jesus saw Mary weep and noticed the tears of the Jews who came with her, He was deeply moved and visibly distressed.

"Where have you put him?" He asked.

"Lord, come and see," they replied, and at this Jesus Himself wept.

"Look how much He loved him!" remarked the Jews, though some of them asked, "Could he not have stopped this man dying when he could open that blind man's eyes?"

Jesus was again deeply moved at these words, and went on to the grave. It was a cave, and a stone lay in front of it.

"Take away the stone," said Jesus.

"But Lord," said Martha, the dead man's sister, "he has been dead four days. By this time he will be decaying. . . ."

"Did I not tell you," replied Jesus, "that if you believed, you would see the wonder of what God can do?"

Then they took the stone away and Jesus raised His eyes and said, "Father, I thank You that You have heard Me. I know that You always hear Me but I have said this for the sake of these people standing here so that they may believe that You have sent Me."

And when He had said this, He called out in a loud voice, "Lazarus, come out!"

And the dead man came out, his hands and feet bound with grave-clothes and his face muffled with a handkerchief.

"Now untie him," Jesus told them, "and let him go home."

JESUS' MIRACLE LEADS TO DEADLY HOSTILITY

After this many of the Jews who had accompanied Mary and observed what Jesus did, believed in Him. But some of them went off to the Pharisees and told them what Jesus had done. Consequently, the Pharisees and Chief Priests summoned the Council and kept saying, "What can we do? This man obviously shows many remarkable signs. If we let him go on doing this sort of thing we shall have everybody believing in him. Then we shall have the Romans coming and that will be the end of our Holy Place and our very existence as a nation!"

But one of them, Caiaphas, who was High Priest that year, addressed the meeting. "You plainly don't understand what is involved here. You do not realise that it would be a good thing for us if one man should die for the sake of the people —instead of the whole nation being destroyed." (He did not make this remark on his own initiative but, since he was High Priest that year, he was in fact inspired to say that Jesus was going to die for the nation's sake—and in fact not for that nation only, but to bring together into one family all the children of God scattered throughout the world.) From that day then, they planned to kill him. As a consequence Jesus made no further public appearance among the Jews but went off to the countryside on the edge of the desert and stayed with His disciples in a town by the name of Ephraim. The Jewish Passover was approaching and many people went up to Jerusalem out of the country before the actual Passover, to go through a ceremonial cleansing. They looked for Jesus there and remarked to one another as they stood in the Temple, "What do you think? Surely he won't come to the Festival?"

It should be understood that the Chief Priests and the Pharisees had issued an order that anyone who knew of Jesus' whereabouts should tell them, so that they could arrest Him.

AN ACT OF LOVE AS THE END APPROACHES

12
1 Six days before the Passover, Jesus came to Bethany, the village of Lazarus whom He had raised from the dead. They gave Him a supper there, and Martha waited on the party while Lazarus took his place at table with Jesus. Then Mary took a whole pound of very expensive perfume and poured it out on Jesus' feet and then wiped them with her hair. The whole house was full of the fragrance of the perfume. But one of His disciples, Judas Iscariot (the man who was going to betray Jesus), burst out, "Why on earth wasn't this perfume sold? It's worth thirty dollars, which could have been given to the poor!"

He said this, not through any concern for the poor, but because he was dishonest and when he was in charge of the purse used to help himself from the contents.

But Jesus replied to this outburst, "Let her alone, she has saved this for the day of My burial. You have the poor with you always—you will not always have Me."

The large crowd of Jews discovered that He was there and came to the scene—not only because of Jesus but to catch sight of Lazarus, the man whom He had raised from the dead. Then the Chief Priests planned to kill Lazarus as well, because he was the reason for many of the Jews' going off and putting their faith in Jesus.

JESUS EXPERIENCES A TEMPORARY TRIUMPH

The next day, the great crowd who had come to the Festival heard that Jesus was coming into Jerusalem, and went out to meet Him with palm branches in their hands, shouting, "God bless Him, Hurrah for the man who comes in the name of the Lord, hurrah for the King of Israel!"

For Jesus had found a young ass and was seated upon it, just as the Scripture foretold—

Fear not, daughter of Zion: behold, thy King cometh, sitting on an ass's colt.

(The disciples did not realise the significance of what was happening at the time, but when Jesus was glorified, then they recollected that these things had been written about Him and that they had carried them out for Him.)

The people who had been with Him when He had summoned Lazarus from the grave and raised him from the dead were continually talking about Him. This accounts for the crowd who went out to meet Him, for they had heard that He had given this Sign. Seeing all this, the Pharisees remarked to one another, "You see?—There's nothing one can do! The whole world is running after him."

Among those who had come up to worship at the Festival were some Greeks. They approached Philip (whose home town was Bethsaida in Galilee) with the request, "Sir, we want to see Jesus."

Philip went and told Andrew, and Andrew went with Philip and told Jesus.

Jesus told them, "The time has come for the Son of Man to be glorified. I tell you truly that unless a grain of wheat falls into the earth and dies, it remains a single grain of wheat; but if it dies, it brings a good harvest. The man who loves his own life will lose it, and the man who hates his life in this world will preserve it for eternal life. If a man wants to enter My service, he must follow My way. And where I am, My servant will also be. And My Father will honour the man who enters My service.

"Now comes My hour of heart-break, and what can I say, 'Father, save Me from this hour'? No, it was for this very purpose that I came to this hour. 'Father, honour Your own Name!' "

At this there came a Voice from Heaven, "I have honoured it and I will honour it again!"

When the crowd of bystanders heard this, they said it thundered, but some of them said, "An angel spoke to him."

Then Jesus said, "That Voice came for your sake, not for Mine. Now is the time for the judgment of this world to begin, and now will the spirit that rules this world be driven out. As for Me, if I am lifted up from the earth, I will draw all men to Myself." (He said this to show the kind of death He was going to die.)

Then the crowd said, "We have heard from the Law that Christ lives for ever. How can you say that the Son of Man must be 'lifted up'? Who is this Son of Man?"

At this, Jesus told them, "You have the light with you only a little while longer. Go on while the light is good, before the darkness comes down upon you. For the man who walks in the dark has no idea where he is going. You should believe in the light while you have the light, that you may become the sons of Light."

Jesus said all these things, and then went off out of their sight. But though He had given so many Signs, people in general did not believe in Him, so that the prophecy of Isaiah was fulfilled, which said,

Lord, who hath believed our report?
And to whom hath the arm of the Lord been revealed?

Thus, they could not believe, for Isaiah says again—

He hath blinded their eyes, and he hardened their heart:

Lest they should see with their eyes, and perceive with
    their heart,
And should turn,
And I should heal them.

Isaiah said these things because he saw the glory of Christ,
and spoke about Him. Nevertheless, many even of the
authorities did believe in Him. But they did not admit it for
fear of the Pharisees, in case they should be excommunicated.
They preferred the approval of men to the approval of
God.

But later, Jesus cried aloud, "The man who believes in Me,
is believing in the One Who sent Me: and the man who sees
Me is seeing the One Who sent Me. I have come into the
world as Light, so that no one who believes in Me should
remain in the dark. Yet, if anyone hears My sayings and does
not keep them, I do not judge him—for I did not come to
judge the world but to save it. The man who rejects Me and
will not accept My sayings has a judge—at the Last Day, the
very words that I have spoken will be his judge. For I have
not spoken on My own authority: the Father Who sent Me
has commanded Me what to say and what to speak. And I
know that what He commands means eternal life. All that
I say I speak only in accordance with what the Father has
told Me."

JESUS TEACHES HIS DISCIPLES HUMILITY

Before the Festival of the Passover began, Jesus realised 13
that the time had come for Him to leave this world and return   1
to the Father. He had loved those who were His own in this
world and He loved them to the end. By supper-time, the
devil had already put the thought of betraying Jesus into
Judas' mind. And Jesus, with the full knowledge that the
Father had put everything into His hands and that He
had come from God and was going to God, got up from the
supper-table, took off His outer clothes, picked up a towel
and fastened it round His waist. Then He poured water into
a basin and began to wash the disciples' feet and to dry them
with the towel around His waist.

So He came to Simon Peter, who said to Him, "Lord, are
You going to wash my feet?"

"You do not realise now what I am doing," replied Jesus, "but later on you will understand."

Then Peter said to Him, "You must never wash my feet!"

"Unless you let Me wash you, Peter," replied Jesus, "you cannot share My lot."

"Then," returned Simon Peter, "please—not just my feet but my hands and my face as well!"

"The man who has bathed," returned Jesus, "only needs to wash his feet to be clean all over. And you are clean—though not all of you."

(For Jesus knew His betrayer and that is why He said "though not all of you.")

When Jesus had washed their feet and put on His clothes, He sat down again and spoke to them, "Do you realise what I have just done to you? You call Me 'Teacher' and 'Lord' and you are quite right, for I am your Teacher and your Lord. But if I, your Teacher and Lord, have washed your feet, you must be ready to wash each other's feet. I have given you this as an example so that you may do as I have done. Believe Me, the servant is not greater than his master and the messenger is not greater than the man who sent him. Once you have realised these things, you will find your happiness in doing them."

JESUS FORETELLS HIS BETRAYAL

13
18   "I am not speaking about all of you—I know the men I have chosen. But let this Scripture be fulfilled—

He that eateth my bread lifted up his heel against me.

From now onwards, I shall tell you things before they happen, so that when they do happen, you may believe that I am the One I claim to be. I tell you truly that anyone who accepts My messenger will be accepting Me, and anyone who accepts Me will be accepting the One Who sent Me."

After Jesus had said this, He was clearly in anguish of soul —which was shown in his next words,

"I tell you plainly, one of you is going to betray Me."

At this the disciples stared at each other, completely mystified as to whom He could mean. And it happened that one of them, whom Jesus loved, was sitting very close to Him.

So Simon Peter nodded to this man and said, "Tell us who He's talking about."

Leaning forward, as he was, on Jesus' shoulder, he said, "Lord, who is it?"

And Jesus answered, "It is the one I am going to give this piece of bread to, after I have dipped it in the dish."

Then He took a piece of bread, dipped it in the dish and gave it to Simon's son, Judas Iscariot. And after he had taken the piece of bread, Satan came into his heart. Then Jesus said to him, "Be quick about this business!"

No one else at table knew what He meant in telling him this. Indeed, some of them thought that, since Judas had charge of the purse, Jesus was telling him to buy what they needed for the Festival, or that he should give something to the poor. So Judas took the piece of bread and at once left the room and went out—into the night.

When he had gone, Jesus spoke, "Now comes the glory of the Son of Man, and the glory of God in Him! God is glorified through Him and God will glorify the Son of Man—and that without delay. Oh, My children, I am with you such a short time! You will look for Me and I have to tell you as I told the Jews, 'Where I am going, you cannot follow.' Now I am giving you a new command—love one another. Just as I have loved you, you must love one another. This is how all men will know that you are My disciples, because you love one another."

Simon Peter said to Him, "Lord, where are You going?"

"I am going," replied Jesus, "where you cannot follow Me now, though you will follow Me later."

"Lord, why can't I follow You now?" said Peter. "I would lay down my life for You!"

"Would you lay down your life for Me?" replied Jesus. "Believe Me, you will disown Me three times before cock-crow!

JESUS REVEALS SPIRITUAL TRUTHS

"You must not let yourselves be distressed—you must hold on to your faith in God and to your faith in Me. There are many rooms * in My Father's House. If there were not, should I have told you that I am going away to get a place

14

1

* See Appendix, Note 5.

ready for you? It is true that I am going away to get a place ready for you, but it is just as true that I am coming again to welcome you into My own home, so that you may be where I am. You know where I am going and you know the road I am going to take."

"Lord," Thomas remonstrated, "we don't know where You're going and how can we know what road You're going to take?"

"I Myself am the Road," replied Jesus, "and the Truth and the Life. No one approaches the Father except through Me. If you had known Who I am, you would have known My Father. From now on, you do know Him and you have seen Him."

Then Philip said to Him, "Show us the Father, Lord, and we shall be satisfied."

"Have I been such a long time with you," returned Jesus, "without your really knowing Me, Philip? The man who has seen Me has seen the Father. How can you say, 'Show us the Father'? Do you not believe that I am in the Father and the Father is in Me? The very words I say to you are not My own. It is the Father Who lives in Me Who carries out His work through Me. Do you believe Me when I say that I am in the Father and the Father is in Me? But if you cannot, then believe Me because of what you see Me do. I assure you that the man who believes in Me will do the same things that I have done, yes, and he will do even greater things, for I am going away to the Father. Whatever you ask the Father in My name, I will do—that the Son may bring glory to the Father. And if you ask Me anything in My name, I will grant it.

"If you really love Me, you will keep the commandments I have given you and I shall ask the Father to give you Some- one else to stand by you, to be with you always. I mean the Spirit of Truth, Whom the world cannot accept, for it can neither see nor recognise that Spirit. But you recognise Him, for He is with you now and will be in your hearts. I am not going to leave you alone in the world—I am coming to you. In a very little while, the world will see Me no more but you will see Me, because I am really alive and you will be alive, too. When that day comes, you will realise that I am in My Father, that you are in Me, and I am in you.

"The man who knows My commandments and obeys them is the man who really loves Me, and the man who really loves Me will himself be loved by My Father, and I too will love him and make Myself real to him."

Then Judas (not Iscariot) said, "Lord, how is it that You are going to make Yourself real to us but not to the world?"

And to this Jesus replied, "When a man loves Me, he follows My teaching. Then My Father will love him, and We will come to that man and make Our home within him. The man who does not really love Me will not follow My teaching. Indeed, what you are hearing from Me now is not really My saying, but comes from the Father Who sent Me.

"I have said all this while I am still with you. But the One Who is coming to stand by you, the Holy Spirit Whom the Father will send in My name, will be your teacher and will bring to your minds all that I have said to you.

"I leave behind with you—peace; I give you My own peace and My gift is nothing like the peace of this world. You must not be distressed and you must not be daunted. You have heard Me say that 'I am going away and I am coming back to you.' If you really loved Me, you would be glad because I am going to My Father, for My Father is greater than I. And I have told you of it now, before it happens, so that when it does happen, your faith in Me will not be shaken. I shall not be able to talk much longer to you, for the spirit that rules this world is coming very close. He has no hold over Me, but I go on My way to show the world that I love the Father and do what He sent Me to do. . . . Get up now! Let us leave this place."

JESUS TEACHES UNION WITH HIMSELF

"I am the real vine, My Father is the vine-dresser. He 15 removes any of My branches which are not bearing fruit and 1 He prunes every branch that does bear fruit to increase its yield. Now, you have already been pruned by My words. You must go on growing in Me and I will grow in you. For just as the branch cannot bear any fruit unless it shares the life of the vine, so you can produce nothing unless you go on growing in Me. I am the vine itself, you are the branches. It is the man who shares My life and whose life I share who proves fruitful. For the plain fact is that apart from Me you can do nothing at all. The man who does not share My life is like a branch that is broken off and withers away. He becomes just like the dry sticks that men pick up and use for firewood. But if you live your life in Me, and My words live in your hearts, you can ask for whatever you like and it will come true for you. This is how My Father will be glorified—in your becoming fruitful and being My disciples.

"I have loved you just as the Father has loved Me. You must go on living in My love. If you keep My commandments you will live in My love just as I have kept My Father's commandments and live in His love. I have told you this so that you can share My joy, and that your happiness may be complete. There is no greater love than this—that a man lays down his life for his friends. You are My friends if you do what I tell you to do. I shall not call you servants any longer, for a servant does not share his master's confidence. No, I call you friends, now, because I have told you everything that I have heard from the Father.

"It is not that you have chosen Me; but it is I Who have chosen you and I have appointed you to go and bear fruit that will be lasting; so that whatever you ask the Father in My Name, He will give it to you.

"This I command you, love one another! If the world hates you, you know that it hated Me first. If you belonged to the world, the world would love its own children. But because you do not belong to the world and I have chosen you out of it, the world will hate you. Do you remember what I said to you, 'The servant is not greater than his master'? Where they have persecuted Me, they will persecute you as well, and where they have kept My teaching, they will also keep yours. They will do all these things to you as My disciples because they do not know the One Who sent Me. If I had not come and spoken to them, they would not have been guilty of sin, but now they have no excuse for their sin. The man who hates Me, hates My Father as well. If I had not done among them things that no other man has ever done, they would not have been guilty of sin, but as it is they have seen and they have hated both Me and My Father. Yet this only fulfils what is written in their Law—

They hated me without a cause.

But when the Spirit of Truth, Who comes from the Father
and Whom I Myself will send to you from the Father, comes
to help you, He will speak plainly about Me. And you yourselves will also speak plainly about Me for you have been
with Me from the first.

JESUS SPEAKS OF THE FUTURE WITHOUT
HIS BODILY PRESENCE

"I am telling you this now so that your faith in Me may not   16
be shaken. They will excommunicate you from their syna-   1
gogues. Yes, the time is coming when a man who kills you
will think he is thereby serving God! They will act like this
because they have never had any true knowledge of the
Father or of Me, but I have told you all this so that when
the time comes for it to happen you may remember that I
told you about it. I have not spoken like this to you before
because I have been with you; but now the time has come for
Me to go away to the One Who sent Me. None of you asks
Me, 'Where are you going?' That is because you are so distressed at what I have told you. Yet I am telling you the simple truth when I assure you that it is a good thing for you that
I should go away. For if I did not go away, the Divine Helper
would not come to you. But if I go, then I will send Him to
you. When He comes, He will convince the world of the
meaning of sin, true goodness and judgment. He will expose
their sin because they do not believe in Me; He will reveal
true goodness for I am going away to the Father and you will
not see Me again; and He will show them the meaning of
judgment, for the spirit which rules this world will have been
judged.

"I have much more to tell you but you cannot bear it now.
Yet when that One I have spoken to you about comes—the
Spirit of Truth—He will guide you into everything that is
true. For He will not be speaking of His own accord but
exactly as He hears, and He will tell you about the things
that are to come. He will bring glory to Me for He will be
drawing on My Truth and showing it to you. Whatever the
Father possesses is also Mine; that is why I tell you that He
will draw on My Truth and will show it to you.

"In a little while you will not see Me any longer, and again,
in a little while you will see Me."

world just as You sent Me to the world and I consecrate Myself for their sakes that they may be made holy by the
Truth.

"I am not praying only for these men but for all those who
will believe in Me through their message, that they may all be
one. Just as You, Father, live in Me and I live in You, I am
asking that they may live in Us, that the world may believe
that You did send Me. I have given them the honour that
You gave Me, that they may be one, as You and I are One—
I in them and You in Me, that they may grow complete into
one, so that the world may realise that You sent Me and have
loved them as You loved Me. Father, I want those whom You
have given Me to be with Me where I am; I want them to see
that glory that You have made Mine—for You loved Me
before the world began. Father of Goodness and Truth, the
world has not known You, but I have known You and these
men now know that You have sent Me. I have made Your
Self clear to them and I will continue to do so that the love
which You have had for Me may be in their hearts—and that
I may be there also."

JESUS IS ARRESTED IN THE GARDEN

18   When Jesus had spoken these words, He went out with His
1   disciples across the Cedron valley to a place where there was
a garden, and they went into it together. Judas who betrayed
Him knew about the place, for Jesus often met His disciples there. So Judas fetched the guard and its officers
which the Chief Priests and Pharisees had provided for him,
and came to the place with torches and lanterns and weap-
ons. Jesus, fully realising all that was going to happen to
Him, went forward and said to them, "Who are you looking
for?"

"Jesus of Nazareth," they answered.

"I am the man," said Jesus. (Judas who was betraying
Him was standing there with the others.)

When He said to them, "I am the man," they started back-
wards and some of them fell to the ground. So Jesus asked
them again, "Who are you looking for?"

And again they said, "Jesus of Nazareth."

"I have told you that I am the man," replied Jesus. "If I
am the man you are looking for, let these others go." (Thus

fulfilling his previous words, "I have not lost one of those whom You gave Me.")

At this Simon Peter, who had a sword, drew it and slashed at the High Priest's servant, cutting off his right ear. (The servant's name was Malchus.) But Jesus said to Peter, "Put your sword back into its sheath. Am I not to drink the cup the Father has given Me?"

Then the guard, with its captain and the Jewish officers, took hold of Jesus and tied His hands together, and led Him off to Annas first, for he was father-in-law to Caiaphas, who was High Priest that year. Caiaphas was the man who advised the Jews "that it would be a good thing that one man should die for the sake of the people." Behind Jesus followed Simon Peter, and one other disciple who was known personally to the High Priest. He went in with Jesus into the High Priest's courtyard, but Peter was left standing at the door outside. So this other disciple who was acquainted with the High Priest went out and had a word with the woman at the door and brought Peter inside. The young woman remarked to Peter, "Are you one of this man's disciples, too?"

"No, I am not," retorted Peter.

In the courtyard, the servants and officers stood about; they had made a charcoal fire because it was a cold night, and they were warming themselves. Peter stood there with them, keeping himself warm.

Meanwhile the High Priest interrogated Jesus about His disciples and about His own teaching.

"I have always spoken quite openly to the world," replied Jesus. "I have always taught in the synagogue or in the Temple where all Jews meet together, and I have said nothing in secret. Why do you question Me? Why not ask those who have heard Me what I told them? Obviously, they are the ones who know what I actually said."

As He said this, one of those present, an officer, slapped Jesus with his open hand, remarking, "Is that the way for you to answer the High Priest?"

"If I have said anything wrong," Jesus said to him, "you must give evidence about it, but if what I said was true, why did you hit Me?"

Then Annas sent Him, still with His hands tied, to Caiaphas the High Priest.

PETER'S DENIAL

18 In the meantime Simon Peter was still standing keeping
25 himself warm. Some of them said to him, "Surely you too
are one of his disciples, aren't you?"

And he denied it and said, "No, I am not."

Then one of the High Priest's servants, a relation of the
man whose ear Peter had cut off, remarked, "Didn't I see you
in the garden with him?"

And again Peter denied it. And immediately the cock crew.

JESUS IS TAKEN BEFORE THE
ROMAN AUTHORITY

18 Then they led Jesus from Caiaphas' presence into the
28 Palace. It was now early morning and the Jews themselves
did not go into the Palace, for fear that they would be con-
taminated and would not be able to eat the Passover. So
Pilate walked out to them and said, "What is the charge that
you are bringing against this man?"

"If he were not a rogue, we should not have handed him
over to you," they replied.

To which Pilate retorted, "Then take him yourselves and
judge him according to your law."

"We are not allowed to put a man to death," replied the
Jews (thus fulfilling Christ's prophecy of the method of His
own death).

So Pilate went back into the Palace and called Jesus to
him. "Are you the King of the Jews?" he asked.

"Are you asking this of your own accord," replied Jesus,
"or have other people spoken to you about Me?"

"Do you think *I* am a Jew?" replied Pilate. "It's your race
and your Chief Priests who handed you over to me. What
have you done, anyway?"

"My Kingdom is not founded in this world—if it were, My
servants would fight to prevent My being handed over to the
Jews. But in fact My Kingdom is not founded on all this!"

"So you are a king, are you?" returned Pilate.

"Indeed I am a King," Jesus replied; "the reason for My
birth and the reason for My coming into the world is to witness to the Truth. Every man who loves the truth recognises
My voice."

To which Pilate retorted, "What is truth?" and went
straight out again to the Jews and said:

"I find nothing criminal about him at all. But I have an
arrangement with you about setting free one prisoner at Passover time. Would you like me then to set free the 'King of
the Jews' for you?"

At this, they shouted out again, "No, not this man, but
Barabbas!"

Barabbas was a bandit.

Then Pilate took Jesus and had Him flogged, and the soldiers twisted thorn-twigs into a crown and put it on His head,
threw a purple robe around Him and pretended to come into
His presence, saying, "Hail, King of the Jews!" And then
they slapped Him with their open hands.

Then Pilate went outside again and said to them, "Look,
I bring him out before you here, to show that I find nothing
criminal at all about him."

And at this Jesus came outside too, wearing the thorn
crown and the purple robe.

"Look," said Pilate, "here's the man!"

The sight of Him made the Chief Priests and Jewish officials shout at the top of their voices, "Crucify!
Crucify!"

"You take him and crucify him," retorted Pilate. "He's
no criminal as far as I can see!"

The Jews answered him, "We have a Law, and according
to that Law, he must die, for he made himself out to be the
Son of God!"

When Pilate heard them say this, he became much more
uneasy, and returned to the Palace again and spoke to Jesus,
"Where *do* you come from?"

But Jesus gave him no reply. So Pilate said to Him,
"Won't you speak to me? Don't you realise that I have the
power to set you free, and I have the power to have you
crucified?"

"You have no power at all against Me," replied Jesus,
"except what was given to you from above. And for that
reason the one who handed Me over to you has the greater
sin."

From that moment, Pilate tried hard to set Him free but
the Jews were shouting, "If you set this man free, you are no

friend of Caesar! Anyone who makes himself out to be a
king is anti-Caesar!"

When Pilate heard this, he led Jesus outside and sat down
upon the Judgment-seat in the place called The Pavement
(in Hebrew, Gabbatha). It was the Preparation Day of the
Passover and it was now getting on towards midday. Pilate
now said to the Jews, "Look, here's your king!"

At which they yelled, "Take him away, take him away,
crucify him!"

"Am I to crucify your king?" said Pilate.

"Caesar is our king and no one else," replied the Chief
Priests. And at this Pilate handed Jesus over to them for
crucifixion.

THE CRUCIFIXION

19   So they took Jesus and He went out carrying the cross
17   Himself, to a place called Skull Hill (in Hebrew, Golgotha).
There they crucified Him, and two others, one on each side
of Him. Pilate had a placard written out and put on the
cross, reading, "Jesus of Nazareth, the King of the Jews."
This placard was read by many of the Jews because the site
of the crucifixion was quite near Jerusalem, and it was written in Hebrew as well as in Latin and Greek. So the Chief
Priests said to Pilate, "You must not write 'The King of the
Jews': you ought to put, 'He said, I am King of the Jews.' "

To which Pilate retorted, "Indeed? What I have written,
I have written."

When the soldiers had crucified Jesus, they divided His
clothes between them, taking a quarter-share each. There
remained His shirt, which was seamless—woven in one piece
from the top to the bottom. So they said to each other,
"Don't let us tear it; let's draw lots for it and see who gets it."

This happened to fulfil the Scripture which says—

They parted my garments among them,
And upon my vesture did they cast lots.

JESUS PROVIDES FOR HIS MOTHER,
FROM THE CROSS

19   While the soldiers were doing this, Jesus' mother was
25   standing near the cross with her sister, Mary, Clopas' daugh-

ter, and Mary of Magdala. Jesus saw His mother and the disciple whom He loved standing by her side, and said to her, "Look, he will be your son." And then He said to the disciple, "And she is to be your mother."

From that hour His disciple led Mary to his own home.

After this, Jesus, realising that everything was now completed, said (fulfilling the saying of Scripture), "I am thirsty."

There was a bowl of sour wine standing there. So they soaked a sponge in the wine, put it on a spear, and pushed it up towards his mouth. When Jesus had taken it, He cried, "It is finished!" His head fell forward, and He died.

THE BODY OF JESUS IS REMOVED

As it was the Day of Preparation for the Passover, the Jews **19** wanted to avoid the bodies being left on the crosses over the **31** Sabbath (for that was a particularly important Sabbath), and they requested Pilate to have the men's legs broken and the bodies removed. So the soldiers went and broke the legs of the first man and of the other who was crucified with Jesus. But when they came to Him, they saw that He was dead already and they did not break His legs. But one of the soldiers pierced His side with a spear, and at once there was an outrush of blood and water. And the man who saw this is our witness: his evidence is true. (He is certain that he is speaking the truth, so that you may believe as well.) For this happened to fulfil the Scripture,

A bone of him shall not be broken.

And again another Scripture says—

They shall look on him whom they pierced.

After it was all over, Joseph (who came from Arimathaea and was a disciple of Jesus, though secretly for fear of the Jews) requested Pilate that he might take away Jesus' body, and Pilate gave him permission. So he came and took His body down. Nicodemus also, the one who had come to Him at the beginning by night, arrived bringing a mixture of myrrh and aloes, weighing about a hundred pounds. So they took His body and wound it round with linen strips with the spices, according to the Jewish custom of preparing a body for burial. It happened that on the same hillside where He him. "Happy are the men who have never seen Me and yet believe."

Jesus gave a great many other Signs in the presence of His disciples which are not recorded in this book. But these have been written so that you may believe that Jesus is Christ, the Son of God, and that in that faith you may have Life as His followers.

THE RISEN JESUS AND PETER

21   Later on, Jesus showed Himself again to His disciples on
1 the shore of Lake Tiberias. It was like this: Simon Peter, Thomas (called the Twin), Nathanael from Cana of Galilee, the sons of Zebedee and two other disciples happened to be together.

"I'm going fishing," announced Simon Peter.

"All right," they replied, "we'll go with you."

So they went out and got into the boat and during the night caught nothing at all. But just as dawn began to break, Jesus stood there on the beach, the disciples having no idea that it was Jesus.

"Have you caught anything, boys?" Jesus called out to them.

"No," they replied.

"Throw the net on the right side of the boat," said Jesus, "and you'll have a catch."

So they threw out the net and then found they weren't strong enough to pull it in because it was so full of fish! At this, the disciple that Jesus loved said to Peter, "*It is the Lord!*"

Hearing this, Peter slipped on his jacket, for he had been naked, and plunged into the sea. The other disciples followed in the boat, for they were only about a hundred yards from the shore, dragging in the net full of fish. When they had landed, they noticed that a charcoal fire was burning, with fish and bread placed on it. Jesus said to them, "Bring Me some of the fish you've just caught."

So Simon Peter got into the boat and hauled the net ashore full of large fish, one hundred and fifty-three altogether. But in spite of the large number, there was no tearing of the net.

Then Jesus said to them, "Come and have your breakfast."

None of the disciples dared to ask Him Who He was; they knew it was the Lord.

Jesus went and took the bread and gave it to them and gave them all fish as well. This was the third time that Jesus showed Himself to His disciples after His resurrection from the dead.

When they had finished breakfast Jesus said to Simon Peter, "Simon, son of John, do you love Me more than these others?"

"Yes, Lord," he replied, "You know that I am Your friend."

"Then feed My lambs," returned Jesus.

"Simon, son of John," He said for the second time, "do you love Me?"

"Yes, Lord," returned Peter, "You know that I am Your friend."

"Then look after My sheep," replied Jesus.

Then for the third time, Jesus spoke to him and said, "Simon, son of John, *are* you My friend?"

Peter was deeply hurt because Jesus' third question to him was "Are you My friend?" and he said, "Lord, You know everything. You know that I am Your friend!"

"Then feed My sheep," Jesus said to him. "I tell you truly, Peter, that when you were young, you used to dress yourself and go where you liked, but when you are an old man, you are going to stretch out your hands and someone else will dress you and take you where you do not want to go."

(He said this to show the kind of death by which Peter was going to honour God.)

Then Jesus said to him, "You must follow Me."

Then Peter turned round and noticed the disciple whom Jesus loved following behind them. (It was the one who had his head on Jesus' shoulder at the supper who had asked, "Lord, who is the one who is going to betray You?") So he said, "Yes, Lord, but what about him?"

"If it is My wish," returned Jesus, "for him to stay until I come, is that your business, Peter? You must follow Me."

This gave rise to a saying among the disciples that this disciple would not die. Yet, of course, Jesus did not say, "He will not die," but simply, "If it is My wish for him to stay until I come, is that your business?"

ALL THE ABOVE WAS WRITTEN BY
AN EYE-WITNESS

21   Now it is this same disciple who is hereby giving his
24 testimony to these things and has written them down. We
know that his witness is reliable. Of course, there are many
other things which Jesus did, and I suppose that if each one
were written down in detail, there would not be room in the
whole world for all the books that would have to be written.

APPENDIX

Note 1.

"Scribes."

There is no modern English word by which "Scribes" can be fairly translated. It is therefore necessary to explain that the "Scribes" of the Gospels were the interpreters of the Divine Law (or Torah), for the people of Israel. The Torah was a kind of textbook for both the religious and civil functions of the community. Since in process of time this had become a highly complex matter, the Scribes had to be expert both in knowledge, interpretation and administration. Consequently their position was one of considerable authority and, though there were doubtless noble exceptions, they tended to become both legalist and theological in outlook, and were therefore unprepared to accept the revolutionary teaching of Jesus.

"Pharisees."

The Pharisees were a class of zealous Jews whose chief characteristic lay in their separation from the heathen and from all that they considered evil. They were the Puritans of their day, and emphasised the spiritual rather than the nationalistic side of Judaism. We might fairly say that they were Churchmen rather than statesmen. And, again, though there were good men among them, they tended to concentrate upon rigid outward observances, to the exclusion of human sympathy and understanding. It was this tendency, and the conviction that they alone were right, which brought them into conflict with Jesus.

"Sadducees."

The Sadducees represented the aristocratic conservative element in the Jewish priesthood. Their conservatism, with its desire to maintain things as they were, led them to compromise politically with the Roman occupying power, and thus their moral authority became weakened. Moreover, in clinging to the tenets of the past, they failed to develop in their religion and did not, for example, believe, as the Pharisees did, in the coming Kingdom of God, and only in a very shadowy way did they believe in the immortality of the human soul.

Note 2.

Matthew 5, 22—Raca.

"Raca" means a fool or empty-headed fellow, but the Greek word used in the previous sentence means much the same thing. If however it is, as some suggest, a transliteration of the Hebrew "morēh," then we have a further stage of uncharitable condemnation, for this word means "a persistent rebel against God," and thus makes much better sense.

Note 3.

Luke 16, 1–13—The Parable of the Unjust Steward.

This story recorded by St. Luke is well-known for its difficulty of interpretation. Most commentators suggest that the lesson to be learned is that the follower of Christ should be as shrewd about his spiritual future as the rascally steward was about his own immediate security. Personally, I do not feel satisfied with this view as it introduces a note of careful calculation for the future which is quite at variance with Christ's teaching elsewhere. Moreover, the passage in question goes on to state categorically that dishonesty in earthly things is bound to mean dishonesty in the greater, or spiritual, things, and this seems a very odd conclusion to be drawn from the parable!

I am myself somewhat attracted by the suggestion of Professor C. C. Torrey, who is a specialist in Semitic Languages at Yale University, that the original words of Jesus were spoken in Aramaic, and suffered some alterations when written down in Greek. Professor Torrey, in his own translation, makes the two difficult remarks in verses 8 and 9 into questions, viz. "Did the lord of the estate praise his faithless manager . . . ? and do *I* say to *you* . . . ?"

If the above interpretation is true, then the parable is one of faithfulness, illustrating the fact that since even in worldly matters men cannot "get away with it"—how much more essential is faithfulness in spiritual matters. My translation then would read:

"Now did the employer praise this rascally agent because he had been so careful for his own future? For the children of this world are considerably more shrewd in dealing with the people they live with than the children of light. And do you think I am recommending you to use the false means of money to make friends for yourselves, so that when it fails you, they could welcome you to houses fit for eternity? No, the man who is faithful in the little things will be faithful in the big things, and the man who cheats in the little things will cheat in the big things too. If you are not trustworthy with the tainted wealth of this world, how can you be trusted with the true riches? And if you have not been honest with other people's property, who will entrust you with some of your own? No servant can serve two masters. He is bound to hate one and love the other, or give his loyalty to one and despise the other. You cannot serve God and the power of money at the same time."

But to be fair to the Greek that we possess, one cannot translate the statements by questions, and I have therefore tried to make the best of it by suggesting that our Lord says, in effect, that the Christian must "outsmart" the "smart," by turning money, which has so many potentialities for evil, into a spiritual opportunity. But this still leaves the following verses about faithfulness rather "in the air."

Note 4.

John 7, 53-8, 11—The Woman taken in Adultery.

This passage has no place in the oldest manuscripts of John, and is considered by most scholars to be an interpolation from some other source. Almost all scholars would agree that, although the story is out of place here, it is part of a genuine apostolic tradition.

Note 5.

John 14, 1—Many rooms.

I am of course well aware that the word translated "mansions" in the A.V. is a word frequently used to mean "resting places," commonly applied to stations on a journey affording accommodation for the night. Commentators make much of this, but it appears to me that they forget that our Lord is stating that such places exist within the Father's *House*. To bring out the sense of resting places on a journey as existing inside a house seems to me to raise a confused picture to the mind. I have therefore translated the word "rooms," which can certainly be used for rest and refreshment, and are normal parts of a house.